Letters from Revolutionary France

LETTERS WRITTEN IN FRANCE TO A FRIEND IN LONDON,
BETWEEN THE MONTH OF NOVEMBER 1794,
AND THE MONTH OF MAY 1795

Watkin Tench in the uniform of a Captain of Marines, artist unknown, exact date unknown (1782–93). Reproduced by permission of the Misses Grylls, from copies held at the Mitchell Library, State Library of New South Wales.

Letters from Revolutionary France

LETTERS WRITTEN IN FRANCE TO A FRIEND IN LONDON, BETWEEN THE MONTH OF NOVEMBER 1794, AND THE MONTH OF MAY 1795

WATKIN TENCH

edited by

GAVIN EDWARDS

UNIVERSITY OF WALES PRESS
CARDIFF
2001

© Introduction and Notes, Gavin Edwards 2001

All rights reserved. No part of this book may be reproduced, stored in a retrieval system, or transmitted, in any form or by any means, electronic, mechanical, photocopying, recording or otherwise, without clearance from the University of Wales Press, 6 Gwennyth Street, Cardiff CF24 4YD.
www.wales.ac.uk/press

British Library Cataloguing in Publication Data
A catalogue record for this book is available from the British Library.

ISBN   0-7083-1692-1 (hardback)
           0-7083-1691-3 (paperback)

Cover illustrations:

Front cover:
(*main picture*) *HMS Alexander . . . ten minutes before she struck her colours to a French Squadron . . . on the 6th November 1794*, detail from an aquatint by J. Wells, after an original by T. Guest, published by T. Guest 20 June 1800. Reproduced by permission of the National Maritime Museum, London
(*top*) Heading to a letter from the Quimper Committee of Surveillance (for complete letter see pp. 114–15). Reproduced by permission of the Archives départementales du Finistère.
(*bottom*) Watkin Tench's signature on a letter of 1819. Reproduced by permission of the Mitchell Library, State Library of New South Wales.

Back cover:
Watkin Tench in the uniform of a Captain of Marines, date unknown, artist unknown. Reproduced by permission of the Misses Grylls, England, from copies held in the Mitchell Library, State Library of New South Wales.

Cover design by Chris Neale

Typeset at the University of Wales Press
Printed in Great Britain by Dinefwr Press, Llandybïe

CONTENTS

Acknowledgements	vii
List of Plates	ix
A Note on the Text	x
Chronology	xi
Introduction	xv
Notes to the Introduction	xxxvi
THE LETTERS	1
Preface	3
Letter I	5
Letter II	19
Letter III	22
Letter IV	25
Letter V	44
Letter VI	53
Letter VII	62
Letter VIII	74
Letter IX	91
Letter X	99
Letter XI	121
Letter XII	127
Notes to Letters	135
Appendix I: Charles Pougens's 'Translator's Note' to *Relation d'une expédition à la Baye Botanique*	163
Appendix II: A Letter from Rear-Admiral Bligh to the Admiralty, November 23, 1794	165
Appendix III: Review by Mary Wollstonecraft in the *Analytical Review* of Tench's *Letters Written in France*	168

Notes to Appendices	173
Bibliography	174
Index	179

ACKNOWLEDGEMENTS

I am grateful to Iain McCalman at the Australian National University's Humanities Research Centre for his encouragement and practical support at an early stage of this project, and to Jenny Newell at the ANU's Centre for Cross-Cultural Research who provided important technical and moral support. At the University of Sydney, successive Heads of the Department of English – Margaret Clunies Ross, Margaret Harris and Geraldine Barnes – put themselves out to provide me with facilities for my work and I am most grateful to them.

More recently, my work on this edition has benefited from a visit to the Archives départementales du Finistère at Quimper. I am most grateful to the Research Committee of the University of Glamorgan's School of Humanities and Social Sciences for the award of a grant which made the visit possible, as well as to the staff of the Archives – especially Daniel Collin – for their friendly helpfulness. I am similarly glad to have the opportunity to record my gratitude to Jennifer Broomhead and her colleagues at the State Library of New South Wales, and to librarians and archivists at the Musée des beaux-arts de Quimper, the National Maritime Museum, Greenwich, the Royal Marines Museum, Portsmouth, and the Chester and Cheshire Record Offices. The edition has also benefited from the map-designing skills of Catherine Evans and Mike Davies at the University of Glamorgan's Media Centre.

Among colleagues, friends and correspondents in Britain, France and Australia who have provided me with information or practical support, I particularly wish to thank John Barrell, Jacqueline Belanger, Patricia Clark, Deirdre Coleman, Mary-Anne Constantine, John Creasey, Barbara Dennis, William Doyle, Chris Evans, Geraint Evans, Anne Ferris, Percy Ferris, Michael Flynn, Helen Fulton, Ceris Gruffudd, Danielle Guillou-Beuzit, Terry Hale, Ivor Indyk, Owen Jackson, Wallace Kirsop, Stephen Knight, Joel Le Bec, Anthony Mandal, Jon Mee, Adrian Mitchell, Adrian Price, Marc Simon, David Skilton, Andy Smith, Nicholas Thomas, Diana Wallace and Gordon Williams. Gerard Goggin kindly drew the Wollstonecraft review to my attention, while Deborah Ferris and

ACKNOWLEDGEMENTS

Sharif Gemie have come to the aid of my halting French repeatedly, at short notice and without complaint. The interest and hospitality of Mike, Sue, Ossie and Daisy in London has been sustaining throughout, and I thank them for it.

The sad news of the death of Bernie Martin reached me as I was completing this project, the early stages of which benefited so much from the range of his knowledge and the pleasure of his company. This edition of Tench's *Letters* is dedicated to his memory.

Gavin Edwards
University of Glamorgan
May 2001

LIST OF PLATES

Watkin Tench — frontispiece

1. Southern Britain and northern France in 1764 — xvii
2. *Département du Finistère* — xix
3. Title-page of Watkin Tench's *Letters Written in France to a Friend in London* (1796) — 1
4. Letter from Admiral Richard Rodney Bligh to Representatives Guesno and Guermeur, dated Quimper 21 February 1795 — 69
5. The renaming of Quimper's streets and squares — 75
6. Bilingual French/Breton decree: 'Concerning expenses for the removal of royal symbols in churches and other public monuments' — 77
7. Letter from the Quimper Committee of Surveillance to Representative Prieur de la Marne at Brest, undated — 114–15

A NOTE ON THE TEXT

The text reproduced here is the first and only edition of Tench's *Letters Written in France*, published in 1796. Apart from removing the 'long s', I have faithfully reproduced the 1796 edition's orthography. Although the original spelling has not been modified, very occasional silent emendation of typographical errors, including some clearly incorrect punctuation and clear inconsistency in spelling, has been undertaken. Where the spelling of French names or words is consistently and clearly incorrect in the text, especially in the use of accents, I have noted the correct spelling in my textual notes at the first occurrence. The paragraphing of the original has been retained, but running quotation marks have been removed.

CHRONOLOGY

Date	Britain	France	World
1787	*May*: Convict fleet sails for Botany Bay.		
1788	Centenary of 'Glorious Revolution'. Anglo-French trade treaty.		*Jan*: British reach Botany Bay; French under La Pérouse reach Botany Bay. *July*: Tench's *Narrative* leaves New South Wales
1789	*April*: Tench, *A Narrative of the Expedition to Botany Bay*.	*17 June*: Third Estate declares itself the National Assembly. Tench: *Relation d'une expédition*. *14 July*: Fall of the Bastille. *26 Aug*: Declaration of the Rights of Man and Citizen. *2 Nov*: Confiscation of Church property.	
1790	*Dec*: Burke, *Reflections on the Revolution in France*; Helen Maria Williams, *Letters Written in France*.	*19 June*: Nobility abolished *12 July*: Civil Constitution of the Clergy *Sept*: Revolutionary mutiny at Brest.	*3 June*: News of the Revolution reaches NSW

Date	Britain	France	World
1791	*Feb*: Paine: *Rights of Man*		*Aug*: Slave uprising in St Domingue. *18 Aug*: Tench leaves NSW. *27 Aug*: Declaration of Pilnitz between Austria and Prussia. *Oct*: United Irishmen founded
		1 Oct: Legislative Assembly established.	
1792	*Jan*: London Corresponding Society founded. *Feb*: Paine, *Rights of Man*, II.		
	May: Proclamation against seditious publications.	*28 April*: France and Austria at war.	
	June: Tench reaches Spithead.		
		12 June: Girondin ministers dismissed. *Aug*: Royal family imprisoned; National Convention established. *2 Sept*: 'September Massacres' begin. *20 Sept*: France defeats Prussia at Valmy. *21 Sept*: Monarchy abolished.	
		YEAR I	
		22 Sept: Republic declared.	*6 Nov*: France defeats Austria at Jemappes.
	Dec: Militia embodied.		
1793		*21 Jan*: Louis XVI executed. *Feb*: Declaration of war against Britain and Holland;	British take Tobago, part of St Domingue, Pondicherry.

Date	Britain	France	World
1793		Decree conscripting 300,000 men. *11 March*: Revolt in the west begins. *15 April*: Assignats established. *4 May*: First price 'maximum' imposed. *June*: Fall of Girondins. *13 July*: Assassination of Marat. *5 Sept*: Government by terror begins. YEAR II	*Aug*: Alliance between black and Republican forces on St Domingue.
	Tench, *A Complete Account of the Settlement at Port Jackson*. *Oct*: Tench joins Channel Fleet.	*5 Oct*: Republican Calendar adopted. *16 Oct*: Execution of Marie-Antoinette. *10 Nov*: Festival of Reason in Notre-Dame. *22 Nov*: Paris churches closed.	
1794	*Jan, March*: Scottish treason trials. *April*: 'Scottish martyrs' sentenced to transportation to NSW. *May*: suspension of Habeas Corpus. Wollstonecraft, *Historical and Moral View of the French Revolution*.	*Jan*: Repression in the west. *4 Feb*: Decree emancipating slaves in French colonies. *Feb-March*: Renewal of Chouan revolt in Brittany. *1 June*: 'Combat de prairial'/'Glorious First of June'. *8 June*: Festival of the Supreme Being. *27 July*/*9 Thermidor*: Fall of Robespierre. YEAR III	British take Martinique, Guadaloupe, St Lucia.
	Oct: English treason trials.	*6 Nov*: Capture of HMS Alexander. *12 Nov*: Jacobin Club closed. *8 Dec*: Girondin deputies reinstated. *24 Dec*: Price 'maximum' abolished.	

Date	Britain	France	World
1795		*17 Feb*: Tench arrives in Quimper. *21 Feb*: Freedom of worship re-established. *April*: Germinal uprisings defeated; Peace with the Chouans at La Prévalaye.	*Jan*: British take Cape of Good Hope, Malacca, Ceylon. *20 Jan*: French occupy Amsterdam.
	10 May: Tench reaches Plymouth.	*July*: Defeat of Quiberon invasion.	
		YEAR IV	
	Nov: Gagging Acts.	*26 Oct*: End of the Convention. *Nov*: Directory established.	
1796	*Jan*: Wollstonecraft, *Letters from Sweden*.	*19 Feb*: Abolition of the *assignat*.	
			March: Bonaparte appointed commander in Italy.
	May: Tench, *Letters Written in France*.		
		YEAR V	
			Oct (to *Jan 1800*): Tench in Channel and Atlantic Fleets.
1797		*March*: Execution of Charette.	*Jan*: Withdrawal of Irish expedition under Hoche. *Feb*: British naval victory at St Vincent.
	April–May: Channel Fleet mutinies at Spithead. *May–June*: North Sea Fleet mutinies at the Nore.	*May–June*: *Fragmens du dernier voyage de la Pérouse*. *Aug*: Laws against clergy repealed. *Sept*: British peace overtures rejected.	*11 Oct*: British naval victory at Camperdown.

INTRODUCTION

TENCH'S STORY

When *Letters Written in France to a Friend in London* was published in 1796, the *Gentleman's Magazine* reminded its readers of where they would have come across its author – 'Major Tench of the Marines' – before:

> MAJOR Tench, who gave the first account of the new settlement at Botany-bay, and since extended it on a larger scale, here relates . . . the incidents to which he was witness during his captivity, after he was taken, in admiral Bligh's ship, by the French; between whose treatment of prisoners, and that which they experience in England, these letters show the strong and striking contrast; as well as paint the horrid excesses to which a civilized people in the 18th century have been transported.[1]

Tench's first-hand reports on the founding of New South Wales as a convict colony are available in paperback, under the title *1788*,[2] in every Australian bookshop. His equally vivid and astute account of life in another new society – Revolutionary France – is virtually unknown in either hemisphere.[3]

Watkin Tench was born in 1758 in Chester, where his parents ran a boarding-school. Tench is very much a Cheshire name, while he was probably called Watkin after Sir Watkin Williams Wynn (1749–89), Wales's wealthiest landowner, MP for the county of Denbigh and sometime mayor of Chester. *A Complete Account of the Settlement at Port Jackson* is dedicated to Williams Wynn's eldest son, also called Sir Watkin (1772–1840) 'in gratitude to a family, from whom I have received the deepest obligations'.[4] We do not know what those obligations were, though since commissions in the marines were acquired by influence it may have been Williams Wynn influence in Tench's case. We know nothing about his life before his commission as second lieutenant in June 1776, aged seventeen. However, the range of his knowledge – Latin and French literature, English literature (especially Shakespeare and Milton), political and social theory as well as

INTRODUCTION

professional knowledge of naval and military matters – suggest an education at an endowed grammar school, a culturally and socially ambitious home-life and, possibly, participation in amateur theatricals held in the Williams Wynn's private theatre at Wynnstay ('so many of my happier days', Tench tells us in the *Letters*, 'have been passed in Wales', p. 87[5]).

Tench's service career was determined from the start by the global rivalry between Britain and France, and all through the *Letters* he writes as a marine – a sea-soldier – conscious of that rivalry as a central element in his own and his country's history. The French had sided with the American colonists in the War of Independence and Tench spent some months as a prisoner of the French in Maryland in 1778. He tells us in the *Account* that at some early point of his career – we do not know when – he 'lived in the West Indies' (p. 186), where control of the sugar-colonies and their slave labour-force was contested between the two principal European powers. He sailed for Botany Bay on the *Charlotte* in 1787, arriving just three days before a French exploration party under La Pérouse (for the officers on both sides it was a gentlemanly encounter in an interlude of peace between the two countries).

A Narrative of the Expedition to Botany Bay was published in London in 1789, while Tench was still in New South Wales. A translation (*Relation d'une expédition à la Baye Botanique*) appeared in Paris later the same year with a remarkable introduction by its translator, Charles Pougens (see Appendix 1), which links the founding of the penal colony and the work of 'la Nation assemblée' (the new National Assembly) as comparable acts of enlightened social innovation.

When news of the Revolution reached the social innovators in New South Wales a year later, they were close to starvation and the local Aboriginal population had been devastated by smallpox. Tench sailed for England on 18 December 1791, arriving at Spithead six months later (June 1792) into a society increasingly divided by the radicalization of the Revolution in France and soon to be shaken by French military victories. Britain and Holland joined the war against revolutionary France in February 1793, fighting it at first as a naval war – to disrupt French overseas commerce – in the Channel, the Atlantic and the West Indies.

On 22 October 1792, Tench married Anna Maria Sargent, daughter of a Devonport surgeon, Robert Sargent, and his wife Hannah Hill. *A Complete Account of the Settlement at Port Jackson* was published, by subscription, the following year, and in October 1793 Tench joined the

INTRODUCTION

Plate 1: Southern Britain and northern France in 1794.

INTRODUCTION

Channel Fleet, the principal task of which was to blockade the French naval port of Brest.

In June 1794, the fleet – not including Tench's own ship, *HMS Alexander* – achieved a kind of victory over the French, in an engagement called 'the Glorious First of June' by the British, 'le combat de prairial ('the battle of Prairial') by the French. Arguments between British and French officers about what really happened on that day – when five French ships-of-the-line were captured, but a vital American grain convoy eluded British attempts to prevent it reaching Brest – surface regularly in the letters that Tench wrote from French ships in Brest harbour; while many of the British prisoners already in Quimper when Tench arrived there in January 1795 were veterans of the 'First of June' and its immediate aftermath.

HMS Alexander was itself captured later the same year, following a battle off the coast of Brittany. The *Letters* begins with this battle, referring us also to the more detailed account written by his commanding officer, Admiral Richard Bligh, and published in the official government *Gazette* (see Appendix 2).

Tench was taken prisoner on 6 November 1794; or – we might more appropriately say – on 16 Brumaire, Year III. The new Republican Calendar had started time afresh, measuring it not from the birth of Christ but from the birth of the Republic on 22 September 1792. The new Republican years were secular, divided into ten equal months that honoured, in quasi-classical fashion, nature and the agricultural seasons.

Tench, a fluent French speaker, was quickly appointed '*aid de camp* [sic] *and interpreter*' to Bligh (p. 22). But he was not moving into a familiar French world; rather, it was a new Republican world with its own meanings and terminology (what Tench calls 'the vocabulary of French patriotism', p. 81). Moreover, the French Republic was not a securely established new world: it was itself subject to radical, repeated and unpredictable transformation. Indeed, in one important respect Tench did not arrive into a French world at all. When he tried to talk to a group of Breton country people on the coast near Quimper, he found that they 'conversed entirely in the Breton language, the sound of which, had I not forcibly felt from other circumstances where I was, would have made me swear I was in Wales'. He found, 'upon trial, that not one in ten of the peasants could speak French, or even understand it when spoken to them' (p. 59).

It was three months after his capture before Tench and his fellow officers were taken ashore. His first five letters are dated from ships in

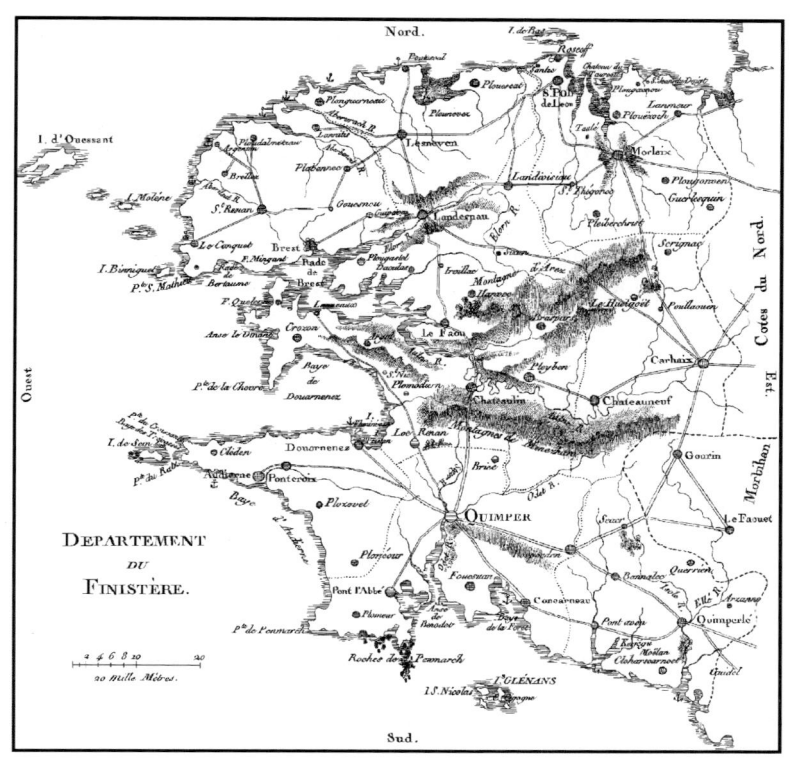

Plate 2: Map of 'Département du Finistère', from Jacques Cambry, *Voyage dans le Finistère ou état de ce département en 1794 et 1795* (1799). Source: Private collection of D. Guillou-Beuzit.

Brest harbour, *le Marat* and *le Normandie*. Then, in mid-February 1795, Tench and Bligh were taken in a small boat round the coast of Brittany and up the river Odet to Quimper, recently designated as the principal town of the new 'department' of Finistère. The reason they were taken by boat was probably that the overland route might not be safe. From 1792 to 1795 rural areas of the north-west were the principal locations of popular French counter-revolution. Tench's letters from Quimper report news and rumours of the struggle between Republican forces and the so-called Chouan guerrillas or their allies in the department of La Vendée immediately to the south. Furthermore, the coast of Brittany was the most likely (or, in Tench's mistaken view, the no longer likely) point on the French coast at which the British

INTRODUCTION

might try to land their own or *émigré* forces so as to link up with internal counter-revolutionaries.

Quimper seems to have been, as Tench asserts, the main holding place for prisoners of war from the western departments. When he arrived in early 1795, there were between 2,000 and 3,000 of them, kept in what had been an Ursuline convent on the edge of the town, suffering hunger, disease and the bitter cold of 'le grand hiver', the coldest winter of the century.[6] However, while Tench reports on these conditions and on attempts to ameliorate them, he did not suffer them himself. Tench and Bligh were comfortably lodged, with their servants, in the house of a Mademoiselle Brimaudière, and allowed considerable freedom of movement in the town and the Breton-speaking hinterland. Finally, after lengthy negotiations for an exchange with French officers of similar rank held in Britain, Tench and Bligh returned home in May 1795. *Letters Written in France to a Friend in London between the month of November 1794 and the month of May 1795* was published later the same year in London by Joseph Johnson. Mary Wollstonecraft's review (see Appendix 3) appeared later in 1796 in Johnson's own journal, the *Analytical Review*.[7]

While *Letters* seems to have marked the end of Tench's career as a writer, his career as a marine continued, first on active service in the Channel and Atlantic fleets, subsequently on home duties in Chatham, Portsmouth and Plymouth. On the *Alexander*, Tench had been a major, the highest rank available to a marine on active service at that time; he ended his career as lieutenant-general, commander of the Plymouth Division of what had by then become (in 1802) the Royal Marines. He died at Devonport on 7 May 1833.

THE LETTERS

Tench's two New South Wales books, while based on his journals, had taken the form of two continuous narratives written from single points of hindsight. However, the *Narrative* had been wholly written in New South Wales (Tench sent the manuscript back to London while he stayed in the colony) and it is evident that a stable position of narrative hindsight had been hard to establish.[8] By changing, in his third book, to the letter form, he is able to dispense with that point of hindsight so as to foreground the contingency and unpredictability of Revolutionary events. The earlier books, it could be said, described 'what I did',

xx

INTRODUCTION

whereas *Letters* describes 'what I did', 'what I have been doing' and even 'what I am doing'. Letters, that is to say, can foreground the present and allow for a direct expression of the author's immediate responses to events in the way that continuous narrative cannot. Furthermore, a part of that present is the present of letter-writing itself. Although the New South Wales books had been written in the first person, they had represented 'I' the marine, but not 'I' the writer. The letter-form draws our attention – as it does in the great epistolary novels of the eighteenth century – to the actual work of writing the letters ('under very adverse circumstances') and of sending them to the 'friend in London'. The correspondence becomes part of the story, sharing in and helping to dramatize the unpredictability of the events it records.

Tench tells us in his Preface that: 'Since his [the author's] return to England they [the letters] have been revised; and would have been earlier sent to the press, had not reasons of a private nature interposed to procrastinate his intention' (p. 3). Should we believe him? Or did that gap allow for more than revision? Are these revised versions of actual letters, or have they been written up as letters from a journal, addressed not to 'Dear Friend' but to 'Dear Diary'? The fact that the 'friend' to whom they are addressed emerges as a serviceman with experiences and interests very like Tench's own can be read either way, as evidence for or against that man's real existence; as can the opening of Letter II, dated 'Normandie, prison-ship, in Brest-Water, 1st Dec. 1794':

> I must continue to write on to you, as if I had the means of regularly transmitting my letters. In the horrid dungeon in which I am now immured, it forms my only consolation to talk to you, although you cannot hear me; and to complain to you, although you cannot succour me. (p. 19)

This uncharacteristic moment of Gothic sensibility is evidently written by a reader of epistolary novels, a fact which however makes it neither more nor less likely to be a fictional contrivance. The passage may be a hint that the letters were all in fact addressed to himself as an imaginary 'friend', but we cannot be sure of this. As Adrian Mitchell has shown,[9] Tench's New South Wales books do display considerable literary contrivance, while the artful imitation of non-fictional verisimilitude is a favourite occupation of eighteenth-century writers.[10]

While Tench's very realistic stress on the hazards of postal communication makes the apparently successful arrival of all his letters in

INTRODUCTION

London something of a miracle, there is certainly evidence that such letters could reach their destination. A letter survives from Sarah Fish, poignantly addressed to her husband 'Captain George Fish, prisener [*sic*] of war in Brest Castle, or elsewhere, Brest', and dated 'yarmouth, march 6 1775'. It begins:

> my dear George, this is to inform you that I received your melancholy letter and was wretched to hear of your deplorable situation but Bless God I know from Glies [Giles] and French Letter that you are removed to Brest prison and that I hope you are better of [off] than when you was on board the ship.[11]

This probably tells us that a letter could get through to England from a prison ship in Brest harbour. But the fact that Sarah's own letter survives in the Finistère Archives at Quimper suggests that her husband George did not receive it. Communication was evidently possible but accident-prone. In only one case do we have reasonably firm evidence that a Tench letter was written and sent: the final letter from Quimper is to be delivered, he tells us, by his fellow lodger at Mademoiselle Brimaudière's, Captain Robinson, on the latter's forthcoming return to England. We know about Robinson from other sources and it is most improbable that Tench would have invented this particular piece of postage.[12]

My own view is that *Letters* is indeed based on letters written in France which Tench sent or tried to send to a friend in London, but copies of which he also kept with him. He had, I believe, the possibility of publication in mind from the start (God willing) and (again, God willing) the desirability of subsequent revision. But the point to emphasize is that Tench has not simply decided to publish some private letters. An established author, who had made arrangements with a publisher before he embarked for New South Wales in 1787, it is very likely that he would have seen the commercial possibilities again as soon as he was captured in November 1794. Mary Wollstonecraft describes Tench as writing 'with the cheerful ease, and in the agreeable and unaffected style, that distinguishes the author and the gentleman'. He is indeed self-consciously an 'author'. These are the letters of a 'man of letters' who draws attention, at the start of his book, to two great predecessors as soldier-storyteller, Caesar and Othello.

As for more specific models, Tench may well have known some of the early volumes of Helen Maria Williams's letters from France, published

xxii

INTRODUCTION

in Britain between 1790 and 1796, perhaps particularly (as a model for his title), the first of them, *Letters Written in France, in the Summer of 1790, to a Friend in England* (Joseph Johnson, 1790). However, Tench's book does not often, as Williams's earlier volumes do, use letters as 'registers for the movement of the heart', of private emotional rather than public political turbulence.[13] Neither is he, unlike Williams and unlike the Wollstonecraft of *Letters Written During a Short Residence in Sweden, Norway and Denmark* (Joseph Johnson, 1796), interested in natural description, either for its own sake or as metaphor for psychic and political forces.[14] Consequently – and since Tench defends the poetry of Alexander Pope against the modern cult of sensibility – a more important model may have been the *Turkish Embassy Letters* (1763) of Pope's friend and correspondent Lady Mary Wortley Montagu, those 'sprightly letters' as Tench had called them in his *Account* (*Sydney's First Four Years*, p. 106).

THE REVOLUTION

Letters Written in France to a Friend in London between the month of November 1794 and the month of May 1795 and *Letters Written in France, in the Summer of 1790, to a Friend in England* announce themselves in their titles as the work of what we would call 'foreign correspondents', first-hand reports on a foreign country undergoing rapid, radical and truly world-shaking transformation. These books are published in a context, that is to say, in which the naming of a particular year, season and month is immediately and vividly informative to their contemporary readers. For modern readers, however, this is unlikely to be the case. So that while Tench's book itself provides some of the historical context in which it can be understood and enjoyed, his picture of the Revolution will benefit from reframing so as to illuminate parts which might otherwise remain obscure.

The French Revolution is now commonly thought of as having three principal phases. The first phase, inaugurated in 1789 with the declaration of the National Assembly and the storming of the Bastille, established a constitutional monarchy, abolished feudal privileges and promulgated the Declaration of the Rights of Man and the Citizen. In religion, the Civil Constitution of the Clergy limited the power of the Pope over the Church in France and required all clergy to swear an oath of allegiance to the state.

INTRODUCTION

The Revolution's second phase is associated with the growth of an artisan-based popular movement and control of the state by the radical Jacobin faction with their Montagnard allies. Their rivals, the Girondins (or Brissotins as they were then generally known) were defeated, the monarchy abolished and the monarch himself guillotined. A secular Republic was established. The twin threats of invasion from without and counter-revolution from within then led to the introduction of the highly centralized and often ruthless system known – to its supporters as well as its opponents – as the Terror. This phase of the Revolution is associated with powerful individual revolutionaries, notably Robespierre, Marat and Danton, and with the establishment of a range of new governing institutions: the National Convention; the Committee of Public Safety and the local Committees of Surveillance; and the Representatives on Mission (delegates sent into the regions and into the branches of the armed services to enforce the will of the Convention).

The third phase of the Revolution was inaugurated by the overthrow of Robespierre on 27 July 1794 (or 9 Thermidor) and can be thought of as ending with the downfall of the Convention itself in October 1795. In this period the institutions of the Jacobin Terror – the Committees of Public Safety and Surveillance, the Representatives on Mission, the Convention itself – survived, but the personnel and policies changed. Terror was gradually wound back, or turned against the radicals in a 'white terror'. The surviving Girondin deputies (including the Breton deputy Kervélégan whom Tench meets in Quimper in January 1795) returned to the Convention. There was a move, in economic and social terms, to the right, as price controls on basic foods were lifted. Freedom of religious worship was haltingly restored.

It is from this third period – sometimes known, like its inaugurating moment, as 'Thermidor' – that Tench's letters send back their report. But of course periodizations of this sort always involve simplification and, for the people involved, such periods may only become visible as such in retrospect, if at all. There was no knowing at the time that 9 Thermidor would inaugurate what is now called the 'Thermidoran reaction', that the fall of Robespierre would lead to the collapse of Jacobin power. Although Robespierre was being universally disparaged by Tench's captors when the latter was taken prisoner on 6 November 1794, and the Jacobin Club in Paris was closed a week later on 12 November, it was another five weeks before Tench noticed a change of the official line on board *le Marat*:

INTRODUCTION

> When we were taken, I was perpetually stunned with the exclamations of "*Vive la Montagne! Vivent les Jacobins!*" But suddenly, *La Montagne* is become the theme of execration, and the Jacobin club is cashiered . . . I had observed the disuse of these ridiculous cries for some days, and had overheard a conversation which had raised my suspicions. To ascertain their justness, I bade one of the boys call out as before. "Ah!" said he, "that is forbidden; *à présent il faut crier, au diable la Montagne! A bas les Jacobins!*" which he immediately ran along the deck exclaiming. (p. 42)

It is precisely the volatility and unpredictability of events which Tench evokes so powerfully, in a situation where a new balance of forces is not clearly established. While Tench is in Quimper, the policy of 'dechristianization' is being partially reversed, but the convent is still being used as a prison, the bishop's house as a tavern and as the office of the Representatives on Mission: these buildings do not revert to their original ecclesiastical owners or uses. The cathedral is open for worship, but it still has the Robespierrist slogan, 'the People of France recognize the Supreme Being' over the main entrance and it is still not wholly clear who controls this important symbolic space:

> I went upon Easter Sunday to the cathedral, and found a numerous congregation there. The altar was lighted up by twelve large waxen tapers; the holy water was sprinkled upon the congregants; and the incense was burnt, with the accustomed ceremonies; but even here democratic spleen manifested itself in disturbing what it is no longer allowed to interdict. In the most solemn part of the service, the *Marseillois Hymn* was heard from the organ . . . How incongruous were its notes in the temple of the Prince of Peace! A blackguard-looking fellow close to me, whom I knew, by his uncombed hair, dirty linen, ragged attire, and contemptuous gestures, to be a *veritable sans-culotte*, joined his voice to the music, and echoed, "*Aux armes, citoyens!*" Fear alone kept the people quiet; and of its influence in this country I have witnessed astonishing proofs, which demonstrate, beyond volumes of reasoning, the terror inspired by the revolutionary government. (pp. 123–4)

Tench survived the bloodshed on the *Alexander*, and avoided the brutal incarceration of his fellow prisoners of war in Quimper. What he records are relationships in which insecurity and animosity are intensified by the fear of a violence temporarily in abeyance; a situation in which it is hard to know to which faction it is safest to belong, or whose past Jacobin affiliations will catch up with them. He deciphers the word 'Montagne' through a coat of whitewash on the Statue of Liberty in the market-place at Quimper. Some of the people Tench meets are engaged in similar attempts to cover their tracks. In some cases we have information unavailable to Tench which illuminates the difficult positions in which people could find themselves. Three crucial figures in this respect are Captain Le Franq, who appears in the first letter as Tench's captor; Le Franq's commander, Admiral Villaret-Joyeuse, whom Tench admires and eventually meets in Brest; and Jean Bon Saint-André, the Montagnard Representative on Mission to Brest (gone by the time of Tench's capture, but not forgotten). It is intriguing how these men flit in and out of the pages of Tench's book.

TENCH'S 'POLITICAL PRINCIPLES'

Although Tench vividly communicates the uncertainties of the present, he has a very clear conception of the Revolution's past as dividing into two distinct stages. And while he evokes the transformations of popular opinion, he distinguishes sharply between 'the versatile levity of sentiment' among the French (p. 118) and the constancy of his own 'political principles'. These principles, he tells his friend, are

> unchanged since we parted; and I still think a limited monarchy the best of governments. Had I been born a Frenchman, I should have struggled as hard for the revolution of 1789, as I should have resisted with all my might that of 1792. Much as I hate despotism, I am scarcely less a foe to democracy . . . (p. 100)

In important respects these principles – support for the Revolution of 1789, opposition to the Revolution of 1792 – were commonplace in propertied Britain. They rested upon a commitment to the system of constitutional monarchy established, in the aftermath of the Civil War, by the 'Glorious Revolution' of 1688, a settlement which avoided, its supporters thought, the twin dangers of 'tyranny' and 'democracy' in the state, just as the established Anglican Church could be thought to avoid the twin extremes of Protestant dissent and Roman Catholicism.

But Tench's formulation of these principles is in some respects distinctive. For one thing, writing in 1795, the events of the second Revolution – including the Terror – have not in any way reduced his enthusiasm for the first Revolution, as they did for many propertied people of his broadly Whiggish sympathies. Where Edmund Burke's

INTRODUCTION

Reflections on the Revolution in France (1790) seemed to many such people, by 1795, to have been prophetic in its lurid picture of 1789, Tench believes (with justice) that Burke helped to bring about that radicalization of the Revolution which he claimed only to foresee.

Furthermore, when Tench talks about 'principles' he is talking about principles of action. He immediately thinks not about which side he would have sympathized with in 1789 and 1792 but which side, as a Frenchman, he would have 'struggled' for or 'resisted'. Tench is not just a thinker who happens also to be a military man: he thinks as an active citizen, and specifically as an officer responsible for the deployment of armed force in the public interest. This is a self-consciously 'Roman' posture on Tench's part. He is self-consciously committed to the civic and martial values of classical republicanism as he, like many Whigs, believed these had been embodied, since 1688, in Britain's mixed government of king, lords and commons. He is correspondingly conscious – as I believe his references to Oliver Cromwell and the Restoration of Charles II make clear – that the 'Revolution of 1792' in France has reopened the breach between Monarchism and Republicanism which the 'Revolution' of 1688 in Britain seemed to have closed.[15]

Wollstonecraft complains that 'some of his [Tench's] conclusions are drawn with that hastiness, and that careless ease, for which military men are so often remarkable' (p. 172). And we know what she means, when we read his irritatingly habitual anti-democratic ironies at the expense of plebeian militants – *sans-culottes* – or the '*bourgeois* . . . tinkers and taylors' (p. 129) of the local militias and popular societies. His military character is nevertheless also what gives Tench's book its special place – including, I would argue, its ethical force – in the British literature of what has come to be called the Romantic period.

It is a commonplace – and a largely true one – that British writing produced in the period of the Revolution and the war reflected these upheavals, but did so with very different degrees of explicitness. Many novels of the 1790s have been called 'jacobin' or 'anti-jacobin', linked in sometimes explicit fashion to the political pamphlet wars associated, most influentially, with Edmund Burke and Tom Paine. Even Jane Austen's novels, it has been argued, while they were published two decades later and are far less explicitly political, should be seen in the context of the 1790s, the period of Austen's literary apprenticeship. So that novels which can look to modern readers like studies of manners and moral conduct without historically specific political implication, would have been read by her contemporaries in a political light.[16] As

xxvii

INTRODUCTION

for the poets – on whose work from about 1796 the idea of a Romantic period is principally based – it is widely argued that it was the traumatizing effect of the Revolution and the war which produced a cultural revolution, turning poets decisively away from the dramatic and narrative world of human action and towards the lyric worlds of nature and inner feeling. Wordsworth's poems in particular are now widely read as if they had the collective sub-title, 'poems not about the French Revolution'.

Tench's *Letters* has a unique importance in this literary-political context. Not only is it the only substantial work of the period to record and reflect upon the Revolution and the war from the point of view of an active participant in the fighting; it does so in ways which directly complement and illuminate the more familiar texts. For instance, his political judgements on what he sees in France are in fact made on the basis of moral judgements of personal character which resemble Jane Austen's, but with the political implications of such judgements made explicit. Moreover, in the first half of his book (in the letters written on board *le Marat* and *le Normandie*) he makes these judgements in and about precisely the kind of exclusively male world which Austen chose not to represent but the absence of which she makes so palpable.

Tench explains to his friend that, although he believes 'a limited monarchy the best of governments', he will judge the French system by the personal conduct of its proponents: 'your friend', he writes,

> will not yield his assent to new systems, until he has, at least, scrutinized and weighed their effects upon those who inculcate and practice them; and if, upon this test, he finds the professors of these doctrines to be men of profligate manners and corrupted sentiments, with the words truth, honour, humanity, and generosity in their mouths, while they are estranged from their hearts, you will not suppose his danger of conversion to be imminent. (pp. 41–2)

Many of the French naval officers do turn out to be men of 'corrupted sentiments', a condition linked, in Tench's view, to their 'manners' in a more restricted sense:

> Having established it as a maxim that some degree of information may always be gained by talking to men of their own professions, I am as inquisitive as I modestly can be, about their naval institutions. But, if my question be heard by more than one, such shocking abrupt oppositions of

INTRODUCTION

opinions follow, and so pertinaciously does each party defend his assertion on the most ordinary points, that my only alternative, to prevent a perfect equilibrium of mind, is to place the little confidence left at my disposal in the champion who has been least violent and vociferous . . . (p. 14)

Readers of *Mansfield Park* (1814) may be reminded here of Fanny Price's return to her parents' home in Portsmouth with an ideal of the conversational courtesies of Mansfield Park in her mind. And of course Fanny Price's home is a naval one in a naval town. It is men of Mr Price's class who have displaced the nobly born officer-class of the pre-Revolutionary French navy: Mr Price who had 'no information beyond his profession' and who 'swore and drank'.[17] While Tench is surprised and shocked by their conduct, he clearly has strategies, as a gentleman, for dealing with these people. He has met them before, possibly in Portsmouth, but not in the officers' mess.

Tench sees the dangers of democracy in what he calls the 'democratic manners' of the Commissary of Prisoners at Quimper, whom he refers to contemptuously as '*Citoyen* Precini'. In a remarkable passage (which Wollstonecraft quotes in full) Tench describes Precini's appearance at a carnival-week party where people of bitterly opposed political views are gathered together:

At one of these routs I saw a specimen of genuine democratic manners, which all who aim to become great men in the state affect to imitate. The commissary of prisoners, a man allied to nobility, liberally educated, and once an Abbé, bolted into the room where the company were assembled, humming the *Carmagnole*, with his hat on, which was adorned with a red, a white, and a blue feather, and his hands stuck in his breeches, *not pockets*. In this attitude he stood all the evening, and thrusting himself among the ladies, had the impudence to enter into familiar conversation with the Marchioness de Ploeuc, and other women of rank and delicacy, with all the airs which conscious superiority of power can instil into a reptile. This brutal manner of mingling in society, and addressing women, has become, since the revolution, the *ton* of republican coxcombs, and during the reign of Robespierre set decorum and the restraints of civilized life at defiance. It is now on the decline, except with those who still court the applause of the dregs of that faction. A courtier of Versailles at his toilet, surrounded by paints, patches, and perfumery, was, in the eye of reason, a ridiculous and contemptible animal; but the most effeminate essenced *marquis*, that ever consulted a looking-glass, was surely preferable to this indecent blockhead. (pp. 65–6)

INTRODUCTION

The Commissary of Prisoners is presented to us as a carnival figure, or a figure from political street-theatre, 'held up in effigy' as Wollstonecraft approvingly puts it. But this is not only a powerfully venomous political caricature, it also defines, negatively, the English gentleman and the nation of which the gentleman is the ideal representative.

Tench asks us to look at the courtier of Versailles with 'the eye of reason', but that eye is really focusing this whole scene. It is the eye, supposedly, of dispassionate analysis, and consequently likely to appeal to a writer in the *Analytical Review*. Nevertheless, Tench's 'reason' is not the deified Reason which had been worshipped in Quimper's Temple of Reason on the 'Plateau de la déesse Raison' in Year II. In the context of Tench's caricature, 'reason' is English, 'Reason' is French. This English 'reason' has a lot to do with being reasonable: it is defined less by any specific positive features than by its avoidance of various extreme positions with regard to class, gender and political ideology. And as we enumerate these extreme positions, the person who emerges with the best claim to the 'eye of reason' is the English gentleman.

This English gentleman is defined as being neither a vulgar *sans-culotte* in the manner aped by the well-born Precini, nor exclusively aristocratic in the manner of the courtier at Versailles. The concept of a gentleman is indeed not a class concept, but a concept which derives its meaning from its relationship to class and its ability to facilitate mediation and movement between different propertied classes. Furthermore, a gentleman is very much a man; but he is properly manly, which means avoiding the effeminacy of the 'courtier at Versailles at his toilet' on the one hand and, on the other hand, the machismo of the indecent, thrusting Precini with 'his hands stuck in his breeches, *not pockets*'. As for the political posture commended by reason and adopted by the English, it is the commitment to a balanced constitution, one which is neither absolutist (the aristocrat reduced to a courtier at Versailles) nor egalitarian (the 'democratic manners' of the Republican officers on *le Marat* all speaking at once). The threads of class, gender and ideology are perfectly combined here to produce the English gentleman as a seamless garment.

Should we also call him the British gentleman? Tench himself usually refers to his homeland as 'England', but sometimes uses 'Britain' and 'British'. Linda Colley, in her influential book *Britons: Forging the Nation 1707–1837* argues that it was indeed in the eighteenth century, following the Act of Union which joined Scotland to England and Wales in 1707, that a distinctly British national identity

INTRODUCTION

was formed. And it was formed above all, she argues, by a succession of wars with absolutist and Catholic France which 'brought Britons, whether they hailed from Wales or Scotland or England, into conflict with an obviously hostile Other and encouraged them to define themselves collectively against it'.[18] As we have seen, Tench's participation in these wars defined his adult life. With his belief in limited monarchy, Protestant religion, the rule of law and commercial and intellectual innovation, Tench does embody a powerful British eighteenth-century self-image. And if the identity of Britain and the British gentleman was always essentially relational – defined by its difference from a French 'Other' – then Tench, arriving in France, is encountering directly the source of his own and his nation's identity.

Travel writing almost always foregrounds questions of identity, but it usually does so in two opposite ways, confirming but also questioning those identities that are already established. Tench's *Letters* certainly does both to a remarkable degree. The description of Precini – like the French satirical prints of the British which decorate *le Marat* (Letter I, p. 13) – works to draw 'us' together by exaggerating the gap between 'us' and 'them'. From the description of Precini it would seem that Tench, finding himself in the land of the Other, of 'them', has his sense of that gap powerfully renewed. But this is not the only effect of finding himself 'in a part of France remote from the beaten track in which travellers generally keep' (p. 3). Finding himself in a part of France where many people do not speak French, he is reminded of a part of Britain that is not English. In a similar way, he knows how to deal with the strange behaviour of French Republican officers because it is the familiar behaviour of British men of their class. Differences of class and language cut across those of nation, making 'us' different from ourselves and simultaneously revealing affiliations between us and them.

Linda Colley's version of the dominant British self-image links political liberty, Protestantism and enlightenment. It is a linkage to which Tench was powerfully attached, identifying 'Popery' with 'the sloth, the ignorance and the bigotry' of Rio de Janeiro in the *Narrative of the Expedition to Botany Bay*.[19] But his experience of anti-clerical French Republicanism breaks those links. About a month before the Easter service in the cathedral, the sound of the organ had drawn Tench in to what may have been the first service there since the Terror:

> I... found mass celebrating in the presence of a congregation consisting chiefly of poor people from the country, with a few of the higher ranks,

many more of whom, I was assured, would have been there, could they have believed themselves secure from reproach; but the return of religious worship was yet too young for them to incur the risk . . . I walked the whole length of the church, through rows of people on their knees, which formerly might have been deemed disrespect in a heretic; but I now met with nothing but courtesy and regard, all seeming conscious that the basis of their persuasion and mine was the same, however we might differ in external forms of adoration. (p. 71)

The regrouping of people and the regrouping of ideological elements are two sides of the same coin. The bond between Protestantism, political liberty and enlightenment – which had seemed so natural to Tench a short time before – has been weakened; as has the corresponding bond between Roman Catholicism, tyranny and obscurantism. Here too, in a religious context – as elsewhere with respect to language and class – we can see Tench's experience of the Revolution in Brittany loosening the threads of an established British identity.

And if we bring other knowledge (some of it provided by Tench, some not) to bear on this episode in the cathedral we can see that the ideological realignment is itself underpinned – but also complicated – by the threads of linguistic affiliation that link and separate the different people in the building. The languages of the service would almost certainly be Latin (the language of the sacraments) and French (the language of the sermon) while the 'poor people from the country' would mostly be monoglot Breton-speakers. It is therefore possible that Tench, the Anglican Englishman outsider, is one of the few people in the cathedral who can understand what is being said there.

This scene in the cathedral presents us with a characteristically vivid and evanescent kaleidoscope of people and affiliations. By the time of the Easter service four weeks later the cathedral kaleidoscope has been given another shake: the composition of the congregation has clearly altered, with the Breton-speaking country people departed to illegal ceremonies conducted by non-juring priests (the so-called 'refractories') in private houses (p. 123).

TENCH'S REPUBLICANISM

Despite the insistence on the constancy of his own principles, the letter-form in which he has chosen to write helps to expose the shifts and conflicts in Tench's position as well as in those of the French. He writes as a British officer and gentleman of Anglican and liberal Whig persuasion, and a confident embodiment of his nation. But if this identity is sometimes strengthened in Quimper, it is also sometimes put in question: strengthened when (faced by the 'democratic manners' of Citizen Precini) its elements are confirmed as naturally and inevitably linked; questioned when (in the cathedral) Tench experiences the contingency of those links. But it is French Republicanism which poses the most powerful challenge to the coherence of his own position. In this context, when he refers to the possibility of his 'conversion' to the French 'system', his irony is very defensive, if it is irony at all.

In the Dedication of the *Account of the Settlement at Port Jackson* Tench expressed the hope that the young Sir Watkin Williams Wynn (then aged seventeen) would, like his father before him, 'shine incorrupt and independent in the senate' (*Sydney's First Four Years*, p. 126). Tench is not a patrician – he is speaking across a class divide that is wide and acknowledged – but he is nevertheless speaking as one classically educated gentleman to another, from one part of Britain to another, and on the basis of a shared commitment to the values of liberty and independence – embodied in the Roman senate and the British parliament – which distinguishes Protestant Britain from the absolutist rulers of Catholic Europe and their courtier aristocracies. The values of the Roman Republic are embodied, for Tench, in the British system of constitutional monarchy. But the French Republicans look to the same model. They are rivals for the same Roman mantle. And while Tench's republicanism is quite different from the strictly anti-monarchist republicanism of the French revolutionaries, his is not a position from which such a republic can be condemned out of hand. Indeed, in his own century the Dutch republic was widely admired by enlightened gentlemen who were, within Britain, fully committed to their own constitutional monarchy.

Sharing the same ancient model, Tench normally deals with French Republicanism by assessing the personal qualities and abilities of French republicans and, normally, finding them wanting: 'This people possesses not the stability of character, or the austere self-denying virtues, of the ancient republicans' (p. 121). A republican worthy of the name must, for Tench, combine certain qualities, qualities which are in fact very like those required of a gentleman. For one thing, a real British gentleman like a Roman republican but unlike the new naval-officer class on *le Marat* and *le Normandie*, knows Latin. French Republicanism is represented as a vulgar travesty of the values it claims to uphold: such is the republicanism of the Parisian barber who sits in the Assembly under the name of Brutus (p. 98).

A second response to the neo-classicism of French Republican culture – a response which appears in his discussion of the arts – is to ignore it altogether. Instead, he links the spread of 'gothicism' in France at the expense of the work of Racine and Boileau, on the one hand to the belittling of Alexander Pope in England, and on the other hand to revolutionary politics. What links these tendencies for Tench is the threat which they all supposedly pose to order and restraint: a belief in 'fiery fancy' in the arts is linked to incendiarism in politics.

Tench's commitment to an aesthetic of order and restraint is certainly backed by his own habits of literary allusion. He frequently quotes poetry, and does so often at moments of emotional intensity (the allusions to Milton in his description of the bloody scene in the cockpit of the *Alexander* is a powerful case in point); but while he goes to poetry to help him express feeling, it is to a kind of poetry – dramatic and epic, not lyric – which also controls individual feeling by submitting it to the disciplines of a continuing narrative of public action.

The idea that there is a necessary link between a 'classical' aesthetic of order and restraint and an anti-revolutionary politics is familiar from English literary historiography, which has often, correspondingly, associated 'romanticism and revolt'. However, while such associations can be made to fit some of the British facts, they make very little sense when carried across the Channel to France where the dominant revolutionary aesthetic was precisely an austere neo-classicism. The connection between a style of art and a style of politics suggested by the phrase 'fiery fancy' would find it hard to account for the austerely neo-classical paintings of the Jacobin painter J. L. David.

Nevertheless, there is always, alongside the attempt to denigrate or to ignore the classicism of the Revolution, a part of Watkin Tench which does wish to find in France a republicanism worthy of the name. At a public meeting called to discuss measures to be taken against surviving Jacobin 'terrorists', he hears among the 'orators' a blacksmith who 'was universally allowed to bear away the palm, haranguing with great fluency against the terrorists, and surprising his auditors by the keenness of his sarcasms, and the justness of his observations' (p. 112). This blacksmith – an artisan articulately espousing a constitutional republicanism – unlinks the elements soldered confidently together by the phrase 'democratic manners', demonstrating that a particular social class, a particular political position and a particular

INTRODUCTION

cultural style do not always and necessarily go together. Unlinking these elements, the blacksmith walks off with the classical 'palm' which Tench may have intended only ironically to offer him.

However, that is a brief break in the chain. In general, 'artisans and *sans-culottes*' (to borrow Gwyn A. Williams's cross-channel expression[20]) are not regarded by Tench as proper participants in public political life. It is when, in Brest, he meets republicans in positions of authority who are trustworthy, courteous, well-educated and in some cases nobly born – 'gentlemanly', in fact – that we can see, retrospectively, how much Tench has wanted to find them. Admiral Villaret-Joyeuse is an obvious case, but the meeting with Representative Champeaux, with its allusion to the seventeenth-century Dutch republic, is especially telling:

> At a few minutes before six on the following day I renewed my visit, and waited but a short time before I was admitted to Monsieur Champeaux. He was sitting in his office, in an elbow-chair, dressed in a flannel jacket abominably filthy, and smoking a short black pipe, exactly such an one as the old women in Ireland carry about in their mouths. It brought to my mind Sir William Temple's descriptions of those old burgomasters, who formerly, with so much plainness, wisdom, and integrity, conducted the affairs of the Batavian republic. (p. 132)

At this point it is possible to say that as an Englishman Tench still believes a constitutional monarchy to be the best of all systems, but that as a Frenchman he would probably have struggled for the Republic of 1795.

This is not, I believe, the only moment when Tench can imagine himself fighting for the other side. He is clearly identifying with the black slaves of the West Indies when he describes 'the resistance of a million of men, suddenly awakened to a perception of their rights' (p. 108). The brief comments on slavery in Tench's *Account* of 1793 stood out for their intensity, and the same is true of his brief comments on the topic in the *Letters*. But between 1793 and 1796 the French Republic had abolished slavery in its own territories and allied itself with slave rebellion, putting a patriotic and disciplined British military man like Tench on a collision course with the enlightened principles he thinks of as peculiarly British.[21]

Major Watkin Tench was in many respects a conventional man. But he was a conventional man of intelligence, writing – in New South Wales and France – from circumstances of exposure and upheaval which put the range of conventional eighteenth-century attitudes to which he was attached under unprecedented strain. He presents himself as a man proud to serve a Britain defined by its limited monarchy, Protestant religion, legal equality, ideals of civic duty and of commercial and intellectual innovation. Servant of an imperial power, he wished to see these British values spread around the globe. However, he was increasingly faced with situations in which those cherished values were at odds with one another; in which, for instance, British commercial advantage was in conflict – as he feared it might be in the West Indies – with equality before the law. His commitment to enlightened British principles (and 'enlightened' is a favourite word) is matched by a feeling (which can also be found in the European Enlightenment) for the distinctive strengths of other peoples and systems, a feeling which frequently leads him to doubt the practicability or propriety of British policy in practice, whether in New South Wales, the West Indies or France.

Notes

1. *Gentleman's Magazine*, June 1796, p. 506. For a modern French account of the treatment of French and British prisoners of war, see Philippe Masson, *Les sépulcres flottants: Prisonniers français en Angleterre sous l'Empire* (Brest: editions ouest-France, 1987).
2. *1788*, comprising 'A Narrative of the Expedition to Botany Bay' and 'A Complete Account of the Settlement at Port Jackson' by Watkin Tench, edited and introduced by Tim Flannery (Melbourne: Text Publishing Company, 1996).
3. Excerpts from *Letters Written in France* (hereafter referred to as *Letters*) were included in *English Witnesses of the French Revolution*, edited by J. M. Thompson (Oxford: Basil Blackwell, 1938), pp. 257–62.
4. *Sydney's First Four Years, being a reprint of 'A Narrative of the Expedition to Botany Bay' and 'A Complete Account of the Settlement at Port Jackson' by Captain Watkin Tench of the Marines*, edited by L. F. Fitzhardinge (Sydney: Library of Australian History, 1979, p. 126). All quotations from Tench's two New South Wales books (hereafter *Narrative* and *Account*) are taken from this edition. We get a sense of Tench's Welsh connection from the subscribers' list printed with the *Account* in 1793. Apart from a large number of London-based subscribers, the names are concentrated in the English west (from Liverpool to Cornwall) and north Wales, with Chester and its immediate environs predominating. The names from Wales include prominent members of the English-speaking or bilingual gentry and their associates: the Williams Wynns (and their steward 'Mr Sidebotham, Wynnstay'), Lord and Lady Penrhyn, Philip Yorke of Erddig, and the antiquarian Thomas Pennant (although this selection of well-known names gives an overly patrician impression of the list).

INTRODUCTION

[5] All page references to *Letters* refer to the present edition.

[6] The fullest account of the prisoners of war at Quimper can be found in Adrien Carré, 'La prison-bagne des marins anglais à Quimper 1794–1796: aspects méconnus de la Révolution en Basse-Bretagne', *Bulletin de la Société archéologique et historique de Nantes et de Loire Atlantique* (1982), pp. 9–37. Prisoners of war were held in the convent building from early 1794 to 1796/7.

[7] A favourable review appeared in the Whiggish *Monthly Review* (May 1796, pp. 62–6) and a brief notice in the conservative *British Critic* (May 1796, pp. 570–1). Tench may have been led to Joseph Johnson as a publisher (and therefore to Wollstonecraft as a reviewer for Johnson's journal) by their common connections to Enlightenment scientific and medical circles in Liverpool and the English north-west, in particular to Thomas Haygarth, principal of Chester Royal Infirmary, campaigner for smallpox inoculation, subscriber to Tench's *Account* and a Johnson author. Johnson, despite his reputation as a publisher for religious dissent and reformist politics, had an ideologically broad list which would easily accommodate Tench. However, Tench's willingness, in the polarized circumstances of 1796, to publish with a so-called 'jacobin' like Johnson suggests an admirable ability to distinguish between Jacobins and 'jacobins' (see letter IV, note 36).

[8] On the difficulty of maintaining this position of narrative hindsight in the circumstances of writing the *Narrative* and the *Account* see Gavin Edwards, 'Watkin Tench and the cold track of narrative', *Southerly*, 60, 3 (2000), pp. 74–93.

[9] Adrian Mitchell, 'Watkin Tench's sentimental enclosures', *Australia and New Zealand Studies in Canada*, 11 (June 1994), pp. 23–33.

[10] The possibility that Tench is engaged in the simulation of non-fiction would be increased if it could be shown that he was the author of the *Fragmens* [sic] *du dernier voyage de la Pérouse* (Quimper: P. M. Barazer, Prairial, an V [1797]). A French scientific expedition under Jean-François de Galaup, Comte de La Pérouse (1741–?1788), left Brest on 1 August 1785, encountered the British at Botany Bay in January 1788 and subsequently disappeared in the South Seas. The anonymous 'fragment of the last voyage of La Pérouse' was supposedly stolen from a French officer at Botany Bay in 1788 by an English sailor who claims (in an introduction to the volume) to have 'accompanied captain Watkin-Tenck [sic] on board the Astrolabe'. The catalogue of the Bibliothèque Nationale identifies the editor as the francophone Breton writer Jacques Cambry and a good argument has been made for Cambry being the author of the *Fragmens* itself (see Jacques Gury, 'En marge d'une expédition scientifique: *Fragments du dernier voyage de La Pérouse* [1797]' (the *Fragmens* is reprinted with Gury's essay), *Dix-Huitième siècle*, 22 (1990), pp. 195–237). Cambry would know about

INTRODUCTION

Tench, and his meeting with La Pérouse, through Pougens's 1789 translation of the *Narrative of the Expedition to Botany Bay*; nevertheless, since Cambry was apparently visiting Quimper when Tench was there (during the early months of 1795) it is hard to believe that some sort of transaction did not take place between the two men (see Jacques Cambry, *Voyage dans le Finistère ou état de ce département en 1794 et 1795*, edited by D. Guillou-Beuzit (1799; Quimper: Société archéologique du Finistère, 1999, p. xli); John Dunmore, 'Utopie française, auteur anglais?', *Dix-Huitième siècle*, 26 (1994), pp. 409–506; and Jacques Gury, '*Fragments* en quête d'auteur', ibid., pp. 507–9).

11 Archives départementales du Finistère, 8 L 82.

12 The fact that Admiral Bligh's letter to Mr Stephens at the Admiralty eventually got through (dated 23 November 1794, arrived 30 January 1795) is probably evidence of official French co-operation, the traditional conventions of war still being followed in this respect.

13 Mary A. Favret, *Romantic Correspondence: Women, Politics and the Fiction of Letters* (Cambridge: Cambridge University Press, 1993), p. 57.

14 See Elizabeth A. Bohls, *Women Travel Writers and the Language of Aesthetics, 1716–1818* (Cambridge: Cambridge University Press, 1995), p. 5.

15 See Mark Philp, 'Republicanism', in *An Oxford Companion to the Romantic Age: British Culture 1776–1832*, edited by Iain McCalman (Oxford: Oxford University Press, 1999), pp. 673–4. Tench's sense of participating in this history may owe something to the fact that he was brought up in the house in which Charles I was thought to have taken refuge during the siege of Chester in 1645 (Hemingway, *History of Chester*, 2, pp. 32–3).

16 See Marilyn Butler, *Jane Austen and the War of Ideas* (Oxford: Oxford University Press, 1975).

17 Jane Austen, *Mansfield Park*, edited by John Lucas (1814; London: Oxford University Press, 1970), p. 354.

18 Linda Colley, *Britons: Forging the Nation, 1707–1837* (New Haven and London: Yale University Press, 1992), p. 5.

19 'Let him who would wish to give his son a distaste to Popery, point out to him the sloth, the ignorance, and the bigotry of this place' (*Sydney's First Four Years*, p. 24).

20 Gwyn A. Williams, *Artisans and Sans-Culottes: Popular Movements in France and Britain during the French Revolution* (London: Arnold, 1968).

21 Napoleon restored French colonial slavery in 1802, so that the politics of slavery have changed significantly by the time Fanny Price asks Sir Thomas Bertram about his Antiguan estates in *Mansfield Park*.

LETTERS

WRITTEN IN FRANCE,

TO A

FRIEND IN LONDON,

BETWEEN THE MONTH OF NOVEMBER 1794,

AND

THE MONTH OF MAY 1795.

By Major TENCH, of the Marines,

LATE OF HIS MAJESTY'S SHIP ALEXANDER.

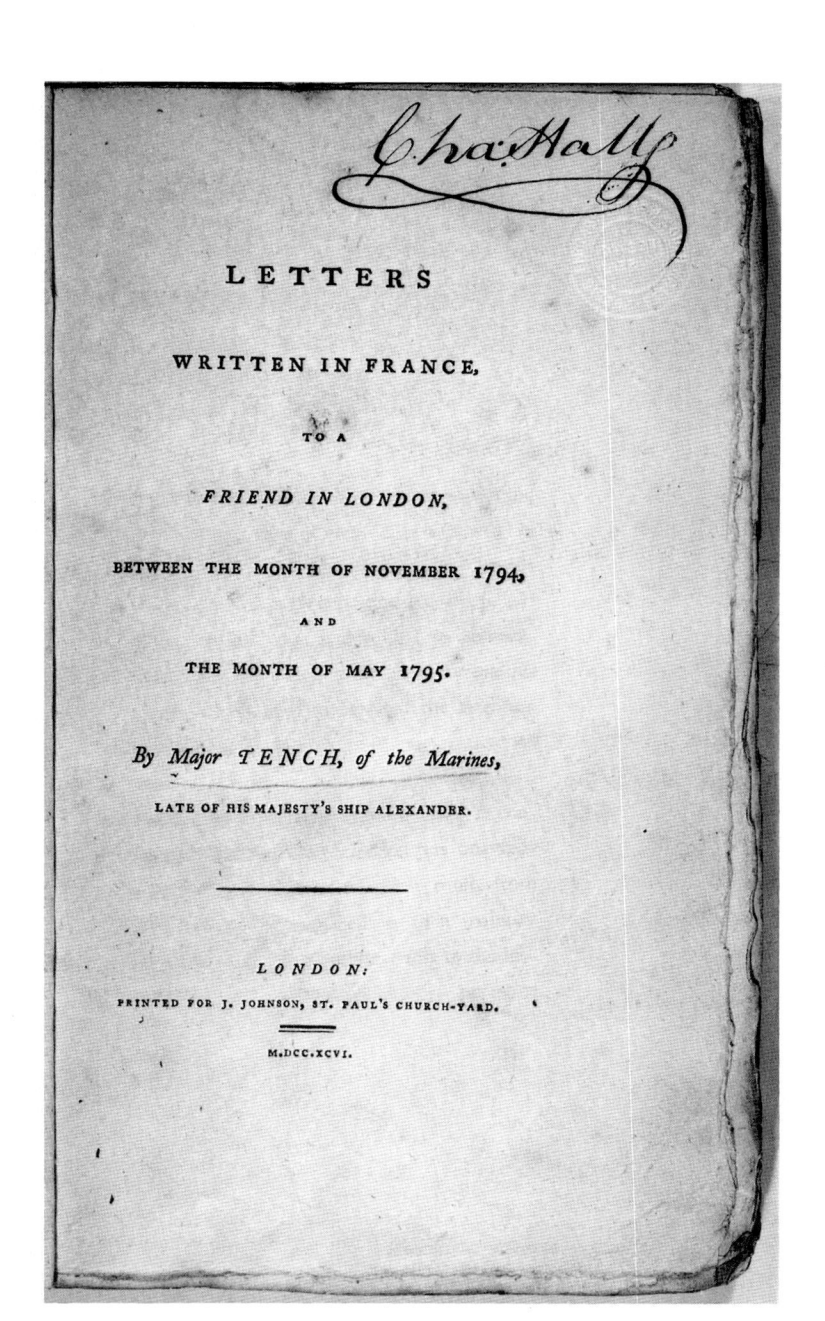

LONDON:
PRINTED FOR J. JOHNSON, ST. PAUL'S CHURCH-YARD.

M.DCC.XCVI.

Plate 3: Title-page of Watkin Tench's *Letters Written in France to a Friend in London* (1796). *Source*: Dixson Library, State Library of New South Wales.

PREFACE

THE following Letters were written under very adverse circumstances, in a part of France remote from the beaten track in which travellers generally keep, and where curiosity has seldom led to observation. As connected with that stupendous object, which has concentrated the attention not only of Europe, but of every quarter of this planet where human communications reach, they are offered to the Public. A considerable part of the collection was unavoidably dedicated to matters which must, from their nature, be uninteresting to a majority of readers; but the author trusts to the importance of the subject to compensate for the poverty of the relation. Since his return to England they have been revised; and would have been earlier sent to the press, had not reasons of a private nature interposed to procrastinate his intention.

LETTER I

On board le Marat,
Brest, 9th Nov. 1794.

My Dear Friend,

A performance of those flattering promises, which we exchanged at parting, to meet for a few days in London, about Christmas next, provided the exigencies of service would permit, must be suspended for the present—to be fulfilled when—is one of those secrets of futurity, which I dare not trust my imagination to anticipate.

The wayward fortune of your friend has again* exposed him to be taken by the "insolent foe,"[1] after an unsuccessful, but I trust not inglorious combat, against very superior force. This disastrous event happened on the 6th instant. † —— —— — —— —— —— —— —— —— —— —— —— —— —— —— —— —— —— —— ——

To our great surprize, the enemy's ships continued to fire upon us after our colours were struck. At first we conceived,

* The writer was taken prisoner in the last war in America.

† Here followed a minute relation of the battle, which the Alexander sustained for two hours and a quarter, against three ships, each of her own strength, and just before she struck against *five*. But as all the circumstances of the action, and of the causes which led to it, have been detailed by him, who like Cæsar, knew not only how to execute, but to narrate deeds of glory,[2] I have thought it right to suppress my description; and beg leave to refer the reader to the official letter of Captain, now Rear Admiral Bligh, which appeared in the Gazette, either about the latter end of January, or the beginning of February, 1795.[3]—The names and force of the squadron by which we were taken, were as follows, under the command of Contre-Amiral Neilly.[4]

	Guns:		Guns:
Le Tigre,	74	La Fraternité,	40
Les Droits de l'Homme,	74	La Gentille,	40
Le Jean Bart,	74	La Charente,	40
Le Pelletier,	74	Le Papillon,	14
Le Marat,	74		

that this unprovoked prolongation of hostilities arose from their not seeing that we had surrendered; but when their knowledge of this event could no longer be doubted, and the firing did not cease, some among us, joining to this conduct a recollection of the decree of the convention, which forbade quarter to be extended to Englishmen,[5] were almost ready to believe, that it was designed to be executed upon *us*; and so irritated were our seamen, by this apparently wanton continuation of attack, that they had once nearly determined to renew the fight, and sell their lives as dearly as possible. At length, however, their firing ceased.

Knowing from sad experience, that in such a situation all distinction of property is confounded, and that the officers and public stores of the ship become at once the indiscriminate prey of the enemy and their own crew, I left the deck, and descended into the bread-room. There I had in the morning deposited one of my trunks, out of which I filled a clothes-bag with such necessaries as I thought would be most useful to me, and left it in the charge of my servant, while I endeavoured to save a part of what a very large trunk, lodged in the marine store-room, contained. But this resolution I was incapable of effecting. The cock-pit, which I was obliged to pass through, presented such a scene of misery, as banished every feeling, but sorrow and pity. I found myself encompassed at once by the dead and the dying. The groans of the latter, joined to the cries of the wounded, on whom operations were performing by the surgeon, and to the blood which overflowed my feet, filled me with horror and disgust.

"Sight so deform what heart of rock could long
  Dry-ey'd behold?"—   MILTON.

It "quelled my best of man;"[6] and, after two ineffectual attempts to penetrate across this stage of woe, I returned to my servant, and made a few farther arrangements of what was left to me.

By this time the French boats had boarded us, and taken possession of the ship. When I attempted to ascend to the deck, I found every hatchway guarded by French sentinels, who refused to let me pass. In vain did I expostulate with them; all the answer I could obtain was, "*Citoyen, tels sont mes ordres. Je suis républicain!*"[7] At length I saw a French officer, and begged his interference, which, after some hesitation, was granted, and on his speaking to the sentinel, I was suffered to proceed to the deck, where I found all that confusion and disorder reigning which I had expected. The Admiral[8] had, I learned, been already sent away. I enquired for the French commanding officer, and was directed to a respectable looking old man, to whom I presented my sword, telling him, at the same time, that I hoped, and trusted, we should be allowed to retain our private property, and be protected from pillage. He answered me, that we certainly should. I had, however, but just turned from him, when a French officer seized on my cross-belt, and demanded it. On my refusing to comply with this mandate, he said it was arms; which I denied, and bade him, if he thought I had not made a full surrender of those, to search me. To all the arguments and protestations which I could use, this gentleman thought proper to answer by force only; so that, finding farther resistance vain, I yielded up the belt to him, when his motive for divesting me of this dangerous implement of war, at once appeared—a large silver plate, which was attached to it, being the bait. This he very composedly took off and put in his pocket, trailing the belt carelessly along after him as he marched away.

The commanding officer being extremely urgent that we should quit the ship directly, I got leave to make another effort to recover some more of my effects; but universal plunder and uproar had now taken place. The store-rooms and cabins were broken open and pillaged, and the most brutal excesses committed. I was surprized to find the French seamen and soldiers even more forward than our own, in searching for wine and spirits, and equally eager to intoxicate themselves: a new trait in their national character.

   About four o'clock I quitted the Alexander, carrying with me my bag, which was all I had been able to save, and was conducted, with several other officers, on board Le Marat,[9] a name of ill omen, and not too predictive, thought I, when I heard it proclaimed, of the virtues of humanity and generosity. Here I found our gallant and respected commander, who introduced me to Captain Le Franq,[10] the commander of the ship, by whom I was civilly received. This gentleman speaks very good English, which he learned in the last war, when he was a prisoner in England and in the East Indies. In a very candid manner, he repeatedly desired us not to be under any apprehensions about the treatment which we were to receive; for that if he, or any of his officers or men, should be found guilty of ill using prisoners of war, the republic would punish the offenders. When we complained to him of having been plundered, he protested, that he had given the strictest orders to forbid it to those who had boarded us; and that he was sure they could not be the authors of our losses, as his officers were all *gentlemen* (he spoke in English) and his men in a state of the most exemplary discipline. We answered, that among the great number of boats which had boarded the Alexander, from every ship in the squadron, it was impossible for strangers to point out either the names or the persons, or the ships to which the parties might belong; and that we chiefly attributed our losses to the precipitancy by which we had been compelled to quit our own ship. Upon hearing this, Captain Le Franq very fairly and honourably proposed, that one of ourselves should be selected, and sent on board the Alexander, in order to bring away whatever could be found belonging to any of us. We thanked him for his offer, and embraced it; but the officer who went on this service was able to obtain very little. Some few articles, indeed, he *did* recover; and to-day, as many more of us as chose to go again on a similar errand, were permitted, and French officers were sent with us, to enforce the order for a search: it was conducted in a very open and liberal manner, although it ended almost as fruitlessly as the former, the possessors of their newly-acquired property having taken effectual means to secrete nine parts in ten of it from our scrutiny. My large trunk, however, I discovered, close to the door of the store-room, wherein it had been deposited. I blessed my good fortune, and sprang to it: but what was my mortification, to find, that of all its former treasures (having closely packed it with my most valuable articles) nothing remained but two bits of black ribbon, serving to fasten my gorget![11]

We had been more than two hours in Captain Le Franq's cabin, without having had any refreshment offered to us, when, at about six o'clock, supper was announced. The captain, inviting Admiral Bligh, and all of us, to follow him, led us into the ward-room, where we found the banquet spread, and all the officers of the etat-major, or ward-room mess, assembled.[12] I was no stranger (as you know) to the customs of the French on land[13] which were never remarkable for delicacy and cleanliness; but I had never before seen their mode of living on board their ships of war. Our entertainment was served up on a large clumsy deal table, which was placed (to speak in sea-language) not fore and aft, but athwart ship, very awkwardly and inconveniently, surrounded by benches and lockers, and in place of a table-cloth was covered by a piece of green painted canvas. Sweet are the joys of hunger, on such an occasion! After a fast of thirteen hours, and that in a day of such unceasing agitation as we had passed, neither this circumstance, nor the garlic with which the meat abounded; nor a want of knives and forks, and a change of plates; nor the battling of the *mousses*[14] (dirty ragged cabin-boys) for the scraps which were left; nor the appearance of the

Letter I: November 1794

company, who all sat with their hats, or red caps, on; nor their vociferation of the word *Citoyen*, the only title they used in pledging each other to republican toasts,[15] could prevent me from making a most satisfactory repast. Nothing short of the evidence of my senses could, nevertheless, have made me believe, that so much filthiness could be quietly submitted to, when it might be so easily prevented. Indeed, a ship is in all situations very unfavourable to scrupulous nicety; but no description can convey an adequate idea to a British naval officer, who has not witnessed it, of the gross and polluted state in which the French habitually keep all parts of their vessels, if I may judge from what I see in this. And to complete the jest, Captain Le Franq has more than once boasted to us of the superior attention which he pays to the cleanliness of his ship.

In the course of our conversation at supper, we learned, that this squadron had been purposely dispatched from Brest, to intercept us on our outward-bound passage, being furnished with exact intelligence of the time we had put into Plymouth, and of our force and destination*.

But to proceed with the adventures of your friend in a regular detail. After supper, Admiral Bligh, and those officers who had saved their beds, went up into the cabin, where places to sleep in were allotted to them, while a sail was spread below, for the majority who had lost their's, in which number I was included. This humble couch, which was as good as circumstances would

---

* The Alexander sailed from Portsmouth on the 13th of September, having under her command the Canada of 74 guns, the Adamant of 50, the Thorn sloop, and a convoy bound to the Mediterranean. Owing to foul winds we put into Plymouth on the 16th, whence we sailed on the 26th of the same month. The Adamant and Thorn, with the merchant ships, parted from us off Cape St. Vincent. The Canada was in company when we were chased, saw us engage, and strike. Her signal was made, to join and support us; but this, which she attempted, a manœuvre of the enemy prevented her from executing: Captain Hamilton, who commanded her, then very properly began his retreat. Malevolence was not wanting to attack his character upon this occasion; but I am happy in bearing my testimony, that farther perseverance on his side was not wished by us, as it would have caused only an useless effusion of blood, and the capture of two British ships of the line, instead of one.

allow our hosts to furnish, or as we could reasonably expect, would have been perfectly satisfactory to us, had we been permitted to retire to it. But our entertainers, no longer checked by the presence of their chief, who had retired, and elated by victory, and by an anticipation of the triumph which awaited them at Brest, on the novel and glorious achievement of capturing a British 74 gun ship, now called for a fresh supply of wine, and began to sing, in a loud key, republican songs, which were interrupted only by questions to us, that delicacy should have withholden them from asking. One of them, taking a candle in his hand, begged me to look at two prints of heads, as large as life, of Pelletier[16] and Marat, "Ah!" said he, pointing to the latter, "behold the friend of the people! he who shed his blood for them!" I looked, as he had desired me, and thought I saw all the diabolical qualities, by which that monster was marked in his lifetime, depicted in this portrait. Prudence, however, kept me silent. Poor Pelletier came in for no share of this gentleman's eulogy; and as to Robespierre,[17] they all spoke of him, and "*his reign*," with great bitterness and detestation.

We were compelled to rise at a very early hour next morning, the sail on which we had slept being wanted. I would willingly have walked on the quarter-deck, according to the English custom; but it was so crowded by the men, and so greasy and slippery, that I found it impracticable. The captain, overhearing us talk on this subject, very gravely said, that he never allowed his people to eat between decks, but always made them do so upon deck, *in order to keep his ship clean*. When we saw that after these meals they neither scraped nor washed the decks, we were at no loss to account for the state in which we found them; and no doubt those whom it professionally concerned, duly noted this curious improvement in the œconomy[18] of a ship of war.

About eight o'clock the boatswain and his mates went to the different hatchways of the ship, and summoned the crew in a loud voice, "*aux prières.*"[19] My ignorance of what these prayers

Letter I: November 1794

might be, did not long continue. The quarter-deck was immediately thronged by men and officers, who with united voice sang the Marseilles Hymn,[20] with a fervor and enthusiasm of manner which astonished me. I had heard it at a distance on the preceding evening; and upon enquiry learned, that it was thus publickly performed twice a day, by order of the government. The sublime music of this fine lyric composition, the gaiety breathed by the *Carmagnole*,[21] and by many other popular airs which are continually in their mouths, during their most ordinary occupations, must produce a prodigious effect on the pliant minds of Frenchmen, and highly contribute to invigorate that spirit of idolatry for a republic, and that hatred and contempt of monarchy, which it is so much the interest of their leaders to encourage. I need not point out to you the good policy of such national establishments, and how deep a knowledge of human nature they manifest; perhaps no other country is so culpably indifferent to the foundation of similar institutions as our own. We fire, indeed, a few lazy guns on the anniversaries of the King's birth, accession, and other similar occasions; but we never stimulate the passions of our soldiery, by recalling to their memories, in periodic exhibitions, the days on which their forefathers won the fields of Agincourt, Blenheim, and Minden;[22] nor re-animate the ardent energy of our seamen, by public recitals of the victories of a Russel, a Hawke, a Rodney, and a Howe.[23] And yet the histories of the greatest nations, both ancient and modern, sufficiently demonstrate the power of such exhibitions over the human mind; and justify me in affirming, that no people ever rose to superlative dominion who did not employ them. How would the flame of heroism be enkindled in our youth, on hearing these celebrations, performed by the veterans of Chelsea and Greenwich![24] And what still more important sentiments would be diffused through the mass of our people, if they were frequently reminded of those glorious æras, when John was compelled to sign Magna Charta; and when the declaration of the rights of the people was made the foundation of William's throne![25]

This digression towards a country, which busy remembrance points to with unceasing anxiety, could not be suppressed. To proceed with my observations here:—The republican spirit is inculcated not in songs only, for in every part of the ship I find emblems purposely displayed to awaken it. All the orders relating to the discipline of the crew are hung up, and prefaced by the words *Liberté, Egalité, Fraternité, ou la Mort*,[26] written in capital letters. The *bonnet rouge*, or cap of liberty, is erected in several places, and crowns the figure on the prow of the ship, which represents the demagogue whose name she bears, and on which is written an extract from the declaration of the rights of man.[27] In the cabin (to which the officers are entitled to resort at all times) *Liberté & Egalité* are pourtrayed in female characters, the former brandishing a sword, and the latter nursing a numerous offspring, with impartial attention to the wants of all. But a picture of another sort also caught my eye: it was pasted on the *outside* of a door, which led to the apartment of an officer, and represented the prime minister of Great Britain conducting to a *guillotine* his blindfolded sovereign. The person to whom it belonged, on seeing me regard it with mingled indignation and contempt, would have begun a conversation on the subject, had I not prevented him by turning my back and walking away. Indeed, next to the poor emigrants, Mr. Pitt,[28] or *"Ministre Peet,"* as they always call him, seems to be the primary object of their abhorrence. Hated name! never breathed but in curses, never coupled but with execrations! To hear them, one would suppose that he is the only man in England hostile to their growing republic. Even Captain Le Franq, who has certainly hitherto behaved towards us with more delicacy than the other officers, did not scruple to call him "a Robespierre." To argue with these people I find impossible; "but to be grave exceeds all power of face."[29] My only resource, on such occasions, is to ask some question foreign to the subject they wish to talk upon: even here I can make no progress; I am either repulsed by want of common knowledge, or bewildered in contradiction. Having established it as a maxim, that some degree of information may always be gained by talking to men of their own professions, I am as inquisitive as I modestly can be, about their naval institutions. But, if my question be heard by more than one, such shocking abrupt oppositions of opinion follow, and so pertinaciously does each party defend his assertion on the most ordinary points, that my only alternative, to prevent a perfect equilibrium of mind, is to place the little confidence left at my disposal in the champion who has been least violent and vociferous; agreeably to the old observation, which says, the still stream is the deepest. Their ignorance, indeed, upon almost every subject which has been stated, is deplorable. One of them, in pure simplicity of heart, asked me if London were as large as Brest? I was contented to answer him, by saying I had never seen Brest. He was greatly surprized, on being informed that London is a sea-port; and, to recompense me for my intelligence, told me Paris did not enjoy that advantage as he had heard, for he confessed he had never been there. A second had read Shakespeare, "and did not like him; he was too *sombre*."—"Pray, sir, do you allude to any particular play?" He seemed confounded; but, after some hesitation, said, "Yes, to *Paucippe*."—"To Paucippe!" exclaimed I; "you mistake the name, there is not any of his plays which bears such a title." He was confident he was right, and therefore I begged to know the fable of the piece, or the names of the other characters; but with them, this critical reader did not pretend to any acquaintance. I need not observe to you, that none of these officers had ever served in the navy of France, but in the most subordinate capacities, under the king's government,[30] except the captain, who had commanded a cutter under Monsieur de Suffrein,[31] but who had nevertheless been bred up in the service of the East India company.

Letter I: November 1794

We anchored in Brest-Water about three o'clock this morning, and I presume to hope we shall very soon be sent on shore; but whether, or not, on parole, does not seem quite clear. They answer with great ambiguity, and apparent unwillingness, to all questions on this head, pretending that they are ignorant of what is customary, but assuring us that we shall be treated well. To be shut up in a prison, in this cold and dreary season that is coming on, is what I dread to look forward to. We frequently describe to them the parole which is allowed to all French officers in England. But, whatever is to be our lot, I shall not wonder at their taking almost any step to rid themselves of so numerous a troop of intruders on their society and table. Their own mess consists of sixteen persons, besides the captain who lives in common with his officers, although this association, they tell me, is forbidden in their naval instructions; but it seems these little deviations are winked at, in certain cases, to prevent the too weighty tax of a separate table. We breakfast every morning at nine o'clock on *Gloucester* cheese (taken out of an English prize[32]) good brown bread, called *pain d'egalité*,[33] which they bake on board, and a thin acid claret, of which the Frenchmen drink very liberally. This does not seem to argue the scarcity of flour among them, which has been so much insisted upon in England. A hint of this was dropped, and great derision followed, on their part, at the idea of starving such a country as France, by cutting off a few casual supplies by sea. We dine between twelve and one, and sup between six and seven o'clock. On all these occasions there is a sufficient quantity of provisions provided, though the dirty state in which it is served up, would disgust a Hottentot.[34] I have mentioned before, that during our meals we are surrounded by filthy ragged cabin-boys, whose appearance, contentions and impertinence, are intolerable. Among this crew of little blackguards, two were pointed out to me as the son and nephew of *Delcher*, who is one of the representatives from the Western Pyrenees to the convention. It is certain, that when I challenged the boys with it, they confirmed it to me, and seemed to glory in their situation. I was also shown a third boy, about eleven years old, who is the son of an *emigrated nobleman*. In him nature is not quite subdued: "*Le petit —— pleure quelquefois*,"[35] said one of the lieutenants to me.

I have forgotten to mention before, that on the day of our being brought on board the Marat, we were shown their furnace (which is the oven) for heating shot. It is well contrived, and the balls, by means of a pair of bellows, would soon be made red-hot; but I doubt not that "even-handed justice" will oftener render this dreadful implement of destruction, like "the ingredients of the poisoned chalice, rather the plague of the inventor," than the destroyer of the objects of its vengeance.[36] The motion of a ship at sea must, I apprehend, not only cause its effect to be very precarious, but its use very dangerous. Be this as it may, every thing here was prepared, the faggots were laid, and the shot were placed between them; and they assured us, that in the moment we had struck, they were just going to heat them for us: a confession which, considering the odds that we had fought against, was not very honourable to republican gallantry. All their ships of war, they told us, were provided with similar furnaces.

In the little time I have been in my new situation, nothing has surprized me more than the quantity of English articles I every where observe. The cheese, as I said before, was *Gloucester*; to which I might have added, that the plates it was served upon were *Stafford*, and the knives it was cut by were *Sheffield*, while the coats, hats, and shoes of those who were eating it, were also chiefly of British manufactures. "*Prize, prize,*" is the only answer we receive to our enquiries. Surely what one of their officers told me cannot be true! Seeing me just now looking up one of the arms which help to form this capacious port, and which is crowded with shipping, he assured me that they were all English, and not less than 400 in number. It is too well ascertained, that the French have been, during the present war, wonderfully successful against our trading vessels. Their frigates, I am informed, cruize in small detached squadrons to the westward of Europe; whilst we confine ours almost totally to the Channel, which I presume to consider a very injudicious disposition of them, in a war wherein the enemy have no privateers, and when consequently the little ports on the French coast, within Ushant,[37] should be less objects of our jealousy than heretofore. Provided our grand fleet can, after a parade off Brest, return into Spithead or Torbay, without being materially damaged by the weather, we seem to be satisfied, and conclude that all is going on well on the waters.

How I shall be able to procure money for bills on London, during my probable term of residence in this country, is not the smallest of my inquietudes. I have hinted the difficulty to Captain Le Franq; but from his real or assumed ignorance, one might be led to suppose, that paper-money had always been the only currency of France. The little cash I had by me, I took care to secure in my pocket, which escaped unsearched. It is, however, very inadequate to administer to my wants, stripped as I am almost to my last shirt. Small as it is, something like an attack was made upon it just now. An old *militaire*,[38] who is captain of the troops on board, came to me, and, with many professions of esteem, offered to serve me, by giving me, in exchange for English guineas, twenty-four livres in paper, each; assuring me that I should subject myself to disagreeable consequences, by offering to purchase with gold, when I might land. He brought the *assignats*[39] in his hand to tempt me: but I begged leave, with a profusion of compliments, to decline this courteous proposal. Surely gold and *assignats* cannot be deemed by all Frenchmen of equal value! *Nous verrons!*[40] At present all is mystery to me.—This said captain has a son on board, a fine youth, who is a corporal in his father's company.

Admiral Bligh is gone on shore to-day with the French captain, in order to be taken before the representatives on mission here.[41] He will probably gain some intelligence of what we are destined to, and we expect his return with impatience. We are too well acquainted with his feelings and sentiments, to doubt that he will hesitate to sacrifice even his own personal comforts to promote ours, and to prevent our being separated from him.

Upon surrendering our swords we were given to understand, that they should be restored to us, agreeably to the usages of war among civilized nations, but nothing has been lately said of this restitution; and the French officers, on being asked about it, only shake their heads, and plead ignorance.—How unlike the polished generosity which once distinguished Frenchmen towards enemies, who, in submitting to the imperious necessity of war, yielded up arms without a stain!—Adieu!

LETTER II

Normandie, prison-ship, in
Brest-Water, 1st Dec. 1794.

I MUST continue to write on to you, as if I had the means of regularly transmitting my letters. In the horrid dungeon in which I am now immured, it forms my only consolation to talk to you, although you cannot hear me; and to complain to you, although you cannot succour me.

Two days after the date of my first letter, we were all, except Admiral Bligh, sent from Le Marat, on board this prison-ship. Such a change did not much surprize us; for the reception which the Admiral experienced from the representatives, was so cold and mysterious, as to afford neither intelligence nor consolation; and Le Franq, who was his introducer and interpreter, affected utter ignorance of their intentions towards us.

Our situation here is extremely irksome. The captain of the vessel and his lieutenants are men of ferocious manners and brutal behaviour, high-flying patriots, whose supreme delight consists in blaspheming all revealed religion, and in abusing the English nation. In the day-time we have nominally the liberty of walking upon the deck; but this privilege is frequently so curtailed, by the caprices of our gaolers, as to amount almost to a prohibition. At night we are crowded into a small cabin, and hardly allowed light enough to undress ourselves by. Luckily, however, I have recovered my mattress and a couple of blankets. We eat with the officers of the ship, who are allowed a *traitement*,[1] or table-money, of three livres six sols a day, besides a ration of provisions, for each of us; so that the fault does not seem to be imputable to the government. But either the markets of Brest are extravagantly dear, or these patriotic gentlemen make an advantage of us; for hardly a day passes in which we have a sufficiency of any thing but coarse brown, or rather black, bread, so full of sandy particles as to be almost uneatable. Our breakfast at first was bread and butter, and a small red wine; but of late the butter has been taken away, and either Newfoundland salt-fish, or salt herrings, substituted in its place. These, indeed, are petty grievances, which would be easily tolerated, were they not incessantly aggravated by the disagreeable tempers, and debased sentiments, of those with whom we are obliged to live and converse. We are surrounded by American vessels, but cannot hold with any of them the smallest communication. A hope of hearing from England, or of conveying aught to it, must not be indulged. We have been told, that if we choose to venture the experiment of sending open letters by the post through Switzerland, we may do it; but that they must be first taken to the representatives, who will order them to be read, and forward them, if they contain information of a private nature only. This precaution is reasonable enough; but I have been assured by an officer of the ship, who is in a civil capacity, that I may spare myself the trouble of sending any, for that to his knowledge they are always thrown aside, and forgotten, in the office to which they are carried.[2] The number of prisoners on board is about four hundred, nearly all of whom are English; and three more vessels appropriated to a similar use, which also seem quite full, are moored close to us. On the return of some frigates from a cruize, a few days since, we received an accession to our number which surprized me:—twenty emigrants—who for the crime of being Englishmen were taken out of an *American* ship at sea, after which the vessel was suffered to proceed on her voyage to Philadelphia and the rest of the cargo remained unmolested.

    I find that I acted prudently in not parting with my guineas. Since I have been here, my brother-officer from Le Marat has honoured me by a second visit, and offered *thirty* livres for a guinea, pointing out one of the serjeants of the guard, through whom the business might at any time be transacted. I again begged permission to decline this benevolent gentleman's proposal, and also two others of a similar tendency, which were made to me here. Nor did the event deceive my expectation; for to-day a little Jew, who mounts a cockade,[3] and belongs to a frigate in the harbour, came on board, and secretly gave me two hundred and fifty livres for five guineas, declaring it to be the market price on shore. What think you of these specimens of republican honour and delicacy to children of misfortune, like us? I was so transported by indignation at those who had thus endeavoured to cheat me, that I could not help asking them, on their attempting to renew the subject, if the law did not forbid the depreciation of paper, when bartered for gold. This regulation, they pretend, relates to French gold only. To exchange a *louis* for more than its nominal value in *assignats* were criminal: but mark the curious distinction! An English guinea, and a Portugueze johannes,[4] are articles of merchandize, whose worth depends on the election of the buyer. Well! I have yet four English guineas left! Let me look at them! Oh "ye ever-young, loved, and delicate wooers! whose blush doth thaw the consecrated snow on Dian's lap;"[5]—and before whom even, the sternness of modern republican virtue melts into thin air,[6]—tenaciously will I treasure ye up!—Adieu!

LETTER III

Normandie, prison-ship,
Brest-Water, 7th Dec. 1794.

ADMIRAL BLIGH has been allowed to visit us twice or thrice since our separation took place. He still remains on board Le Marat, with his son, a little boy of ten years old, and two young midshipmen, who are also permitted to be with him. Until this day he has been unable to give us any information, and was even ignorant of what was to be his own lot. He is now promised to be sent, on his parole, to Quimper, in Bretagne;[1] and in addition to innumerable proofs of kindness and regard, which I have experienced from him ever since I have been under his command, he has honoured me by obtaining leave for me to accompany him, as his *aid-de-camp*[2] *and interpreter*. Since my last letter he has been on board La Montagne,[3] to see Vice Admiral Villaret de Joyeuse, the commander in chief of the fleet here, and who acted in that capacity against Lord Howe on the first of June.[4] He told me that he was very politely received, and was pressed to accept of pecuniary assistance, which he declined; but Admiral Villaret plainly hinted to him, that he was obliged to suppress much of the regard which he wished to show to him, from the delicacy of his situation, in the present temper of the times. Monsieur Renaudin, late commander of the Vengeur, who was taken, after the sinking of his ship, on the first of June, and is just returned from England, has visited him on board Le Marat. This gentleman declares, in loud terms, the humanity of the English, and the polite attentions he received from many of our most distinguished naval officers, whose generosity left him no want: Of this list, I remember the names of Lord Howe, Admiral McBride, Captain Bentinck, and Captain Schomberg. Monsieur Renaudin also made a tender of

Letter III: December 1794

his purse to Admiral Bligh; but I have reason to believe, that it was not done with that explicit frankness, which could hope to supersede the offer of Monsieur Villaret, even had it been made previously to it. By the way, the re-appearance of Renaudin, does not a little astonish the French; for the convention, in order to gratify the national vanity, and inflame the minds of the people, against the English, had publickly announced, that Le Vengeur, with *all her crew*, sunk with colours flying, disdaining to accept of quarter from slaves whom they despised; and a decree was even passed, to perpetuate this heroic resolution, by erecting a monument to the memory of the event.[5]

I am sorry to say, that Monsieur Renaudin echoed the profession of his commander in chief, in lamenting that the political prejudices which reign here will prevent him also from acting up to the extent of his wishes, in attending to the English, and the Admiral in particular. What evils do not these political phrenzies generate? Be this as it may, I am all alive at the thought of the scene about to burst upon me; and there are moments when I am almost tempted not to regret a captivity, which opens an inlet into this extraordinary country at such a period as the present; but these momentary illusions flit before the memory of the scenes I have left behind. Can curiosity, all-powerful as it is, stand in opposition to love and friendship? Let me, however, but quit La Normandie, and then we will strike the balance. Tomorrow I am to bid adieu to her darksome round:[6] how joyfully! And yet I shall not leave without a tear of commiseration those gallant comrades, with whom I have so lately fought, and so severely suffered.[7]

The few remarks I have been able to make are entirely nautical. I shall detail them to you when I can revise them at my leisure at Quimper. From a fear of being searched, I have used some extraordinary precautions to secure them; and if they be found they will not be easily understood, for I have so transposed the natural order of the sentences, and so intermixed words from all the languages which I could recollect (not excepting that of New Holland) that it would puzzle the interpreter of the convention to decypher them.[8]—Adieu.

LETTER IV

Le Marat, Brest-Water,
15th Dec. 1794.

THAT leisure which I so lately looked forward to at Quimper, seems likely to be afforded to me here. I was removed from the prison-ship on the 8th instant, and allowed to bring my servant with me, expecting to be sent immediately on parole; but this event, like the resolutions of the Dutch councils, seems to be put off *ad referendum*.[1] We receive daily assurances that it is to take place, and are daily disappointed of seeing it arrive. I enjoy, however, the society and conversation of the Admiral; and as he does not speak French, I am the chief medium through which he communicates with those who surround him, Captain Le Franq, who is married, living almost entirely on shore. So that here I remain, with nothing to do but to ask and answer questions from morning to night. These are chiefly nautical; and as you know my sentiments on the consequence of all naval concerns to Englishmen, I am induced to believe you will concur with me in thinking the subject momentous, however trite the remarks, or unimportant the observations of your correspondent may prove.

Whether Selden's assertion, that "we have an hereditary uninterrupted right to the sovereignty of our seas, conveyed to us from our earliest ancestors, in trust for our latest posterity," be perfectly deducible either from the nature of things, or from the authority of history, I shall not stay to enquire.[2] But I will venture to affirm, that when we suffer this right, however acquired, to depart from us, the sun of England may be truly said to be set for ever.

When the question of the relative naval strength of the two nations is agitated, which it often is, I am tempted to cry out to my country, in the words of the Grecian oracle,—"Trust to your wooden walls."³—I am the more confirmed in this opinion, from reading every day in the *bulletins* of the astonishing successes of this people, both in the Pyrenees, and on the frontier of Holland. They openly boast of being able, in a short time, to penetrate to Madrid; to force the German powers to peace; and to totally subdue the Dutch.—And then *"Delenda est Carthago."*⁴ I accuse not those with whom I converse of using this, or any other Latin phrase; but you will smile on being told that they habitually call us Carthaginians, and themselves Romans. They pay us, however, the compliment of declaring, that we are the only enemies worth combating. They stigmatize the Spaniards as cowards: at German tactics, when opposed to the energy and enthusiasm of republicans, they laugh: Dutch apathy can alarm no one. But this respect is confined to our naval character. Our impotent interference and puny attempts on the Continent they treat only with ridicule and derision. This spirit is not new: A noble lord, now high in rank in the British army, told me nearly twenty years ago, when we were on service together in America, that when he was very young, and travelling in France, a general officer, on hearing him relate that he was designed for the army, expressed his surprize that any Englishman, to whom the choice was left, should hesitate to prefer entering into the navy. Are the scorn and contempt of our enemies necessary to teach us in what our true grandeur, our real national pre-eminence, consists? It is certain that at present we far surpass them in the number of our ships, in the dexterity of our seamen, and in the interior regulations of our service; but I am persuaded, that they will hereafter strain every nerve to equal and exceed us. I know, that by very high authority the naval power of France has been denominated "forced and unnatural;" but let those who apply to it epithets so devoid of knowledge and reflection, remember the short period in which Louis XIV. created this navy, and its resurrection in 1778, when, to the astonishment of all Europe, notwithstanding its wasted and disastrous condition but fifteen years before, it suddenly started up, singly, to contest the empire of the sea with Britain, and for four years (until the 12th of April 1782) poised the scale of victory against its formidable antagonist.

Nature has denied to France a port in the Channel, capable of receiving large ships; but if art can supply the deficiency, they seem determined to employ it to its utmost extent. Whether the works at Cherbourg are proceeding or not, I cannot exactly learn; but it is certain, that the scheme of rendering it secure for line-of-battle ships is not utterly abandoned; and who can doubt, that it will either be carried on there, or in some neighbouring port, with accelerated vigour, on a return of peace?[5] Their warlike spirit now runs so high, and is so universally diffused, that many years must elapse ere it will subside. It is a train of gun-powder, to which, in the present temper of the people, a spark will give fire. A hatred of England is fostered with unceasing care. In nothing does this inveterate spirit against us demonstrate itself so bitterly, as in the abhorrence with which they always mention our taking possession of Toulon: "You gained it like traitors; you fled from it like poltroons."[6] On the celebrated measure of making them a present of four ships of the line, and six thousand of their best seamen, which were sent to Brest and Rochfort from the Mediterranean, they often make themselves merry, and us serious, by pointing out the ships as they now lie near to us, equipped and ready for sea; and by affirming, that the supply of men thus received enabled them to fit out those cruizing squadrons which have so sorely distressed our commerce.

How incumbent upon us, then, is it become to guard against the effects, which a propagation of this principle will inevitably produce! Naval perfection is, I am well aware, like all other perfections, placed beyond human reach; but the road to excellence is open. In it we have advanced before our rivals in all branches of naval superiority but one: I mean ship-building. Our vessels want length, and in the construction of their bottoms are undeniably very inferior to those of our enemies. Hence the continual escapes of the French fleets from ours, by superior sailing, when we want to bring them to action, which no skill, diligence, or bravery in our commanders can surmount. We possess models from which we might learn to correct our errors, and supply our deficiencies; but these patterns we are more ready to destroy than to imitate, as if fearful lest comparison of them with our own productions should demonstrate our inferiority. Thus do we continue obstinately to grope on in a dark and superannuated track, merely because our ancestors preceded us in it. The truth is, the art of ship-building has been cultivated in France by men of science, enlightened by a previous study of its theory: whereas in England it has been committed to the management of those, who for the most part have certainly had no room to boast of a scientific education, or a laborious examination of principles; and who could justifiably lay claim to the merit of observation only. In a country so eminent for mathematical acquirements as ours, is it not extraordinary, that this most useful branch of knowledge should have been so rarely applied to national advantage? What treatises on this important subject can we oppose to those, which have been published by French academicians, and by Bouguier in particular?[7]

"Oh! for a bridge to pass over two hundred thousand *sans-culottes!*"[8] I hear often exclaimed. Not that bridge which, according to Milton, Death consolidated across Chaos, could be more fatal to the remaining innocence of our first parents, than such a structure, in the shape of a superior fleet, would prove to their English descendants.[9] To prevent its erection, or to have a chosen band of pioneers ready to destroy it, must be our concern. I am, however, well convinced, that hitherto they have never seriously intended to invade us. This bug-bear has now for more than a century been employed to affright us; to cramp our foreign efforts; to diminish our sum of productive labour, one of the most important of national considerations; and to debauch the manners of our artisans and peasants in camps and barracks*.

I have been curious to hear their account of the signal defeat, which they experienced on the first of June.[11] This ship was not in their fleet, having been *launched since*; but Captain Le Franq commanded on that day L'Entreprenant of 74 guns, and some of the other officers were also parties concerned. Not the invincible superiority of British seamen in fighting and managing their ships, but "Treason! treason! joined to the ignorance, obstinacy, and cowardice of Jean Bon St. André,[12] caused the loss of the day." This naval dictator, who from a Hugonot curate at the foot of the Pyrenees was raised to be a member of the convention, and delegated by that body to superintend the equipment, and direct the manœuvres, of a great fleet, is never mentioned but with execration. His star set with that of his master, Robespierre. I have heard an officer assert, that he *saw* him, in the heat of the engagement, seized with a sudden emotion, start from Admiral Villaret, near whom he was standing, in the stern-gallery of La Montagne, and run pale and breathless down to the lower gun-deck, under a pretence of encouraging the men; nor could he be drawn thence, until the danger was over. "His seamanship," continued this gentleman, "consisted in having made one short passage. He might be a good *ecrivain ou secretaire*;[13] but for the marine! Oh! le vilain ———!"[14] But for him, they say, the action would have been renewed, agreeably to the wishes and representations of Monsieur Villaret; for "*the English were beaten, and might have been*

---

* Since the above was written, I have read Major Cartwright's opinion on this subject;[10] and am only more thoroughly convinced from his arguments, that neither a "*Saxon militia*," or any other militia, beyond the regular establishment of the kingdom, is necessary for our preservation from invasion, which can be effected by a strong naval force only.

destroyed."—I cannot help thinking, that if *Jean Bon St. André* really did prevent a renewal of the battle, he is not altogether so obnoxious to the reproaches of his fellow-citizens as they describe him to be. France is not the first republic which has profited, by declining to combat a victorious enemy.—A second cause of the disaster of the day arose from Lord Howe having gained possession of a copy of the French signals, which was procured by "the guineas of Pitt;" so that he was enabled to divine all their intentions, and to counteract them. It is certain, that some of their captains were guillotined, after the return of the fleet to Brest, but whether on a suspicion of cowardice, or perfidy, I know not. How consolatory to French vanity are these satisfactory solutions of this dreadful overthrow! Happy people! who, in all your conflicts against other nations, conquer by superior skill and bravery only; and are never vanquished but by disparity of number on the side of your enemy, or by treachery among yourselves!

An error, which you with myself, and all other Englishmen, have fallen into about this engagement, I must beg leave to correct, or at least to offer you my reasons for believing it to be one.—Lord Howe's account of the action states, that *two* ships of the enemy were sunk. Of Le Vengeur we will not speak: here proof is positive. But I am persuaded she was the only one. This the French positively assert; and I beg leave so far to join with them, as to observe, that when in Admiral Montagu's[15] squadron (of which the Alexander formed a part) we were chased, on the *ninth of June*, by the shattered remnant of their fleet, which was steering to Brest, it was composed of *nineteen* sail of the line. Now, I apprehend it to be certain, that on the day of battle this fleet consisted but of twenty-six ships, *six* of which were captured and brought into England; so that it should appear the *seventh*, Le Vengeur, made up the original number. But beside the strong presumption which this circumstance affords, I have received assurances from so many quarters (and particularly

Letter IV: December 1794

from one not remarkably friendly to the present system) that I am convinced one ship only was sent to the bottom on the first of June. Indeed, in matters of this nature, owing to the passions of those engaged, and the innumerable causes which obstruct vision, we should always receive similar relations *cum grano salis*.[16] In Lord Rodney's[17] action of the 12th of April 1782, a French ship, said to be Le Diademe, was supposed to be sunk; but I believe subsequent accounts clearly evinced that such an event did not happen. However, the French are more than even with us upon this head; for I have heard some of them positively affirm, that they saw three, and others four of our ships, among which was the Queen Charlotte, go down on the first of June. And when I assured the gentleman who furnished me with this last piece of information, "on the evidence of his own senses," that he had been deceived, he only shook his head, and continued, like your friend, a sceptic.

The remainder of this letter shall be dedicated to a detail of those detached parts of their naval institutions, customs, and present state, which I have been enabled to pick up. In general, I think them inferior, because less easily practicable, to our own, but many of them deserve consideration. *"Fas est et ab hoste doceri."*[18]

The discipline of their men struck me at the first view as contemptible; and yet I must confess that I was surprized by the state of subordination in which I afterwards found them. The seaman or soldier addresses his commander by the title of *Citoyen*, and receives in return the same appellation;[19] but in the five weeks I have lived among them, I have witnessed only one instance of disobedience. The offender was a soldier, who refused to assist in performing some of the ordinary duties of the ship. A court-martial, or *conseil de discipline*[20] as they call it, was immediately holden upon him, by order of Captain Le Franq, who prosecuted. It consisted of a lieutenant of the ship and three seamen, and of two serjeants and a corporal of the troops.

Letter IV: December 1794

The prisoner pleaded ignorance of the law on this head; and that when he had voluntarily enrolled himself to serve as a soldier, it was under an idea of not being *compelled* to do that which *ought to be the result of inclination* only. This defence was deemed so unsatisfactory, that the offender was sentenced to three months imprisonment on shore.

All the judicial institutions of their navy, and the punishments allowed to be inflicted, as well as the cases to which they apply, are strictly defined. The *conseil de discipline* is impowered to try only inferior officers and men. The officers of the *état major* (answering nearly to those of our ward-room) and all above them, can be tried only by a board of officers, who assemble in the admiral's ship. Neither of these courts has the power of condemning to death: all offences of a capital nature must be tried before the revolutionary tribunal. The punishments enjoined are flogging in certain cases, the number of lashes being limited; running the gantlope;[21] ducking from the yard-arm; confinement on shore, or in the lion's den (boatswain's store-room); stoppage of pay; and degradation.[22] The three last extend to officers. A prisoner's allowance of wine is always stopped. No man can be punished but by a sentence of the *conseil de discipline*; and, in carrying on the service of the ship, it is positively directed, that no "French citizen" shall, on any account whatever, be struck; but he may be *pushed* as violently as may be found necessary. For giving a box on the ear an officer would be cashiered; but to dash a man's head against the ship's side, so as to crush his nose, or beat out his teeth, by rushing suddenly upon him, is allowable.

The ranks of officers differ from ours: those only who command line-of-battle ships, and frigates carrying 18-pounders, are properly styled captains. Other frigates are commanded by lieutenants; and vessels of 20 guns or under by ensigns. Common courtesy, however, with them, as with us, annexes the title of Captain to all commanders. Agreeably to this classification the pay is regulated, but it is at present found so grievously inadequate, as to cause great complaints; and yet the French are unanimous in affirming, that all ranks are not only better paid, but better fed, clothed, and treated, than under the old government. Besides his pay, every officer, including the warrant officers and midshipmen, is allowed a *traitement*, in lieu of the table which was formerly kept at the king's expence. The *traitement* of admirals and captains is very handsome, and suited to their rank, as they are enjoined to keep separate tables: that of Captain Le Franq is 24 livres a day. No half-pay has yet been settled upon, or even promised to, the French officers. The seamen are divided into four classes: the pay of the highest class is $40 \frac{1}{2}$ livres a month; of the second $36 \frac{1}{2}$; of the third $33 \frac{1}{2}$; and of the lowest $30 \frac{1}{2}$.

Their gradations of command are very similar to our own, from the captain to the lieutenants, ensigns, and boatswain. The office of *pilote*, which formerly answered to that of master with us, is abolished. It is particularly enjoined, that the officers be put at five watches, if the state of the ship will allow of it. The lieutenant of the watch is stuck up on a little pedestal, which overlooks the helmsman, whence, except in emergencies, he never stirs during his guard, the ensign appointed to assist him, who is distinguished by wearing a gorget, being charged to superintend the execution of his orders.

The general uniform of both their navy and army is a blue coat with a red waistcoat and breeches: the naval facing is white edged with red, and that of the soldiery red; both services wear gold epaulettes. The naval button is an anchor, surmounted by the cap of liberty, and encircled by the words "*La République Française.*"

Of the minute regulations established for dividing prize-money, I cannot speak; but the general principle on which its distribution is founded appears to me worthy of attention. Two-thirds of every prize are put into a common stock, which is shared by the whole navy, and the remaining third is divided among the captors. A captain receives but in a proportion of 5 to 1 to a foremast-man;[23] a captain of troops, and a naval lieutenant, as 4 to 1; a naval ensign, subaltern of troops, surgeon, and commissary, as 3 to 1; midshipmen, boatswains, gunners, &c. as 2 to 1; and quarter-masters, and the lowest rank of officers, as $1 \frac{1}{2}$ to 1. The first part of this system, which relates to the common stock, were valuable, if it could be impartially carried into execution; but from the daily fluctuation of the parties concerned, I do not see how it could be reduced to practice among us, without giving rise to perpetual lawsuits. Some modification of the latter part would render its adoption very desirable in a country where, hitherto, this important part of the reward of naval toils has been apportioned with the most cruel and insulting contempt of the feelings and necessities of the lower orders.[24]

Drugs and instruments of surgery are, I apprehend, very scarce at present in France, as hand-bills are distributed over the fleet, enjoining the officers who may board prizes to be particularly careful in preserving them for the use of the republic. Those belonging to our surgeons were seized upon this pretence; and, notwithstanding representations were made to reclaim them, as private property (which they were) they were neither restored, nor an equivalent for them offered. Every French 74-gun ship is allowed a surgeon and five assistants. How many lives might be saved in our fleets, were our medical establishment equally liberal! Permit me here to observe to you, that the faculty owe obligations to the revolution. It is well known that they were heretofore, in France, treated in many instances highly unbecoming the regard so justly due to a profession, whence mankind derive so many benefits. Surgeons on board (and I am told on shore) are now considered with all the respect due to gentlemen, and live in the society of the principal officers.

The French marine corps, which, similarly to ours, was instituted for the service of the navy, is abolished, and troops of the line embarked in their room, who are subjected, by an express order, which I have read, to all the general regulations of the crew, and placed under the absolute command of the sea-officers. The detachment on board this ship belongs to a regiment in the Western Pyrenees: it is composed of stout healthy young men, who, if not formidable from discipline and knowledge of tactics, are full of energy and republican enthusiasm. I must here remark a vulgar error, which prevails too much among Englishmen who have never travelled out of their own country—that the lower orders of the French are puny debilitated creatures, inferior to ourselves in physical powers.[25] Could these persons be present at a muster of the seamen and soldiers of this ship, they would find their size and strength the same as their own, and in hardihood they are certainly superior to us. I never before saw people support cold so well; this is owing to their having no stoves on board to heat themselves by, a privation which extends to the officers, not from election but necessity; for Admiral Bligh's stove was immediately transported to La Montagne, for Admiral Villaret, and one which belonged to the ward-room of the Alexander, became the prey of Monsieur de Nieully.[26]

All their men seem to be well supplied with clothing. It is furnished to them by the government at an easy price, which has remained the same, while on shore it has been trebled. Of this they are obliged to keep up a stated quantity, and whenever men are turned over from one ship to another, a list of their clothes is sent with them, and if it falls short of the prescribed regulation, the men are forbidden to be received. Each man is supplied with a hammock and two rugs, but no bed. In case men belonging to ships are compelled by bad weather, or any other cause, to remain for the night on shore, there is a receiving-house, to which they can retire, where they are both fed and lodged until they can be sent on board.

The allowance of every person in the fleet, without distinction, is as follows, and like every thing else is *decimalized*, or regulated by periods of ten days.[27] On four of them they have half a pound of fresh beef, on two of them half a pound of salt beef, on two of them half a pound of salt pork, and on the remaining two four ounces of salt fish, with oil and vinegar to eat with it; one pound and a half of soft bread daily—no butter or cheese: on fresh-meat days, a soup for dinner made of the beef, with a little thickening in it; every evening a soup composed of four ounces of rice, pease, or beans, and oil; a wine quart of thin claret daily—such is the ration in port. At sea, salt beef and pork are served on the fresh-meat days, and, except in exceedingly bad weather, bread is every day baked; when this cannot be done, the same quantity of biscuit, of an excellent quality, is issued. I have seen them grin, when grinding it, at a recollection of its superiority over the black unpalatable stuff, which, they say, bore the same name under the former government. You, who well know the allowance served in our navy, may, if you please, compare the two institutions, and decide which is preferable. I am of opinion that this is best calculated to preserve health, particularly in long voyages and hot climates; but how far British seamen could be brought to relish its adoption, is not so evident. Observe that these pounds are *French*, which exceed our common weight by full two ounces; and that nominal or purser's pound, which is used by order on board our ships, by a great deal more.

I remember to have formerly treated the measure of sending a frigate off Brest, to count the number of the fleet, or to see whether it had sailed, more lightly than it deserved. I now see that both roads[28] may be inspected, particularly the outer one; and even of the inner one a sufficient degree of information may be generally gained by a good glass. The French boast of the holding-ground in Brest-Water; but if I may judge from the frequent dragging of anchors which happens in moderate weather, it must be far inferior to that of Spithead. The truth is, they are in general shamefully careless in mooring their ships: they overlay each other's anchors, and thereby cause foul berths, without reflection or ceremony.

Of real seamen they have few left, many thousands of their best having been drafted early in the war, and sent to serve as soldiers on the frontiers. Robespierre (whose execution was certainly the triumph of humanity, but not of the allies) by annihilating their foreign commerce, destroyed the only nursery which can ever supply the consumption of a numerous navy. Their ships are, therefore, filled, with landmen, who, previously to their being drafted for actual service, are sent on board certain vessels fitted on purpose, where they are taught all the elementary parts of practical seamanship. The number of boys on board is likewise very great, and for their instruction (as also for that of such men as may be desirous of improvement) a schoolmaster is allowed to every ship, whatever be her size. It is enjoined, that these preceptors be capable of teaching the theories of navigation, gunnery, fortification, and the common parts of the mathematics; and farther, that they be men of good moral characters, and great suavity of manners.

They have a naval committee for examining of midshipmen and inferior officers, to determine whether they be qualified to take charge of prizes. Nothing short of irremediable necessity will justify a commander for entrusting a prize to the direction of any person who has not undergone this examination.

They water their ships in the roadsted from floating tanks, which are brought alongside, whence the water is forced by pumps through hoses into the casks on board.

Every ship is furnished, at the public expence, with a superb set of charts of every part of the known world: those of our country are particularly excellent: there is hardly a little harbour in Britain or Ireland which is not laid down in them. With us this important charge is left to the prudence and honesty of a master;

and how many accidents have befallen our ships by a neglect of it, need not be here enumerated.

I am assured, that there are in the dock-yard here three covered docks, under which the workmen can carry on their operations in all weathers.

An experiment, of covering by a strong wooden case the rudders of ships to the water's edge, which leaves them only just room to work, is now trying on two or three of their frigates. It is intended to prevent the rudder from being unshipped, if struck by a sea.

The ponderous guns with which they used to overload their ships are displaced for others of a size more manageable. No ship now carries heavier metal than a French 36-pounder. Their first rates have sixteen ports on the upper and middle deck, and fifteen on the lower, except La Montagne, whose upper and middle deck are pierced with seventeen ports, and her lower with sixteen; so that, exclusive of those on her quarter-deck and forecastle (twenty in number) she mounts exactly 100 guns. They do not, however, in any of their ships, turn their quarter-decks to so much advantage as they might. In this ship the five aftermost and most useful ports are blocked up by standing cabins, and have no guns provided for them.

When the fleet weighs anchor, each ship's signal to heave up is made in succession. This method prevents the confusion which we experience in weighing all together; but, on the other hand, it precludes that emulation to be first, which a competition causes; they are accordingly very tedious in performing this operation.

Official *bulletins* of all public events, which the convention find it their interest to promulge, are printed on board La Montagne, from a copy transmitted from Paris, and distributed, at the expence of the government, to the officers and seamen of every ship. This is a popular measure, which wonderfully flatters the lower orders, who deem themselves in possession of all the secrets of state, and conclude that politics are no longer a mystery. I frequently read these chronicles, which are always filled with details of victories over their foreign enemies, and addresses to the convention from the departments. I was greatly diverted in reading one of the latter, from the "Popular Society"[29] at Brest, on the occasion of the Alexander's colours being presented to the convention, by the Major of Admiral Nieully's squadron, who was dispatched expressly to Paris on this important mission.—"Behold," says the orator, "*Pitt* himself virtually brought to the bar of the convention, when the British banner is prostrated before your august assembly!" Notwithstanding this flourish, and fifty more of the same sort, I am told that the inhabitants are strongly suspected of incivism,[30] and closely watched.

It has been customary to extol the French signals, as superior to our own; but any man capable of judging, who will compare the two codes, must be convinced, that those now in use in the English fleet are more simple in their principle, more exact in their arrangement, and more easy in their comprehension. The French were long our masters in this art which lately our naval officers have certainly carried beyond them. Their superior dexterity in making and answering them must not be confounded with the signals themselves. In this respect, from being earlier and more closely trained, I fear it will be found (though with many exceptions on our side) that they surpass us. There is on board every French ship a class of youths, called *pilotins*,[31] who attend solely to this part of naval duty. They are placed under the direction of an experienced quarter-master, and hold a rank immediately below that of midshipman, into which body they are promoted from time to time, according to their merit.

Of their deficiency of naval stores every day furnishes me with fresh proofs. The ships by which we were taken had, after a cruize of a few weeks, scarcely a coil of rope to repair their running rigging, or a stick to supply any loss which a sudden gust of wind might have occasioned. But how desperate must the state of France have been, had the American convoy been intercepted by Admiral Montagu! You know already in part my sentiments on that extraordinary failure. Let me now give you fresh cause for amazement; but remember, that I quote the words of another person without asperity, and without pretending to assign to what quarter the culpability of that shameful miscarriage on our side attaches:—Admiral Villaret said a few days since, to a British officer, who was in Admiral Montagu's squadron: "*Were you not astonished to see me chase you, on the 9th of June last, with my crippled fleet?*"—"*Yes,*" was the answer.—"*My only reason for it was, if possible, to drive you off our coast, as I momently expected the appearance of the great American convoy, the capture of which would have ruined France at that juncture. Why you did not return to the charge, after running us out of sight, you best know. Had you kept on your station two days longer, you must have succeeded, as, on the 11th of June, the whole of this convoy, beyond our expectation, entered Brest, laden with provisions, naval stores, and West Indian productions.*"

If my cheek reddens on recording this declaration of an enemy, it is with indignation only.

Hitherto I have not witnessed among the French, either here or in the prison-ship, a single trace of divine worship. The *Decadis*[32] are indeed distinguished by a more than ordinary chanting of republican songs, a display of the tri-coloured flag[33] on the tops of the churches in the town, and by a party of officers going on shore to the play. Thus, it seems, liberty wants perpetual resuscitation, while the adoration, or even the confession, of a Deity, is left to the unassisted operations of the human mind. From the pompous flimsy reports and orations on this subject made in the convention; from the *condescension* of Robespierre, who *decreed* the existence of a Deity,[34] to the hardy denial of Dupont,[35] who proclaimed himself an atheist; must I deduce all I know of the present state of religion in France. It is, however, worthy of remark, that a book, intitled "The Republican Catechism," which is in universal circulation, and expressly composed for the instruction of the youth of the community, does not once acknowledge, or even hint at, the being of a God; and the public instructor of the prison-ship assured me, that, although the minds of men be now somewhat returning to their former bias, six months ago an inculcation of this principle, so far from being prescribed by the legislature, would have subjected the teacher to punishment. God forbid! that, on such slender *data* as I profess, I should stigmatize all Frenchmen, with the horrid appellation of atheists, or even suppose that a belief in revelation is universally subverted: it were almost to affirm that it had never existed. I have, indeed, in many conversations, had the misfortune to hear innumerable blasphemies uttered, and innumerable sarcasms thrown on all worship; but as they have proceeded from none but weak and ignorant men (to the honour of my friend the schoolmaster, he always reprobated them) who possibly take this method of recommending their republican zeal; I shall be very cautious, until able to acquire better information, of asserting what are the general sentiments of the French on this head. Whenever the subject is started, the people, among whom I am condemned to live, fasten immediately upon some of the monstrous absurdities of the Romish church, and the impositions of the priesthood, which in truth offer but too secure a hold for derision and contempt. This trick, of attempting to confound the impositions of knaves, and the reveries of fools, with the spirit of Christianity, is too stale and despicable to deserve confutation. I will not even quote the noble and decisive simile of Hamlet, which seems to have been conceived on purpose to expose it.[36] Tremble not, therefore, for the faith of your friend, from such puny opponents. He will not yield his assent to new systems, until he has, at least, scrutinized and weighed their effects upon those who inculcate and practice them; and if, upon this test, he finds the professors of these doctrines to be men of profligate manners and corrupted sentiments, with the words truth, honour, humanity, and generosity in their mouths, while they are estranged from their hearts, you will not suppose his danger of conversion to be imminent.

And now to terminate this long desultory epistle, which I have written by snatches, when, and how, and as, I could.—Suffer me, however, before we part, to say a word or two of the political changes which I perceive to be working. My residence among the French is not yet six weeks old; and in this short space of time, wonderful has been the alteration of opinion. When we were taken, I was perpetually stunned with the exclamations of "*Vive la Montagne! Vivent les Jacobins!*"[37] But suddenly, *La Montagne* is become the theme of execration, and the Jacobin club is cashiered. I gained a confirmation of these events oddly enough. I had observed the disuse of these ridiculous cries for some days, and had overheard a conversation which had raised my suspicions. To ascertain their justness, I bade one of the boys call out as before. "Ah!" said he, "that is forbidden; *à présent il faut crier, au diable la Montagne! A bas les Jacobins!*"[38] which he immediately ran along the deck exclaiming. The memory of Robespierre they have uniformly affected to hold in abhorrence; but if I may trust to a hint, which was imparted to me on board the prison-ship, very different was once the tone of Captain Le Franq, and all his officers. They now load the character of this extraordinary man, before whom, not six months since, they prostrated themselves like reptiles, with all the assassinations and misery which have overspread France during the last two years. To him alone, it seems, every crime which stains the national character is imputable. At present I will not venture any opinion; but when I get on shore, I shall direct my enquiries to develope the character of this celebrated demagogue.

The fleet is preparing to sail; and as all the line-of-battle ships are known either to the Admiral, his two young gentlemen, or myself, I shall be enabled, by observing which sail, and which do not, to note down exactly its strength, provided we be not gone before it. But to-morrow we are assured we are to be landed.— Adieu.

LETTER V

La Normandie, prison-ship,
Brest-Water, 5th Feb. 1795.

Could what I write reach you in due course, my present place of date might surprize you, after the assurances which my last held out of going forthwith to Quimper. Admiral Bligh has been meanly and cruelly treated: their violated promises to me are of less consequence.

On the day after I last wrote to you, matters respecting our departure seemed to be drawing to a favourable conclusion. An officer from Admiral Villaret waited on Admiral Bligh, to beg his acceptance of a loan of one thousand livres in paper (offering at the same time as many more as might be wished) and to assure him, that we were to be landed on the following day. The livres were accepted; and, as we now deemed our departure certain, we put ourselves, at day-light next morning, in a state of preparation for our removal. Removed, indeed, we were, not to Quimper, but to this horrid receptacle, where we have been closely immured ever since, suffering every mental punishment which low-minded rancour and brutal ignorance could inflict; and every physical hardship which this rigorous winter,[1] and occasional deficiencies of food, could produce. I have not seen a fire during the whole month of January; and on Christmas-day I was one of *fifteen* English officers, with the Admiral at our head, whose dinner consisted of *eight* very small mutton-chops, and a plate of potatoes. This last circumstance, exciting both hunger and indignation (as we knew that a *traitement* was paid for us by the government, and as we had lately from our encreased number lived by ourselves) we determined not to bear it without remonstrance, especially as for several succeeding days our treatment had been little better; and I was

Letter V: February 1795

delegated to inform the officers of the ship, that if they should not use us hereafter more liberally, we would write a complaint against them to Admiral Villaret. This produced a good effect; and henceforth we were more amply supplied. In justice to Monsieur Villaret, I must observe to you, that his character is eminent for honour and justice; and in spite of appearances against him at first, on our not being sent to Quimper, we now know, that had his ability been equal to his disposition, Admiral Bligh would not be here. Of Le Franq I cannot speak in similar terms. He exhibited a mean exultation at our disappointment, not altogether unaccompanied with insult; and his whole behaviour, for some time before we left him, had entirely altered our first impression of him.

Our detention has, however, been productive of a very desirable event to the Admiral. In consequence of a late decree of the convention, directing that all women and children who had been captured shall be liberated, and permitted to return home, he was enabled to send away his son, under the auspices of Lady Anne Fitzroy, who had been a prisoner for many months at Quimper.[2]

The fleet sailed from the outer road on the 30th of December, consisting of the following ships, under the command of Vice-Admiral Villaret, who was assisted by the Admirals Bouvet,[3] Vanstable,[4] Nieully, and Renaudin, and controlled by several representatives.

	Guns.		Guns.
La Montagne,	120	Le Jean Bart,	74
Le Majestueux,	110	La Convention,	74
Le Terrible,	110	La Revolution,	74
Le Revolutionnaire,	110	Le Scipion,	74
Le Neuf Thermidor*,	84	Le Nestor,	74
L'Indomptable,	84	Le Mutius Scævola,	74

* Formerly Le Jacobin, the ship supposed to be sunk on the first of June.

	Guns.		Guns.
Le Tigre,	74	Les Droits de l'Homme,	74
Le Montagnard,	74	Le 31 de Mai,	74
Le Tourville,	74	Le Neptune,	74
Le Pelletier,	74	L'Eole,	74
L'Acquilon,	74	L'Entreprenant	74
Le Temeraire,	74	Le Trajan,	74
Le Zele,	74	Le Patriote,	74
L'Audacieux,	74	Le Gasparin,	74
Le Marat,	74	Le Superbe,	74
Le Tirannicide,	74	Le Redoutable,	74
Le Jemappe,	74	Le Fougueux,	74

And the Alexander, of 74 guns, with at least a dozen frigates, and several corvettes.

Le Republicain, of 110 guns, was intended to constitute a part of the fleet; but on the night of the 24th of December she broke from her anchors, was driven on a rock, and bulged, in a manner which does very little credit to French seamanship. Here she lay until the 9th of January, when her remains were burned, her main-mast and mizen-mast being then standing, and her main-top-sail yard across.

When the fleet sailed, the wind was nearly at E. and it continued to blow here between the points of N.E. and E.S.E. until the evening of Sunday the 25th of January, when it shifted to South, and next day blew fresh at S.W. On Thursday the 29th of January it returned to S.E. and continued in the Eastern quarter until the evening of the 31st, when it backed to S.W.

On the 12th of January Le Redoutable singly came back into port; on the 28th seven sail more of two-deckers returned, having parted three days before in a fog from the body of the fleet, which, to the number of twenty sail, arrived on the second and third of this month, and two others have got into l'Orient:[5] no less than the following five having either foundered, or been purposely run on shore, to prevent their sinking.

	Guns.
Le Scipion,	74
Le Superbe,	74
Le Neuf Thermidor,	84
Le Temeraire,	74
Le Neptune,	74

The condition even of those which have escaped, is deplorable: among others Le Majestueux had four pumps going when she entered the port. Two days ago I held a long conversation with the Captain of Le Jean Bart, who execrated the planners of this destructive expedition to their navy. He assured me, that it had been remonstrated against in the strongest terms by the naval officers, and its pernicious consequences foretold; but the orders from Paris were positive. The fleet cruized in three divisions, the easternmost of which kept but just outside of Scilly and Ushant; and the westernmost was once driven as far as 18° W. in the latitude of 45°; the central division occupied the intermediate space. I learned these particulars from some masters of English merchantmen who were taken, and have been sent to this prison. A more effectual plan to interrupt our commerce could not have been devised. Of its practicability, had I not lived to see it executed, I should at least have doubted; but this is an age of political phænomena on the water, as well as the land. Between fifty and sixty prizes were captured by this fleet, among which was a transport bound from Ireland to Bristol, having on board 120 soldiers of a new-raised regiment, who are now confined here, and do so little credit, by their appearance, to British troops, that I have more than once blushed, when they have been pointed at by the French; and I have been asked with a sneer, "Are these the men who are to march to Paris?" In the list of prizes were also six or seven of the homeward-bound Oporto fleet, all of which they sunk, with their cargoes; deeming, I presume, that honest beverage (to use the words of one of their authors) "a heavy stupifying liquor, fit to be drunk by Englishmen only."

Cut off as I am from all communication with English politics, I shall not presume to guess at the causes which have retained our fleet in harbour. But some of those which have not retained it, I shall venture to state. It was not the weather, for that was uninterruptedly fine until the 25th of January. It was not the wind, for that during the same period was always easterly, here at least, and our distance from Plymouth is barely 45 leagues. It was not a want of information, for (to my knowledge) exclusive of other channels, two English gentlemen, who escaped from this place in a boat at least as early as the 8th of January, must have arrived in England by the 12th or 13th. The rigid caution observed by the French, in not hazarding engagements at sea, is notorious. In the present instance it has been exchanged for a hardy audacity. They now boast that they have challenged us to the lists, which we have not dared to enter against them; but, during the time of their fleet being out, I have seen them tremble at the probability of such an event. Had the month of January been as tempestuous as it commonly is in this climate, our assistance would hardly have been required to destroy their leaky and crazy ships, in want of naval stores and able seamen. One hard gale of wind at S.S.W. would have cost them at least a dozen sail of the line.

What then shall we say? "There is," my friend, "a tide in the affairs" of nations, as well as of men:[6] the page of history every where records it. Hannibal, after the battle of Cannae, instead of marching to Rome, turned aside to Capua;—from that moment the Carthaginian fortune ebbed, never to flow again. The series of rapid conquests, which distinguished the brilliant campaign of 1776, was finished, not by taking Philadelphia, dispersing the Congress, and breaking up the new government, but by occupying winter cantonments in Jersey, where our victorious army was beaten in detail;—and America was lost. The allies, after the surrender of Valenciennes, divided their forces;—and since that fatal separation how has their career of conquest been turned into retreat, marked only by overthrow, consternation and despair![7]

Letter V: February 1795

On the 31st of December, the Admiral was again reduced to my society, and that of his youngsters, all the other officers of the Alexander being sent on shore to the Château, where, according to accounts which I have received from them, by some letters privately conveyed to me, they are treated in a manner shocking to humanity.—But I must be contented with telling you my own story.

On their departure we who were left were again taken into the mess of the officers of the ship. The military part of this assembly are a set of worthless wretches; but two of those who fill civil posts are men of honourable characters, ever ready to pity our situation, and to give us every reasonable degree of intelligence of the state of the country, and what is going on; to which *I* add the advantage of reading daily some of the Paris news-papers, which are brought on board.[8]

Through these channels I draw not only abundant matter for reflection, but frequently obtain diversion. "Moderation, and down with the Terrorists!" resound, I believe, from one end to the other of the republic. It is in all respects our interest to wish that such sentiments may be more than nominal. It is certain that a general dismission of the creatures of Robespierre is taking place. The indiscriminate advancement of unqualified candidates to offices of trust and dignity, which to court popular applause universally prevailed until lately, furnishes to those, who are not over-friendly to a democratic cause, an inexhaustible fund of merriment and ridicule. Among others who have just experienced the instability of honours is Tribout, who commanded the troops at Brest. This man, from beating a drum, and officiating as a regimental barber, under the old government, had been advanced by the revolution to the dignity of a drum-major, whence, by an easy gradation, he at once rose to the rank of a general officer, for intrepidity displayed in a battle on the frontiers. His elevation, however, only exposed him to derision in the district wherein he was delegated to command.

Like the unfortunate cat, who at the request of her master was metamorphosed by Jupiter into a young woman, and who still retained her feline appetites, some unlucky trait, it seems, was for ever occurring in this poor man's behaviour, to remind the spectators of his earlier professions.[9] When he was on the parade he had all the flourishes of the drum-major, and at table all the busy curiosity and oily language of the *frizeur*.[10] After exciting universal contempt against himself and his employers, during the period of his command here, he has been suddenly stripped of his full-blown honours, and condemned to vegetate hereafter on a small pension, which has been assigned to him; with permission, however, to retain the title of *General* Tribout.

    The 21st of January was the anniversary of the execution of Louis XVI. an event which will be annually commemorated by very different ceremonies and emotions from what distinguished this day, when the political phrenzy that now agitates Frenchmen shall be evaporated. A play analagous to the occasion was performed at the theatre, *gratis*; the towers and forts on shore, and all the ships in the harbour, displayed their colours; and lastly, to prove their civism, the *keepers* of this dungeon put on their best clothes, and provided the best dinner I have seen since I have been taken. I ate of it, but not without a sigh for the cause which gave birth to this savage exultation over the manes[11] of a mild and generous, though irresolute, monarch. And even here I feel pleasure in saying, all sensations of pity are not extinguished, all distinctions which should regulate the administration of justice are not obliterated. This very day a Frenchman whispered in my ear, "His death (the king's) in spite of the veil which the convention threw over the real sentiments of the people, struck the hearts of the majority of Frenchmen with amazement and horror." Of the memory of the queen he spoke less affectionately. He recounted to me some of the extravagant tales, which have been so industriously propagated against her; but in defiance of them, what unprejudiced mind can hesitate to pronounce, that the cruel and ignominious rigour of her confinement; the brutal and unmanly spirit that dictated the charges upon which she was tried; and the mockery of all justice with which she was prosecuted; joined to the violent death inflicted upon this unhappy princess (against whom report has been so loud, and proof so feeble) have fixed upon the annals of the revolution a stain, which will be indelible, while sentiments of tenderness and generosity towards women, and principles of equity towards the accused, are cherished in the human breast?[12]

The news of the entire conquest of Holland has caused great rejoicings. But when the wildness of joy and congratulation had subsided, what think you was the first reflection which I heard on the subject?—A calculation of the advantages which will accrue to their marine. By this acquisition, they hope to be enabled to dispute the empire of the sea with England. It is publickly reported, that a negociation for peace with Prussia is proceeding, and will be speedily completed; but to this I only oppose my silent unbelief.[13]

We often hear of Charette;[14] but the accounts are so extravagant and contradictory, that I know not what to think. About two months ago I was persuaded, from all I read in the news-papers, and from what I was every day told, that he had either surrendered, and sworn fealty to the republic, or was about to do so; but as the most furious republicans among my present associates have lately been silent about him, and answer with reluctance to my questions on the subject, I can only guess, from their reserve, that all is not agreeable to their wishes, and consequently that he is still the rallying point of royalism

I have sometimes my doubts whether it be not their intention to continue us where we are altogether, and that the promise of being sent to Quimper is as delusive as every other part of their conduct; but these are only the suggestions of spleen, on recollecting the frequency of our disappointments; for an order is absolutely received on board, to send us hence to a small armed brig, which is to take some coasters under her convoy to Quimper, as soon as the wind shifts to the N.W. In her, it seems, and not according to the first intention of sending us by land, are we to be conveyed to our place of destination.—There!—but hang gloomy anticipations! the thought alone of being on shore, and able to warm myself by exercise, must give it a decided preference to a prison-ship, in which, during this bitter season, we have been cooped up, and frozen both in soul and body. You would have laughed to see the contrivances we have had recourse to, to keep up a little warmth, and restore circulation to our benumbed extremities. The Admiral twice wrote to the representatives, for permission to walk on shore with the officers of the ship; but of his first letter no notice was taken; and to his second only a verbal answer, that "his request could not be granted," was returned.—Adieu.

LETTER VI

Quimper, Bretagne,
18th Feb. 1795.

My Dear Friend,

Lucky! lucky dog! you will exclaim, when you read the word Quimper at the head of this letter; and are farther told, that I am comfortably lodged, and seated at an English table. This welcome intelligence will, I think, soon reach you through a channel by which I shall venture to send you a packet.

We arrived here yesterday: Admiral Bligh brought with him a letter from an English lady, who accompanied Lady Anne Fitzroy, to Mademoiselle Brimaudiere, a native and inhabitant of the town; and, on presenting it, was obligingly told by her, that she had already received notice to prepare for him, from a gentleman at l'Orient, whose son-in-law, the captain of the America, was a prisoner in England; and that if he pleased to accept of such accommodations as her house, which was a hired one, afforded, they were at his service. This courteous offer, you may be sure, was immediately closed with, and we took possession of our new apartments. Here we were also welcomed by two of our countrymen, whom we found to be inmates of our house—Lieutenant Robinson, late of the Thames frigate,[1] and Mr. Burley, of the same ship. With these gentlemen we have formed a mess. The good lady of the house condescends to market for us; our servants, assisted by the maid of the house, officiate as cooks; and we live already so much more comfortably than I ever expected to do during my captivity, that I cannot describe to you the joyful sensations I have experienced on this change.

We quitted the prison-ship on the 14th instant, to our unspeakable satisfaction. From our military acquaintances there we parted without an adieu, from our civil ones not without sentiments of esteem. For the last nine days before our departure we had separated from their mess, and lived entirely by ourselves, owing to the following circumstance:—On some English prisoners being brought on board, one of the officers of the ship, who is a Provençal, and speaks so indistinctly, that his own countrymen cannot, without difficulty, understand him,[2] desired one of our young midshipmen to interpret for him, which request he would readily have complied with, as he had often done before, had he comprehended it; but not possessing the gift of understanding inarticulate sounds, he turned round to his companion, and said, "Monsieur —— asks me some question, but as usual I don't know what it was." The other not hearing himself called upon, and not supposing the matter to be very important, smiled, and both of them, in all the gaiety and thoughtlessness of fourteen, walked away. For this enormous offence they were immediately sent for into the cabin, and, without being suffered to urge a syllable in explanation, were told, that they were not any longer to consider themselves as entitled to eat at the table of the officers. The young gentlemen communicated this to me, and I lost no time in informing the Admiral of it; who finding, on examination, that they had not committed an intentional incivility, desired me to explain the business, and to assure Monsieur —— that the apparent slight had proceeded from misapprehension. This I attempted to do, and in return for it was honoured with several scandalous appellations, as an instigator and abettor of the offenders, although it happened that I had not been present when the crime was committed. Our two friends in the civil department also attempted to interfere in their favour, but were silenced by authority, the insult being deemed of a public nature, and striking at the dignity of the republic. Admiral Bligh now declared, that if the young gentlemen were to be thus driven from the mess, he and I should look upon ourselves as included in the expulsion. This they would willingly have prevented, and wished to draw a line of distinction; but the Admiral's manly resolution cut short debate, and, on their refusing to yield the point, he and I directly quitted them with contempt; and with two spoons belonging to our servants, and a pocket-knife each, which constituted our whole stock of utensils, we set up our mess forthwith, demanding our rations, but refusing to receive any more *traitement*. Now was to be seen, for the first time, in a civilized enemy's country, a British Admiral, whose seat was a trunk, and whose table was a trunk, eating a salt herring laid on a scrap of paper, from want of a plate; or supping at the same board, with a candle stuck in an ink-horn, on a second herring; or dipping his spoon in a tub that held our soup, which was part of that made for the ship's company, sometimes of beef, and sometimes of horse-beans and oil. Breakfast, however, by having a little tea and brown sugar of our own, with the addition of some salt butter, which we had procured from the shore for our servants, was a repast of real luxury. This miserable fare, and want of common necessaries, lasted but two days, when we got leave to employ the cook to market for us, and dress our provisions. It brought me, however, perfectly acquainted with the extent of the French allowance, and likewise with the prices of different commodities on shore, which we found enormously high, and every day rising. To console us, however, the value of gold, in exchange for *assignats*, more than kept pace in its increase.—Here I take my leave of the good ship La Normandie, and her worthy inmates, in full trust that, in the course of our future correspondence, neither her name, nor theirs, will ever again pollute my paper!

My observations since I left Brest could not be numerous; but, as I feel an interest in them, they shall not be suppressed.

The little vessel which conveyed us hither was extremely inconvenient, and ill-fitted for the purpose; but her commander, Monsieur Conseil, and his officers, treated us with great civility

Letter VI: February 1795

and regard. She had been a Jersey privateer, and retains her English name, the Betsy. About noon, on the day before yesterday, we anchored just within the mouth of the river that leads to Quimper, within twenty yards of the shore. After so long a residence on ship-board, amidst men of coarse and ferocious manners, I could not withdraw my eyes from the scene before me. It was a clear frosty day, but the deep snow of the winter had been melted by intervening thaws, and the fields bore that fresh and verdant hue, which is so re-animating to the human heart. The river was of a moderate breadth, and on each side stood a parish-church, surrounded by a few scattering houses. Notwithstanding the keenness of the weather, the peasantry were dancing in circles in the open air. The small space which I could see bore no trace of distress or devastation; and so transported was I with the appearance of all around me, heightened by a recollection of the past, that I was almost ready, with the shipwrecked philosopher of antiquity, to cry out to my companions, "Courage, my friends! from these marks I know we are thrown among civilized beings!"[3]

Our commander, who was of a pleasant unsuspicious temper, begged that the Admiral would defer going up to Quimper until the next morning; and offered, if we pleased, to accompany us on shore after dinner for a walk. This was a welcome invitation, and eagerly embraced. About two o'clock we landed with our conductor, and set out for a large handsome looking house, the *château* of the Marquis de Kersalaun about a mile off, which we had seen in the morning, in running along-shore, before we entered the river. We passed through thick woods, and when we reached the *château* found there an engineer,[4] who is stationed on the coast in the service of the republic, and is a friend of the Marquis. This gentleman is permitted to reside here, and also two of the Marquis's old female servants. He received us very politely, and led us up large stone staircases, through various apartments lined with old tapestry, and half illumined "by rich windows, which almost exclude the light."[5] He shewed us also a small chapel within the house, which, though commonly kept shut up, bears marks of the fury of the times. The *château* is long and low, with a turret, which resembles a pigeon-house, on its centre, and has a fine old avenue leading up to it from the seaside. Before we left the house, the gentleman presented to us some excellent cyder, and lamented, with evident signs of mortification, that he possessed not a drop of either wine or brandy. From the house he took us into two large walled gardens, forming oblong squares. In the disposition of these, and the other grounds surrounding the house, no mark of taste appears, but they exhibit the hand of wealth and labour. In the centre of the largest garden stands a circular bason or fountain of considerable size, "which once," said our civil and sensible conductor, "was thought an embellishment to the *château*. Here," continued he, "ran the leaden pipes which supplied it, and here were fixed the plates of iron which secured it; but, as you see, all the former are dug up, and cast into bullets, and all the latter have been torn off in wantonness. Mark too the breaches in that wall, through which the cattle and pigs enter; and how the espaliers[6] are either broken, or rooted up. No means to prevent these depredations are left in my power. The *château* was lately converted into a temporary prison, to contain a party of Englishmen, who, under the guard of a detachment of soldiers, were sent to cut down the Marquis's woods, for the use of the republic. I have less cause of complaint against the English than against their guards, who were to the last degree insolent and destructive. Twice did they set fire to the house by their carelessness"—(we had seen the marks on the floors and tapestry)—"I complained and remonstrated against them, in vain, to our municipality: I obtained no redress. But this evil was temporary. The fatal change which has taken place in our manners, and the wide-extended spirit of rapine, which it has introduced, has infected our peasantry. The farmers and tenants of the Marquis, who formerly pressed forward to serve him (for he was a kind and generous landlord) are now eager to promote the devastation, and to share in his spoils. This and this," (pointing to different marks of fury and ravage) "have they committed."—As we went homeward he made us observe, that all the trees of the avenue were marked, for the use of the republic; "and," added he, "are all to be cut down soon, with the rest of the wood on the estate, in order to be sent to Brest, the whole being in a state of requisition." I saw some large groupes of stately firs, many of which were felled and squared on the spot. I put some questions to him about the Marquis and his fortune. "He is," said he, "between eighty-one and eighty-two years old, and is now at Paris, where he is obliged to reside, and, in return for stripping him of his estate, he has been *promised* a pension. Perhaps, as matters are certainly softening among us, he may be enabled to make better terms. It is not pretended that he has committed any crime; but he suffers for those of his two sons, who have emigrated; and, at the age of fourscore years, he was thought too dangerous a person to be permitted to dwell on his hereditary estate, where he offered to remain tranquil, and submissive to the ruling powers. He was formerly *Doyen* of the States of Bretagne. In a letter, which he lately wrote to a friend, he states himself to be in good health, and to have borne the excessive cold of the winter very well; but complains that wood was 400 livres a cord, and meat three livres a pound. The value of his estate was between sixty and seventy thousand livres *per annum*; but of this to the amount of not more than twelve thousand lies contiguous to the house. The timber, however, on this latter part was so valuable, as to be reckoned at twice the worth of the land."—It appeared to me, indeed, to be very thickly wooded.

We bade adieu to our obliging informer, and returned towards our ship, by a different way from that which we had come. On this road I observed three or four stone crosses, broken and thrown down. When we reached the landing-place, the peasants were again dancing, with some soldiers, sailors, and fishermen. We went close to look at them, and, except from one lady, who told us, in broken French, she did not like the English, met with neither rudeness nor insult. The figure of their dance was very simple, consisting only of describing a circle, through various parts of which, with joined hands, they threaded from time to time; and notwithstanding their wooden shoes, I thought they executed it with more spirit and less awkwardness than our clowns[7] generally perform. None of the women were handsome, but they had all healthy cheerful countenances, and were coarsely but cleanly dressed; their long white caps, which form a sort of hood behind, giving to the younger ones a very sober and matron-like appearance. A publick-house, which the dancers of both sexes frequently visited, was close by, where cyder and small acid red wine were retailed. These people conversed entirely in the Breton language, the sound of which, had I not forcibly felt from other circumstances where I was, would have made me swear I was in Wales. I found, upon trial, that not one in ten of the peasants could speak French, or even understood it when spoken to them.[8] I asked if the gaiety which I saw was continual, or only occasional; and was told, that this was the week of the *carnival*, a period of festivity, which the Bretons of all ranks, notwithstanding the austerity of the times, have never failed to celebrate in revelry and dissipation.

I went into several houses. They form a medium between the neatness of an English, and the filthiness of an Irish cottage; they are dark and gloomy like the latter, but the walls are strongly built of stone, the roofs well thatched, and none of them are without a chimney. There was a moderate quantity of necessary household utensils in all, and a good fire burning, over which, in most of them, hung large pots boiling. Here was no indication of want or distress. "Destruction to the *châteaux*, peace to the cottages,"[9] is an aphorism, which has been often repeated in the convention, to instigate the poor to plunder the rich.

The church-door being open, I walked in, and found it converted into a barrack for the soldiers belonging to a small fort which stands at a little distance. There was a large fire burning in it, and it was filled by the bedding and other effects of the men; but I observed that the altar was entire. A serjeant, seeing me regard it with attention, whispered me, that it owed its preservation to him: a piece of intelligence of which I could not doubt the truth, when he carried me into a little vestry, which he unlocked with a key that he took from his pocket. There he showed me the images of our Saviour and the Virgin, which were here deposited uninjured. I commended the zeal of this honest halberdier, and we parted good friends, it being time to return on board.

Next morning after breakfast we were conveyed hither, in one of the ship's boats. The distance is about three leagues; and a cold easterly wind blowing strongly against us, made the passage tedious and disagreeable. The river winds very much, and gradually narrows, until it becomes contracted at Quimper to a freshwater brook, deep enough, however, to permit vessels, which do not draw more than eleven feet, to reach the town at high water. Its banks are highly picturesque, very woody, and rather wild and bold than fertile. They are besides adorned by many gentlemen's houses, on a smaller scale than the Marquis de Kersalaun's *château*, but built in the same taste, and surrounded by plantations of fir-trees. Like the *château* too, they all bear marks of the unhappy state of the country, the windows being broken, the garden-walls and fences destroyed, and an air of desolation spread around them.

About one o'clock we reached Quimper, and were taken to the house of the commissary of prisoners, whose reception of us did not forebode the pleasing consequences which followed; for this man of power, when acquainted with our names and ranks, neither did us the honour to return our salute of the hat, or to ask us to sit down. However, after having given a receipt for us to the captain of the vessel, he condescended to conduct us in person to the house of Mademoiselle B— (to whom he is related) whose polite and obliging reception of us, soon caused us to forget the republican manners of *Citoyen* Precini.[10]

We have found here abundance of our countrymen, this town being the principal *depôt*[11] of prisoners of war in the Western departments. In this unfortunate list are Captain Kittoe,[12] of l'Espion sloop of war, and his two lieutenants; Colonel Caldwell, who is a native of Ireland, and in the Portugueze service; with many other officers and gentlemen, and several hundred British seamen.

LETTER VII

Quimper, 2d March, 1795.

ALTHOUGH placed in a part of France very remote from the capital, and unfrequented by travellers, I find in all I hear and see abundant matter of wonder and reflection; and as I advance in my enquiries, the scene continues to open upon me. To witness the meridian blaze of the revolutionary government, I am arrived six months too late; its disastrous lustre is eclipsed. When I testify emotions of astonishment, I am always cut short by the exclamation of, "Ah! if you had been here in the reign of Robespierre, or even during the first three months after his death!"

I am not upon any parole, either written or verbal, but I am *cautionné*,[1] that is, the lady of the house is bound for my appearance at all times, in the sum of 3000 livres. Upon this consideration I have leave to go into all parts of the town, and have ventured to deviate, in every direction, into the surrounding country, to the distance of two or three miles, without having hitherto met with interruption.

Nothing could happen more fortunately than our coming here at the beginning of the carnival-week, during which parties meet every night at each other's houses. The evening of our arrival the meeting was held at Mademoiselle Brimaudiere's, and was attended by all her friends and acquaintances, who, as she is a woman well born and connected, are of the better order, though, as I found in the sequel, of very opposite political opinions. Formerly these assemblies were closed by sumptuous suppers; but in the present poverty of the times, they meet only to play at *passe-dix*.[2] Into this circle I was introduced, and found the greater part of it composed of well-dressed people of both sexes, who surrounded a large table, on which the dice were rolling, and the spirit of betting as keen as it could have been at any former period; handfuls of *assignats* shifting their owners every moment; and even children, of not more than seven or eight years old, were encouraged to stand by, and receive lessons in this instructive seminary:—"*Ma mère! dix sols pour!—Ma tante! quinze sols contre!*"[3] resounded from infant mouths on every side. Among the women were several whom I thought very agreeable in person, particularly Mademoiselle Kérvélligan,[4] and la Marquise de Ploeuc. The latter is extremely elegant in her manners, but beams "with faded splendor."[5] I could not bear to hear the boorish and disgusting title of "*Citoyenne*" applied to a fashionable woman; and therefore, whenever I addressed myself to the marchioness, I called her "*Madame la Marquise,*" and the rest of the company *Mademoiselle*, or *Monsieur*. Indeed to this I had acquired a sort of right, by being myself honoured with the appellation of "*Monsieur le Major,*" when I was invited to play, which I at once accepted, and formed one of the circle. These good old-fashioned courtesies also fell occasionally from the rest of the company; but I observed that they were spoken in a low voice, and not without trepidation: they are, however, I am assured, fast returning into vogue.

At a play-table the common centre of union must be the stake, and to that I found here, as elsewhere, all cares anxiously directed; but, during some short cessations of the game, I remarked that the company divided into knots, which seemed jealous of each other. The operation of a more powerful passion being suspended, their political prejudices were now revived. I was among royalists, federalists, and fierce republicans one and indivisible.[6] The fathers, mothers, brothers, and sisters of emigrants, for whose desertion they had been punished, collected with *bons citoyens*,[7] and *enragés*.[8] Of these last, from not mixing in their groupe, I can say nothing, except that the dress of some of them was affectedly mean, and their conversation marked by a boisterous and rude familiarity, which I knew before were leading characteristics of their party. If I find myself compelled by necessity to cultivate an acquaintance with any of this faction, while I remain at Quimper, I hope I shall not be constrained to extend to them an observation, which I was forced to pass upon their brethren on ship-board—that I never knew one man, professing to be a fierce and flaming republican, who possessed either the manners which should distinguish a gentleman (setting aside the forms of courtesy) or that common share of probity, which is required to keep the links of society together.

In the little knot of royalists to which, you may suppose, I attached myself, I was not worse received for being an Englishman. Indeed they spoke quite undisguisedly before me, but it was in whispers. A young lady, on seeing me gaze with attention upon one of the republican phalanx, who (like all his colleagues) had worn his hat during the evening, asked me, which I liked best, the tri-coloured cockade I was surveying, or the "*cocarde blanche?*"[9] "The cockade of honour, to be sure," I answered.—"Softly, softly, for God's sake!" said she, "or we shall be overheard and undone."

One of the company, Monsieur Kérvélligan,[10] is a member of the convention, and appeared to me, both on this occasion and since, to be a manly dignified character. I conversed a little with him on indifferent subjects, as he only played occasionally. He is reputed to possess a penetrating mind; and it is certain that he very early discovered the views of Robespierre, and described them faithfully to his friends here. Monsieur Kérvélligan was proscribed, with many other deputies, on the 31st of May, when the Brissotine party[11] was overthrown, and compelled to flee before that of the Mountain.[12] With some of his colleagues, he effected his escape into Normandy, and thence into the wildest part of this neighbourhood, where he took refuge among the peasants, by whom he was known and beloved. These poor people were well aware, that by betraying him they might make their fortunes; but they were too simple and honest to violate the duty of hospitality. He frequently ventured to come into town in disguise, and has often heard himself proclaimed a traitor, and a reward offered to whoever would bring him in, alive or dead, to the municipality. Soon after the execution of Robespierre, he emerged from his retreat, and by a late decree of the convention, is recalled, with others, to his seat in their body; and intends to set out to Paris very soon, to resume his delegation. Monsieur Kérvélligan voted against the murder of his sovereign; and has told his friends here, that in going, on the day of the question being put to the vote, to the hall of the convention, he and many other members were several times stopped, and surrounded by bodies of the lowest class of the people, who clapped pistols to their heads, threatened them, and swore they would sacrifice them on their return, if they did not vote for the death of their sovereign.

During the carnival-week there was a second party, similar to the first, at our house: and, under the auspices of our good hostess, I went also to two others, the last of which, on *Sunday*[13] evening was at Monsieur Kérvélligan's, where the same entertainment was provided, and pursued with the same avidity. Mademoiselle Kérvélligan I have already mentioned as a handsome young woman; and her mother, Madame Kérvélligan, is also very agreeable.

At one of these routs I saw a specimen of genuine democratic manners, which all who aim to become great men in the state affect to imitate. The commissary of prisoners, a man allied to nobility, liberally educated, and once an Abbé, bolted into the room where the company were assembled, humming the *Carmagnole*, with his hat on, which was adorned with a red, a white, and a blue feather, and his hands stuck in his breeches, *not pockets*. In this attitude he stood all the evening, and thrusting himself among the ladies, had the impudence to enter into familiar conversation with the Marchioness de Ploeuc, and other women of rank and delicacy, with all the airs which conscious superiority of power can instil into a reptile. This brutal manner of mingling in society, and addressing women, has become, since the revolution, the *ton*[14] of republican coxcombs, and during the reign of Robespierre set decorum and the restraints of civilized life at defiance. It is now on the decline, except with those who still court the applause of the dregs of that faction. A courtier of Versailles at his toilet, surrounded by paints, patches, and perfumery, was, in the eye of reason, a ridiculous and contemptible animal; but the most effeminate essenced *marquis*, that ever consulted a looking-glass, was surely preferable to this indecent blockhead.

In frequenting these little circles, I see many victims of the tyranny of the government, and hear such anecdotes of it related, as make me shudder. The marchioness has been stripped of two estates, and the best house in this town, which is converted into a prison. Two ladies, who reside in our house, are but just liberated from a close confinement, under which, with many more of their sex, they languished for fourteen months. During their imprisonment, in return for the sequestration of their property, they were allowed *twenty sols* a day, out of which they were compelled to pay two for *house-rent*. Monsieur Brimaudiere, brother of the lady of this house, was *capitaine des gens d'armes*[15] of this district, a post of trust and power. When the party of Brissot fell, he was seized, sent to Paris, and imprisoned for fifteen months in the *Conciergerie*.[16] During the whole of his confinement he was kept in the same room, and saw, during that period, 167 persons go out of it to the guillotine, every day expecting himself to be added to the number. His fate was close at hand when Robespierre was overturned, and soon after the death of the tyrant he was liberated, and sent back hither, to resume his former situation, which he now fills. He describes almost the whole of this assembly of victims to have been so conscious of their innocence, and so reconciled to their lot, from the daily exits of their friends, that nothing but resignation, indifference, or levity, prevailed throughout the prison, death having ceased, from its familiarity, to terrify. It was customary to warn, on the preceding evening, those prisoners who were to be put on their trial the next day; and by a regulation made among themselves, the party to be tried gave a supper on that night to the whole room; and, if he was spared for the present, and remanded back, he was in return treated with a dinner at their joint expence. "Our dinner entertainments," said my informer, "were few indeed; but Oh! the suppers without end which we partook of!"

All my days, however, have not been passed in going to routs, and listening to details of misery. I have paid a visit to two more members of the convention, and have been *at church*. On the afternoon of the 19th instant, the representatives Guesno and Guermeur arrived here in great state, in a coach which had once belonged to their king, drawn by eight horses, and escorted by forty hussars. "*Voila l'egalité!*"[17] cried aloud some (I was told) who saw them enter in this pomp. "And," said my informer, "as if conscious of their power, and the importance of their mission, they neither bowed to the crowd which was assembled to gaze at them, nor spread any lure to engage popular attention, like their brethren who have heretofore been among us." They are both natives of Bretagne, and of good, though not of noble, families.[18] In conjunction with several more deputies, furnished with great powers, they have been delegated by the convention to treat with the inhabitants of La Vendée. Among other avowed objects of their coming hither, is an enquiry into the complaints which have been at different times made by the prisoners of war. Accordingly, two days after, Admiral Bligh, attended by Captain Kittoe and myself, went to the tavern (which once was the *town-palace* of the *bishop* of the diocese) wherein they lodged.[19] We saw them both, and the Admiral, through Captain Kittoe and me as his interpreters, made some representations to them, which, if not quite satisfactorily answered, were at least candidly listened to by Monsieur Guermeur, who was extremely civil; but his colleague Guesno was less friendly, and more elevated, keeping his seat, with his hat on, while we remained in the room, and frequently interrupting our statements. He is said to avow publickly a hatred of our nation, which in this short conference could not be restrained. On the following day I was deputed by the Admiral to wait upon them again, with a letter from him, entreating them to give orders that the other officers of the Alexander (who are still closely locked up in the *château* of Brest, suffering misery and imposition) might be liberated, and permitted to join us here.[20] Upon reaching their hotel, I found a crowd of suitors attending at the foot of the stair-case; but the landlady, on seeing me, assured me I should not wait for an audience, as an order had been given by Guermeur to admit at once all English officers who might wish to see him. I profited immediately by this flattering distinction; and marched through two rows of impatient Frenchmen, who were expecting what I had obtained. I found him alone, and was as politely received as on the preceding day. He read my dispatches with deliberation, and in answer desired me to present his compliments to the Admiral, and to assure him, that he would write to his colleagues at Brest, and beg them to comply with the request.

Listen now to a relation, which will in some degree evince to you the infamous height to which imposition, on the ignorance of the people, is practised in this country.—On the 23d of this month an express arrived, in the middle of the night, from the other representatives on mission in this department to those here, which caused great speculation, affording to one part of the inhabitants of the place as much joy and exultation, as to the other it was productive of grief and dismay:—"*Peace concluded with Charette.*"—An event, at once so momentous and desirable, could not pass without celebration. A drummer was sent in the

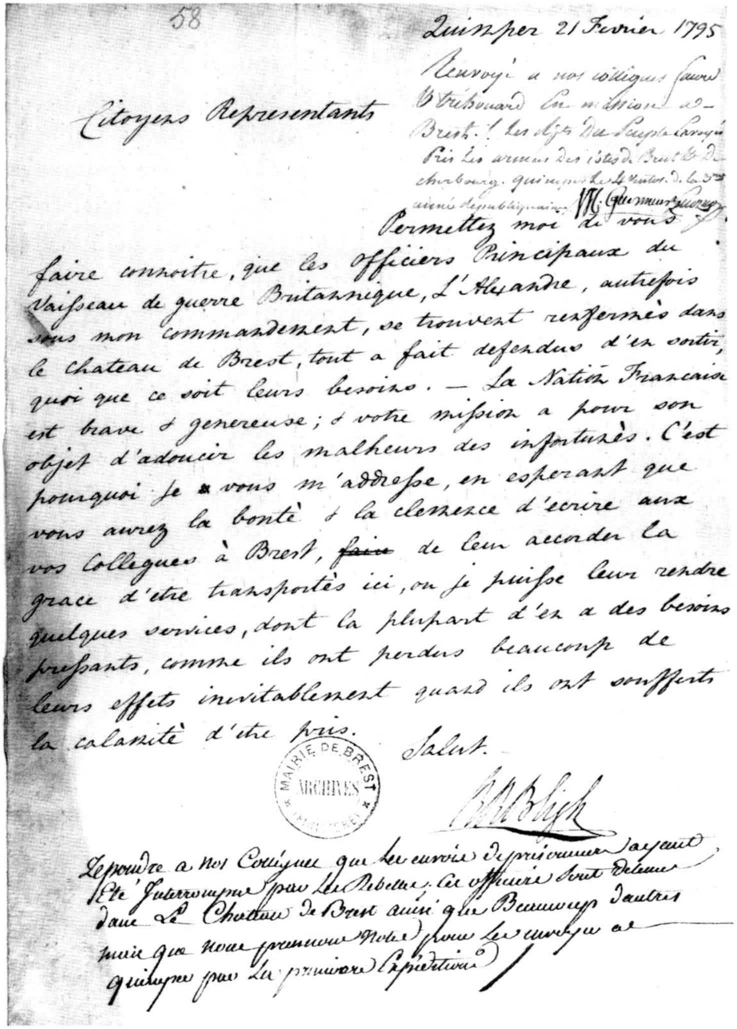

58

Quimper 21 Fevrier 1795

Renvoyé a nos collègues faure & Tréhouard en mission à Brest. / les dép. du peuple envoyés près les armées des côtes de Brest & de Cherbourg. Quimper le 4 ventôse de la 3e année républicaine. Guermeur

Citoyens Representants

Permettez moi de vous faire connoitre, que les Officiers Principaux du Vaisseau de guerre Britannique, L'Alexandre, autrefois sous mon commandement, se trouvent renfermés dans le chateau de Brest, tout a fait defendus d'en sortir, quoi que ce soit leurs besoins. — La Nation Francaise est brave & genereuse; & votre mission a pour son objet d'adoucir les malheurs des infortunés. C'est pourquoi je vous m'addresse, en esperant que vous aurez la bonté & la clemence d'ecrire aux vos Collegues à Brest, ~~faire~~ de leur accorder la grace d'etre transportés ici, ou je puisse leur rendre quelques services, dont la plupart d'en a des besoins pressants, comme ils ont perdus beaucoup de leurs effets inevitablement quand ils ont soufferts la calamité d'etre pris.

Salut.

R R Bligh

MAIRIE DE BREST ARCHIVES

Répondre a nos Collègues que les envois de prisonniers ayant été interrompus par les Rebelles. Ces officiers sont détenus dans le Chateau de Brest ainsi que Beaucoup d'autres mais que nous prenions note pour les envoyer a Quimper par la première expédition

Plate 4: Letter from Admiral Richard Rodney Bligh to Representatives Guesno and Guermeur, dated Quimper 21 February 1795. The letter, delivered by Tench (p. 68), may be in his handwriting, and its French is almost certainly his. The first annotation (top right), signed by Guermeur, forwards Bligh's petition to the authorities in Brest; the second (bottom) is their response, to the effect that the British officers' removal to Quimper is currently prevented by rebel activity in the countryside. *Source*: Archives départementales du Finistère, 8 L 82.

morning into the town, who proclaimed at the corner of every street the important intelligence; and announced, that on the same evening a ball, in honour of it, would be given by the representatives of the people, to which all good republicans were invited to repair. This was a bitter trial to the poor royalists, particularly to those who had been lately liberated from imprisonment. Many of them, rather than go to such a commemoration, chose to submit to the imputation of incivism, and to provoke afresh the arm of power; while others, more compliant, went with aching hearts, to wear the mask of joy on an event, which, if true, quashed their final hope. They all, however, consoled themselves in believing that the information was unfounded. "How," said they, "can we credit any thing which our enemies tell us? How many victories have not we been commanded to celebrate, which were gained only in the fertile inventions of those who fabricated them, and issued the orders! Did they not assure us, that the English fleet was defeated, and almost utterly destroyed, in the engagement of the first of June? Did not ——, and ——, and ——, who were just arrived from Brest, aver with solemnity and oaths, that they had seen, and actually been on board, *three English ships of the line*, in the port of Brest, which were taken in that action? &c. &c."

On these specimens of modern Gallic effrontery I leave you to your own reflections; and shall only observe that in a very few days the intelligence about Charette was contradicted, when the royalists, as far as they dared, returned the laugh upon their opponents.

Be this as it may, the ball was well, or at least fully, attended, by generals, colonels, captains, serjeants, corporals, privates, and drummers, with their wives and children; to whom may be added all the butchers, barbers, bakers, tallow-chandlers, servant-maids and fishwomen in and about Quimper, "whose dress, manners, and vociferation, joined to the offensive smell which proceeded from their persons, drove me," said the lady from whom I borrow this account, "out of the room in about half an hour." The maid of our house (who is not of an ignoble stock, although reduced to service) said, she did not deign to dance, as none but *sans-culotte* partners offered themselves. Water was the only refreshment which was served up at this civic feast, and all the fiddlers of the town were put in a state of requisition to play at it. My curiosity was strong; but it was impossible for an Englishman to be present on such an occasion.

I shall now describe a scene to you, which filled me with very different emotions from this recital.—On leaving the representative, after presenting to him the Admiral's letter, as I was going out of the door, I heard the sound of an organ, proceeding from the cathedral, which was very near the house: I went in, and found mass celebrating in the presence of a congregation consisting chiefly of poor people from the country, with a few of the higher ranks, many more of whom, I was assured, would have been there, could they have believed themselves secure from reproach; but the return of religious worship was yet too young for them to incur the risk—they were all kneeling at their devotions, with great appearance of fervency, while a fine greyheaded respectably looking priest, habited in his pontificals, officiated at the altar. I walked the whole length of the church, through rows of people on their knees, which formerly might have been deemed disrespect in a heretic; but I now met with nothing but courtesy and regard, all seeming conscious that the basis of their persuasion and mine was the same, however we might differ in external forms of adoration. Here I had leisure to contemplate the scene of desolation which this venerable temple presented. At least half the windows of fine old painted glass, "richly dight,"[21] were broken; all the monuments torn down; and the bones of the dead exposed to view, and commingled with the ruins of their tombs, the names and armorial devices being utterly defaced, and the coffins taken away and converted into bullets. When the service was finished, I went within the railing which incloses the altar, to look at a large picture, representing the Ascension, the figures of which are pierced through in more than twenty places, by sabres and bayonets. An old man, who was kneeling near the rails, observing my attention fixed on the painting, told me, that in the vacant side-compartments once stood two other pictures taken from holy writ; "But," said he, "they were so cut and hacked, that *we* were under a necessity of taking them away." A gentleman, who had joined me in the church, informed me, that the altar and confessionals which I saw had been brought hither from another church; for that those belonging to this had been either burnt, or broken into a thousand pieces: nay, that the figures, with which the altar had been adorned, were carefully separated from it, and triumph- antly guillotined in the middle of the great square of the town.[22]

Cold and republican must have been the eye which could survey such scenes of barbarous devastation unmoved, and the heart which could listen to such descriptions of sacrilegious delirium without a sigh!

> "—— Oh! but man! proud man!
> Dress'd in a little brief authority;
> ———— like an angry ape,
> Plays such fantastic tricks before high heaven,
> As makes the angels weep," SHAKESPEARE.[23]

Upon enquiring, I learned that the church had been open for public worship about three weeks, in consequence of a proclamation issued at l'Orient, on the 13th of January, by the representatives Guesno and Guermeur, in which liberty of worship is granted to all men in their own way, on "proper terms," but not as a national worship; the republic disavowing a national religion, although tolerating and permitting the free exercise of all, provided the priests who officiate have taken the oaths of allegiance to the state. To this last stipulation the thinness of the weekly congregations is in part attributable, the rigid catholics holding in detestation the priests who have taken the oaths.[24]—Adieu.

LETTER VIII

Quimper, 4th of April 1795.

I SHOULD not amuse you with a disquisition on the etymology of the name of Quimper, or a research into the date of its foundation, were I capable of furnishing such an entertainment; but I will tell you all I know of its present state, and of the country contiguous to it.

It is unquestionably a town of considerable antiquity, and when it formed a part of the possessions of the dukes of Bretagne (ere those were annexed to the crown of France, by the marriage of Charles VIII. with Anne of Brittany) sometimes sided, in the wars between the English and the French, with one party, and sometimes with the other. A massy stone wall surrounding the old town, the cathedral, and some other buildings, are believed to be the works of our countrymen.[1]

The town stands in a bottom, encompassed by high hills, and the largest part of it is built on a neck of land formed by the confluence of two rivers. I have often thought it like Plymouth; but it is not so large, although even now extremely populous. Its streets are narrow, winding, and dirty; and their former names have been changed into others of a revolutionary sound, such as the street of Voltaire, the street of Mably, the square of Liberty, &c. &c.[2] The greatest part of the houses are very ancient and mean; but a few are large and stately; with walls whose thickness seems intended for endless duration. On entering them, I was surprized to see the unfinished state of most of the apartments, which are uncieled, the bare beams and cross-pieces presenting themselves to view. I shall be within the bounds of truth when I assert, that of 1500 houses, which are perhaps in the town, not fifty have each a cieled room, and not ten, or even five, have the

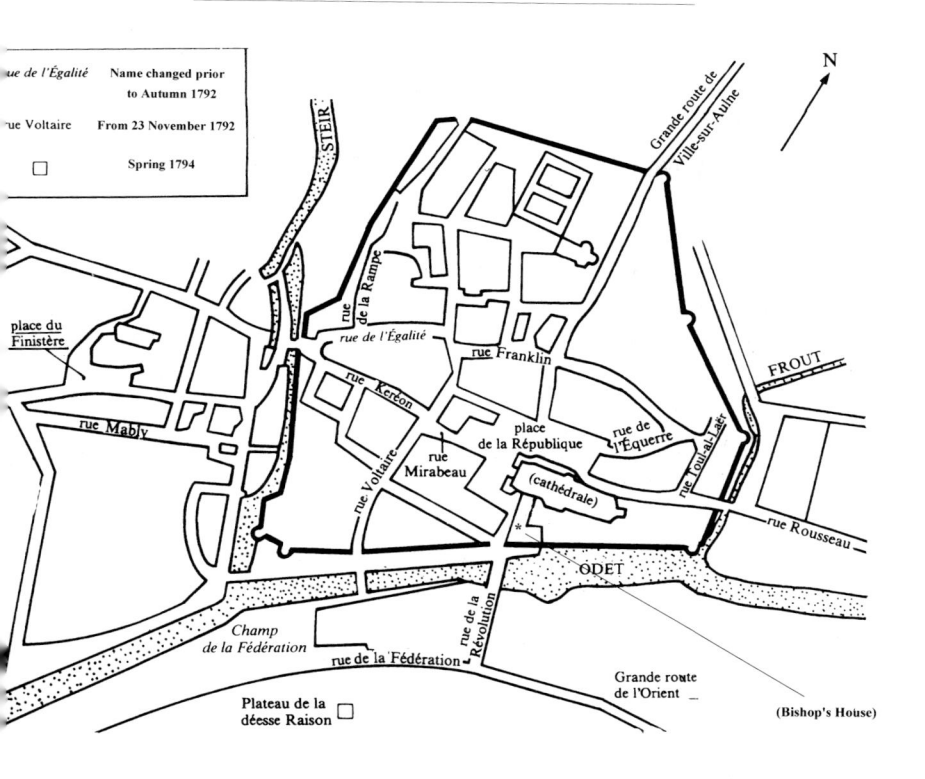

Plate 5: The renaming of Quimper's streets and squares; map adapted from the original of Daniel Collet in Jean Kervervé (ed.), *Histoire de Quimper* (1994).

whole apartments of the ground and first floor cieled. The bottoms of the rooms are as unsightly as the tops, from the gaping chasms of the planks which compose them; and the dirty state in which the floors and furniture are kept, is disgusting. Nevertheless in some respects the interior of these houses deserves regard. The vast mirrors which adorn their best apartments, and the beautiful plate glass of the windows, far exceed what are seen in English houses, except those of the first fashion. The French engravings I prefer to all others, and a few very good ones are still left here, though defaced, by having their dedications to princes, *maréchaux de France*,[3] and other great men, very clumsily erased. Of plate too it is said they formerly displayed sumptuous side-boards; but these have disappeared, having been either buried or committed to the crucible. Indeed it was become necessary to adopt one or other of these measures; for soon after the 10th of August 1792,[4] the democratic lust of destruction rose to such a height, as to order all family distinctions derived from ancestry, and all heraldic emblems whatever, to be erased, not only from the outsides of the houses, but from every article of furniture.[5] Even the armorial bearings engraved on the most trifling toys, a snuff-box, a ring, or a seal, were obliterated; and the post-office took care to detain all letters, of which the seals were impressed with those shocking emblems of aristocracy. I now eat with spoons whence the family marks are carefully expunged, the observation of which led to my enquiries.

A man who has seen only this skirting of France would demonstrate the highest degree of presumption, were he to pretend to draw a parallel between it and England; but, to confine myself to what I have seen here, I may venture to affirm, that civilization, luxury, a general diffusion of the comforts of life, or by whatever other name you please to call it, is more advanced in Cornwall and Wales than it was in this province, even before the revolution.[6]

Formerly there were two public walks on the banks of the river; but the stately elms which formed one of them have been lately cut down, to the great dissatisfaction of the inhabitants, in order to be sent to Brest for keels of ships.

The cathedral is a large edifice, of majestic appearance, but strikingly irregular in its exterior. Over its principal door is written *"Le peuple Français reconnait l'Etre Suprême."*[7] All the other churches and monasteries, which are numerous, have been converted (as the property of the state) into hospitals, stables,

DÉCRET

DE LA
CONVENTION NATIONALE,

Du septième jour du deuxième mois de l'an second de la République française, une & indivisible,

Relatif aux dépenses de l'enlèvement des signes de royauté dans les églises & autres monumens publics.

LA CONVENTION NATIONALE décrète comme article additionnel à la loi du 14 septembre dernier, sur la suppression des armoiries & signes de la royauté dans les églises & tous autres monumens publics, que les municipalités distrairont des dépenses celles faites pour détruire ou changer les signes de la royauté & de la féodalité sur les monumens & édifices déclarés nationaux, entretenus aux frais de la République, lesquelles dépenses seront acquittées sur le trésor public par le ministre de l'intérieur, sur les mémoires réglés par les municipalités & visés par les directoires de district.

Visé par l'Inspecteur.

Signé BOUILLEROT.

DECRED

EUS AR
GONVANCION NATIONAL,

N.° 1807.

Eus ar seis-vet deves eus an eil-mis, eil bloaz a Republic franç, eunan ac indivisibl,

Relatif dan dispignou an anlevamant eus a signou ar roueac'h en ilisou ac er monumanchou all public.

AR CONVANCION NATIONAL a zecret evel articl additionnel da lesen eus ar pevarsecvet deves a vis guengolo divesa, var ar suppression eus an armoniou a signou ar roueac'h en ilisou ac er monumanchou-all public, penaos ar municipaliteou a denno eus an dispignou, ar re great evit distruja pe chench signou ar roueach ac ar feodalite var ar monumanchou ac edifiçou discleriet national, antretenet e mijou ar republic, an evelet dispignou a veso acquittet var an trefor public gant ministr an interieur, var memoriou reglet gant ar municipaliteou a viset gant a directoiret a zistrict.

Viset gant an Inspedour.

Sinet BOUILLEROT.

Plate 6: Bilingual French/Breton Decree (dated 'the seventh day of the second month [Brumaire] of the second year of the French Republic, one and indivisible': 28 October 1793): 'Concerning expenses for the removal of royal symbols in churches and other public monuments'. *Source*: Archives départementales du Finistère, 8 L 82.

magazines, or manufactories of salt-petre. The church applied to this last use is well adapted to the purpose. I went with an English gentleman to see it, and no objection was made by the people whom we found there at work to our inspecting every part of their process, which is very simple.—Against one of the side walls are piled large heaps of wood-ashes, and near them two rows of casks with perforated bottoms, which are filled with the ashes thoroughly wetted. The water, after passing through the ashes, is received into tubs, and constitutes a vegetable alkaline lixivium. The opposite side of the church is filled with the ruins of old houses, and heaps of earth dug out of stables, slaughter-houses, and cemeteries, which last are full of the wrecks of humanity. These, after being macerated and mixed with the liquor drained through the wood ashes, are evaporated over a slow fire, until exhausted of the superfluous watery particles; after which the remaining part is put into large shallow coolers, on the sides of which the salt-petre shoots into crystals.

The workmen employed here are only twelve in number, and the quantity of salt-petre made is about fifty pounds a day, which, according to their account, costs only four livres and a half a pound; but this must not be depended upon, for they did not know the quantity of wood consumed. The wages of these people are inconceivably low, only 50 sols a day, and a ration of bread. Until lately they were paid only 35 sols, the addition having been made in consequence of the increasing dearness of the necessaries of life: even now 50 sols will scarcely buy a pound of the worst veal brought to market. They complained of its insufficiency, and told us, that manufacturers in England were paid as much for two hours work; "but, nevertheless, it is for the republic." Either from this conjecture of the liberality of our country, or from some other cause, they treated us with particular respect, and answered all our questions with the most ready civility: not an interested civility, for they neither received, nor gave us room to suppose that they expected, any gratuity.

Letter VIII: April 1795

I quitted the place with strange sensations. The process which I had witnessed was whimsically shocking. When I saw amidst the earth the bones tossed about, "mine ached at the remembrance." This earth said I to myself, once, perhaps, belonged to men whom these houses sheltered, and against whose descendants in La Vendée it may, when fabricated into the *breath of destruction*, volly forth, in the shape of bullets, the coffins which once enclosed their forefathers. There is certainly no discovery which entitles to higher admiration the inventive genius of man, than that of artillery, in all its wonderful combinations; but, at the same time, it must be confessed, that no stronger proof of our miserable degeneracy and infatuation can be produced, than our application of it.

The bishop's town-house I have mentioned. At a distance of less than a mile down the river stands what was once his country residence; but it is now the property of a naval officer, who bought it at a sale of national domains. I walked out to it the other day, and found it neither very large, nor very magnificent. It commands a good prospect of the river, and is pleasantly situated at the head of a large garden, filled by stone steps and strait walks. I found a gardener at work in it, who shewed me a superb orangery, where, in large wooden cases, stand the finest orange and lemon-trees which I ever saw growing out of their native climes, and bearing ripe fruit in the month of March. I asked the gardener about the last bishop, who was a constitutional one, and was told, that he was guillotined about a year ago, at Brest, for being a federalist. I had heard so before.—"Was not he," said I, "dragged away suddenly, and denied the consolation of taking leave of his family, who were in the house?"—"I believe," answered the gardener, "he was; but those things were so common some time since, that no body attended to them. I mind my work, and ask no questions."—I gave him an *assignat* of small value, which he expected, and went away.

But a building which would have excited my curiosity more than the palaces of bishops and the houses of nobility, I arrived here too late to see—a Temple of Reason, built for the exercise of the new religion of France.[8]—It stood on the summit of a lofty hill, close to the town, and consisted only of a few posts, from which rafters met at the top in a point to support the roof, the sides being open. Within it was adorned by festoons of oak-leaves, and was backed by a tree of liberty. It was the favourite rendezvous of the party of Robespierre, under whose auspicious reign it was erected. Here they swore eternal enmity to kings, and extirpation to aristocrats; and here their dances and sports were held, and the laws were read. In July last (not above ten days before the fatal *neuf Thermidor*[9]) all the unmarried young women, and even all the children of the town, down to seven years old, were compelled to march in procession up the hill, preceded by the mayor and a band of music, and to take an oath never to marry any but true republicans and *sans-culottes*. About three months ago this edifice was either blown down, or its foundation secretly undermined in the night; and only a few broken posts and a little thatch now proclaim, "*Ilium fuit.*"[10]

If the stories which are told of the extravagancies which this place gave birth to did not come from those who witnessed them (both French and English) their possibility might be doubted. I shall trouble you with only one of them.—A young republican of this town, on being ordered as a soldier to the frontiers, took a young woman of the place, and swore her here to be true to him; but even this test of the reality of her intention not being sufficient to quiet his jealous scruples, he absolutely wrote a letter to the convention, which was laid before them, stating his situation, and intreating that the girl might be put in a state of *requisition*, in her maiden capacity, until his return; lest, in his absence, she might be exposed to the allurements and seductions of aristocrats, who went about seeking to injure good republicans and *sans-culottes* like him. Can it be believed that a national congress should afford a serious hearing to such nonsense? Yet so it was; and she was actually commanded to

Letter VIII: April 1795

remain single until the young man should return.—Not a very gallant compliment to the lady's constancy of temper, you will say! To do justice to the French, I must however observe, that all ranks and parties of them now deride the remembrance of these degrading follies.

There are two coffee-houses in the town, which are numerously resorted to by both the English and the French, notwithstanding an inscription placed over the door of one of them, forbidding any but good patriots to enter.[11] The sign of this coffee-house gave rise lately to a refined piece of affectation:—it was a lion devouring a human body, and so exquisitely susceptible are the feelings of the present reigning party become, that they ordered the man of the house to blot out the body, *"it so reminded them of the days of Robespierre."* Accordingly the lion only now is seen. Here I go daily to read the Paris newspapers, and meet not with any interruption. For this privilege it is expected that something be spent: a dish of excellent coffee costs 15 sols, and a glass of *liqueur* from 20 to 40 sols. Persons of all ranks and professions, officers, soldiers, and their wives, and the people of the town, mingle here promiscuously.

The market-place is spacious and convenient. In the centre of it stands, on a square pedestal, a statue of Liberty, with inscriptions on each side, some parts of which have been recently white-washed, to obliterate them. Among these I could decypher the word *"Montagne,"*[12] and a few others of analogous signification, which a change of opinion has suddenly expunged from the vocabulary of French patriotism.—The market-day is still Saturday, when patroles of soldiers are sent on all the roads which lead to the town, to prevent forestalling, by compelling the country people to bring all their commodities into the market-place. Besides large heaps of wooden-shoes, the market generally affords some poultry and game, but not much butchers meat, except lean veal, of which I have never seen a want. Fish would be plentiful, were the boats permitted to go to sea; but, from a fear lest they should give information to the English, the fishermen are either interdicted, or subjected to so many difficulties, by being compelled to give security and take soldiers in their boats, that most of them have given up their employment. Of bread I have not since I have been here seen any deficiency; but I have been informed it was once, in the depth of last winter, so scarce, as to occasion a proclamation to be issued, that whoever sold it to a prisoner of war should be punished. We have always been able to procure it for *assignats*. It is for the most part very brown and coarse, but some whiter and finer is made, and publicly exposed to sale, in spite of the law, ordering only *pain d'egalité* to be used, which every body laughs at, and nobody thinks proper to enforce. The worst quality of all this bread is a grittiness, being full of small sandy particles, arising from two causes—the softness of the grindstones—and the corn not being sufficiently washed, after the oxen have trodden it out, which is practised here instead of thrashing. This may serve to evince, in how small a degree calculous[13] complaints are generated, by swallowing in our food similar materials to those of which stones and gravel in the human body are composed. The Bretons are remarkably healthy, and, I have been assured, are in general free from those diseases. Neither has any symptom of them been found among the English prisoners.

The prices of all articles in the markets and shops are increasing every day rapidly, owing to the depreciation of *assignats*. France is nominally dear, but to a man who possesses gold it is at present, perhaps, the cheapest country in the world. Meat is three livres a pound, and tolerable wine eight livres a bottle; but then a guinea will openly fetch 300 livres, and a *louis d'or* 350; the difference arises from the ignorance of the peasantry in regard to the former, and their consequnt dislike to exchange them.

There is yet a little coasting trade carried on here. It was once more considerable, but they never had any foreign commerce. The shops are numerous, but not overstocked with commodities, and the shopkeepers always recommend their goods, not only to us, but to their countrymen, by saying they are "English," which is too true: they are the spoils of our merchants. I have been well informed, that previously to the war a prejudice in favour of our productions ran so high here, and over all this part of France, that hardly an article of dress and furniture of French manufacture could be sold. You cannot conceive with what avidity those prisoners who are artificers are sought out and employed. You will laugh to be told, that one of the representatives, either Guesno or Guermeur, sent for an English shoemaker to make him a pair of boots, and even prolonged his stay for a day, rather than depart without them. Perhaps a better speculation than to send here a small cargo of our popular manufactures, in a vessel drawing not more than eleven feet, when peace shall be restored, and liberty of exchange unshackled, could not be projected. France will then open her *mines of gold and silver*. In other words, immense quantities of specie and other valuables, which are at this day buried, will be dug up and brought again into circulation. Some part of these concealments will undoubtedly be lost to their owners; who, after having entombed them, have either been chased from their native soil to return to it no more, or else have paid the debt of nature without communicating their secret. Ages hence their children will turn them up from the bosom of the earth; and, on seeing the effigy of the most unfortunate of kings, will recal to remembrance the most calamitous period of the history of their country.

Nothing surprized me more, on my arrival here, than to see beggars in every part of the town. The French officers at Brest had assured me, that there were no longer any in the republic; the government undertaking to make a provision for those, who might have no ostensible means of subsisting. In consequence of this intelligence, I had dressed up a fine speculation, in favour at

Letter VIII: April 1795

least of one change effected by the revolution.—If, said I, the noble and opulent are stripped and have fallen, yet the oppressed and miserable part of the community have emerged from that gulph of wretchedness, into which, under the ancient government, the most numerous class of inhabitants were plunged. The country, which has not in it any citizen so destitute as to want a sufficiency of food and raiment, cannot be so unhappy as we in England are fond of representing it.—What then was my astonishment, on entering Quimper, to find in every street, and in its environs, wretches of both sexes, who, with a livid aspect, and in a faltering voice, solicited of passengers a morsel of bread to appease their hunger, of that of a starving husband, wife, or child! It was in vain to answer me, that these persons, by application to the municipality, might be relieved;—so may all our poor, by applying to the work-house or parish-officer; but who, nevertheless, will venture to affirm, that we have among us no victims of hunger?—As I advance in my actual observations I gain a knowledge of facts, which lay open the real state of the country, and better enable me to appreciate the condition of the people, and the evils derived from equality incorrectly understood.[14]

The inhabitants of this town formerly consisted, besides the working people, only of petty shopkeepers, and of many of the neighbouring gentry, who, though not nominally rich, were able, in this cheap quarter, to keep town-houses, in which, during the winter, they resided in great plenty and hospitality. These patricians are said to have held the *bourgeois* at an immeasurable distance, but to have been very charitably disposed towards the wants of the poor. The taste for gaming, which I have spoken of, is not new. It always flourished here; and formerly, during the week of the carnival, and some other seasons of festivity, it was not uncommon to find adventurers here, who had made a journey from Paris to get a pluck at the *Noblesse Brétonne*.[15]

For two miles around the town I know the country pretty well, having always been fond of walking and making excursions. In these little rambles I keep, however, in the most unfrequented tracks, and always meet with civility from the peasantry, though by the soldiery I have been twice compelled abruptly to return. The parts I have traversed are diversified by hill and dale, and very like the wilds of Devonshire, with a stream dashing through every bottom. There are innumerable copses, but large trees, except firs, are hardly ever seen. The soil is almost universally light and sandy, and abounds in lime-stone. Every cottage has an orchard, but the cyder is not reckoned equal to that of Normandy. I often inspect the labours of the husbandmen, and wish I could talk to them. Except some fine meadows near the town, through which two beautiful streams flow, the ground is chiefly employed to raise corn. The cornfields are very neatly divided into lands,[16] and their implements of husbandry, particularly their wheeled ploughs, are much superior to what I had expected to find. Nevertheless, either from the lightness of the soil, or want of skill on the part of the cultivators, the crops of wheat are very moderate, not above five or six for one.[17]—They raise a few parsnips, and feed their horses with them to great advantage; but I have not seen one field of turnips, cabbages, or carrots, as a winter stock for cattle, and very little clover. I have not yet conversed with any man, who has the least knowledge of what a succession of crops means: to fallow seems to be the only assistance which they give to worn-out grounds. They testify only ignorance and amazement, when an Englishman explains to them the attention bestowed upon this important part of farming, and a cultivation of artificial grasses among us. Potatoes are yet planted only in gardens and small patches; but the culture of them every day extends, having more than once been recommended by authority. They frequently call it *la racine Anglaise*,[18] and many of the young people relish the potatoe; but their fathers and mothers, to whom until lately it was a novelty, prefer the most ordinary vegetable to it. It is a very common practice to irrigate not only

Letter VIII: April 1795

meadows, but higher lands, which demonstrates an intelligent spirit; the little troughs, which steal along through almost every field the streams which the bounty of nature has supplied to the country, are well contrived, and answer, as I have observed, effectually. Upon the whole, what I have been able to see and hear of the management of grounds here, notwithstanding the great deficiency I have pointed out, exalts it above the humble opinion which I at first sight formed of it. You know my fondness of agricultural pursuits, and the impediments which have constantly arisen to prevent my indulgence of it.[19]

The cattle are very small and mean, worse, I think, than any breed I ever noticed in the wildest part of North Wales, and certainly inferior to the moor breed of Devonshire and Cornwall. I speak only of countries[20] which I know. Even in the meadows, though better, they are unaccountably small, considering the pasture. The sheep are proportionably diminutive. Admiral Bligh and I had one day the curiosity to put in the scales a hind quarter of lamb, which was purchased in the market for our table, and it weighed, the kidney and a bit of liver included, exactly—*thirteen ounces and a half*.—At Brest we had remarked the smallness of the meat brought on board, several of the quarters of mutton not weighing more than three or four pounds each. The horses are low and hardy, but, by continual importations from other parts of France, are very superior to the cattle and sheep. The women here ride astride.

The houses of the peasantry are like those I described on my landing. I should oftener enter them were it not for dogs, which are chained close to the doors, by one of which I was seized by the thigh, and bitten through a thick pair of trowsers. Certainly the distresses of the times are greatly felt by all ranks of people in France; but in the cottages I have never seen want. One of the chief articles of the meals of the peasants is a sort of pancake, called *crape*[21] (I spell like an Englishman) made chiefly of buckwheat flour, and eaten with milk. These people are, indeed, a separate race from the body of the French, and have a language and customs of their own, to which they are tenaciously attached. I much lament that I cannot speak Welch, although so many of my happier days have been passed in Wales. As to French, it is of no more use to me among these natives, at the distance of half a mile from the town, than if I were at Ispahan or Delhi.[22] Almost all the gentry can speak this language. The Bretons and Welsh preserve another resemblance:[23] the latter do not love *cwrw* (ale) better than the former do brandy. The evening of a market-day here presents as drunken a scene as I ever beheld in England; but these good folks do not appear to be so quarrelsome in their cups as ours generally are.

The diocese of Quimper stands in a district called Cornwall. The truly old British words *Pen*, and *Caer*, are affixed to the names of innumerable places in the circumjacent country; and mark the origin of this people, were we to seek no other proofs.[24]

The town is surrounded by the *châteaux* of the gentry. Very few of the right owners live in them, and many of them are going fast to decay. Every where I see the dove-cotes demolished, which were the earliest victims of the first revolution; and I cannot lament their overthrow. The game-law now established gives liberty to every one to kill what game he may find upon his own ground, or that which he rents; and if any person, without leave, shoot on his neighbour's ground, he pays for each offence a fine of ten livres. How superior is this simple regulation, conceived in a spirit of equity, to a perplexed and odious code of penal statutes for the preservation of hares and partridges! Let me bring you acquainted with two other laws, which owe their birth to the revolution.—One of them is just passed, and exempts from the punishment of death, even after delivery, women who are tried for any crime when pregnant. "Can a woman so situated," asks the framer of the decree, "become a mother in that tranquil state of mind, which is so necessary to ensure the physical good of her offspring? Besides, could we forget humanity, does not the republic act impolitically in probably preventing the birth of a new citizen; (for women in this condition almost ever miscarry) or in condemning the mother to bring forth a half-formed being, which is usually distorted in mind and body, incapable of serving the state, and of propagating its species?"—I am sure I hear you join me in unqualified applause of the principle of this humane and considerate institution.—The other interdicts a duel, in all cases whatever, under the penalty of death to the survivor or survivors.[25]—The late king of Prussia said, that to determine whether single combat, in certain cases, ought, or ought not, to be abolished, required a congress of all the monarchs in Europe. Had he lived to witness the shocking grossness of speech and manners, which prevail among modern Frenchmen, for want of this or some other curb of a private nature, I think his uncertainty would have vanished, without troubling the crowned heads to assemble.—At least mine has.

The French often boast of the unexplored subterranean treasures of their country; and some among them are sanguine enough to believe that they shall rival England in her collieries. There are near Quimper two veins of what is called *charbon de terre* worked; but I have been assured by an English surgeon, that on analysis he found it to be *not coal.*[26] I picked up a piece, one day, at the mouth of a pit, carried it home, and put it into the fire, where it became red-hot, without consuming. To what use it is applied by those who extract it, I know not. It is, however, certain, that they have several times been industrious in trying to find out miners among the English prisoners; and in a few instances have succeeded in seducing our men to go and work at some mines (of what I do not know) which are said to lie near Brest.

The inhabitants of the town, or troops of the municipality as they are called, are obliged to do the ordinary duties here, when the regular soldiers are absent. In certain cases, however, they are allowed to perform this service by proxy. The present price of a substitute is ten livres a day, which is judged to be more than the worth of a day's labour, though it will not purchase more than a pound and a half of bread, a pound of veal, and a bottle of indifferent wine.

I have not yet said any thing to you of the French regular troops whom I have seen since I have been landed. There is not at present any complete regiment here, but there are detachments of infantry from several. Every day I see the different guards parade, march off, and relieve; and twice I have seen a detachment exercise, and perform their evolutions, which, though few and simple, were very awkwardly executed. Certainly a stranger, who should neglect to calculate the force of other causes, would start, on being told, that before these raw levies (to use Mr. Gibbon's words, as nearly as I can recollect them, on an occasion not very dissimilar[27]) the disciplined legions of Germany, the sons of chivalry of Castille, the gallant nobles of their own country, and even the hardy freemen of Britain, have been compelled to flee. In vain would he look for those usual indications of excellence, and prognostics of success, silence, attention, and the exact performance of movements in a great body, which we find in an individual.—In their room he would see battalions, composed indeed of stout and healthy young men, but clumsily and confusedly drawn up, with uneven ranks and broken files, whose bold looks, slovenly attire, and unrestrained carriage, would seem to proclaim equal defiance of their enemies and their leaders. Talk to them, and they will try to make you believe, that they wish to decide all battles by the bayonet only; and yet at this weapon they would to a certainty be beaten by the English, were the forces on each side in every other respect perfectly equal; for their bayonets, which I have measured, are shorter, and worse fitted for purposes of destruction, than ours. When they charge, nothing is more common than to hear them talk to each other, and fancy an Englishman, an Austrian, or a Spaniard, beneath their point, and crying for quarter.—I acknowledge freely, that the bravery of the French is as unquestionable as the light of the sun; but this in itself is inadequate to the atchievements which we have recently witnessed. To that lively courage which stimulates them to perpetual attacks; to their enthusiastic ardour in the cause of their invaded country; and above all to their undiminishable numbers, must be attributed those extraordinary events, which have confounded all political calculation, and filled Europe with amazement, consternation, and mourning.

The present pay of the common soldier is ten sols a day and a ration of provisions, but no wine when quartered in towns. They are furnished by the state with necessaries; so that the money is for pocket expences only. The name of the general officer now commanding here is Klingly. He is a native of Alsace, and one of the largest men I ever saw, being at least six feet four inches high, and proportionably stout. I have once dined in his company, and sat next to him, when he told me, that he had been in England, and, among other parts of it, at Castle Howard, the seat of Lord Carlisle; but in what capacity he had visited there, he did not explain to me.—His birth is reported to be obscure, and his advancement sudden.—Adieu.

LETTER IX

Quimper, 15th April, 1795.

By a news-paper, which I lately read, I find that the miseries and complaints of the English prisoners here have at length been communicated to our government; and that Sir Morton Eden is absolutely arrived in France, in order to negociate the terms of an exchange.[1] This subject, which I have forborne to touch upon before, is a very serious one; and a relation of the sufferings which the prisoners of war here have undergone, from the injustice and cruelty of their treatment, would form a most afflicting narrative.[2] The following statement, which was drawn up on the spot, by the Honourable Mr. Wesley*, and transmitted to Mr. Pitt, you may depend upon as a genuine and faithful representation.

"Quimper, 18th October, 1794.

In the beginning of July last, the prisons of Quimper contained about 2,800 fine young men, about which period a jail distemper broke out among them, which has already carried off upwards of 1,200. This disease still continues to rage with violence, and is not to be attributed to any general ill state of the air, but to the following local circumstances.

First—Want of cleanliness, from there being no necessaries[3] provided, whence the whole circumambient air becomes contaminated by so many people.

---

* Brother of the Earl of Mornington, who with his sister Lady Anne Fitzroy, was taken in a packet, by French frigate, on their passage from Lisbon.

Secondly—Bad provisions, and those in very small quantities, the daily allowance for seven prisoners being only six pounds of bad black bread; every fourth day these seven persons receive also two pounds of salt pork among them; and on the intermediate days they are served with a scanty mess of horse-beans. They have bad water, and no wine, or any spirits of any kind; nor have even those who possess the means leave to purchase those articles.

Thirdly—Want of bedding and clothes, the commissary of the prison of Pontenazan, near Brest, having stripped the greater part of the victims, who had the misfortune to pass through his hands, of their clothes, bedding, and money*.

Fourthly—Want of proper hospitals and attendance on the sick; the hospital, which is intended for English prisoners, being too small to receive half the number that are seized with the fever. The remainder are carried into a damp room, and laid upon straw, without any covering; and the above-mentioned prison allowance is their only support.

This is a fair and impartial statement of the situation of our unfortunate countrymen. The winter, should they remain here, will open a new scene of distress, as the few who may be spared, will then perish by cold and hunger, as they will be absolutely destitute of clothes, blankets, and other necessaries."

After this it were almost unnecessary to pursue enquiry farther; but as some well-authenticated anecdotes have been told to me, which, besides their relation to the subject, strongly tend to evince the temper of the times at different periods, and thereby become

---

* This commissary was ordered by the representatives then at Brest, to take a blanket from each prisoner who possessed two, and to pay him for it. He executed this commission by turning out of bed, into the court of the prison, all the prisoners, in the middle of the night, when he took away *not half, but all their blankets*, without making any recompence whatever for them. Their complaints of this robbery produced no notice or redress.

in some measure associated with the general politics of the country, I shall give them to you, after first premising, that I believe the greatest part of these nefarious and disgraceful proceedings are attributable not to a deficiency of either proper liberality, or proper directions, on the part of the present French government, but rather to the villany of their subordinate agents, who have violated the latter, in order to profit by the former. We know that a *traitement*, in *assignats*, to officers, who are prisoners, has been decreed by the convention, and its rate settled; although, from the multitude of offices through which it has to pass, and the obstacles and impediments thrown in our way when we attempt to trace the cause of the stoppage, hitherto we have not been able to recover any part of it. It is also fair to state, that since a new commissary of prisoners has been appointed here, the daily ration of provisions, by being equitably issued, is found very tolerably sufficient. Farther, in justice to the people I am among, let me declare, that since I have been landed (except a petty instance or two of splenetic insult) I have had no cause to complain of oppressive treatment, or to lament the want of as reasonable an extension of liberty as I could expect.

I have said, that in the winter bread was forbidden to be sold to the prisoners, and so was fuel, notwithstanding the severity of the season, and although no allowance of it was issued to them. Had not the humanity of some of the inhabitants of the town induced them to step forward to their relief, in defiance of the penalty of imprisonment, many of the English must have perished from cold.

The case of Lieutenant Robinson, of the Thames frigate, will set the conduct of the agents of tyranny in its proper light. This gentleman was taken in the latter end of October 1793, when *terror* was the *order of the day*, and in the engagement, which led to the capture of the ship, lost one of his legs above the knee, and was severely wounded in the other. On his arrival at Brest he was sent on shore to an hospital, and attributes his being now alive to a good constitution only; for he was neglected by the surgeons, and obliged to eat food in the highest degree improper for a wounded man. He once applied to the chief commissary for permission to send a person to buy some eggs, vegetables, and other refreshments for him, and was brutally refused. Mr. Robinson found, however, in some nuns, who were compelled to attend here, tender and careful nurses. These poor women were subjected to the grossest insults, and the harshest treatment. They had accustomed themselves, from motives of religious commiseration towards the sick, to employ their leisure hours in praying by the couches of those who chose to hear them; but this pious and humane practice was interdicted to them, by an especial mandate from the representatives on mission here; and two of them, who were found guilty of transgressing the order, were dragged to prison, amidst reproaches, taunts, and execrations.

Some months after, when his cure was advanced, though far from completed, Mr. Robinson, in a hope of changing for the better, requested to be removed to Pontenazan prison, about two miles from Brest, which was the general receptacle of the English. Thither he was conveyed in a cart, with several more sick prisoners, and thrust into an old rope-house, containing 700 people, who shortly after were increased to 1,400. This room contained no beds for the sick, and his stump was not healed. At first they were allowed to walk for air in the day-time in an inclosed court; but this indulgence did not last long, and thenceforth, on *no occasion whatever*, was a prisoner suffered to go out of the room. Nay the windows were forbidden to be opened, though it was the beginning of summer. However, upon this interdiction being communicated to the representatives at Brest, they ordered the windows to be kept closed on *one side only*. This rigorous crowded confinement soon induced putrid diseases, which swept off twenty and thirty persons a day, who were thrown without covering into a large hole, and quicklime heaped on the bodies. The daily allowance of the prison was a pound and a quarter of black sandy bread, four ounces of salt pork, a pint of sour wine, and at night a soup, of horse-beans boiled in water. The pork they were obliged to eat always raw, for there was neither a kitchen, nor any fire allowed, by which it could be dressed; and the sentinels were strictly forbidden to permit the prisoners to send out and make purchases of fuel, or aught else that they might need.

This huge dungeon contained people of all ages. One day the commissary of prisoners pointed out to Prieur de la Marne (one of the members of the convention on mission)[4] some little children, who were in a destitute miserable condition, and asked what should be done to relieve their wretchedness. "They are young vipers," cried this gentle and compassionate representative, stamping with fury, "turn them out to graze; grass is good enough for the English!"—This same Prieur, who is now "shorn of his beams,"[5] and in arrest, is well known for his severities and oppressions in Brittany. It seems, that he entertained hardly a more favourable opinion of the people of Brest, than of the English; for at one of the meetings of the popular society there, after a great execution, he affirmed that the town did not contain three real patriots; and that all persons who wore mourning for traitors (meaning those who had just been guillotined) were sharers in their guilt.

On the 5th of last May, Mr. Robinson, with other prisoners, was ordered to Quimper, at the distance of forty-five miles from Brest. A man on crutches, who had but one leg, and that crippled, might be supposed to be entitled to the indulgence of a vehicle for his conveyance. But when this unfortunate officer asked how he was to be transported to the place of his destination, he received for answer—"Walk, to be sure!"—In vain did he represent his utter incapacity. He was commanded to set out with the other prisoners; and complied. At the end of a mile he found himself totally exhausted, and must have lain down to perish on the road, or await the casual humanity of passengers, had not the soldiers who formed the escort, lifted him into a cart, which conveyed the baggage. When they reached Quimper in a heavy rain, they were all put, without distinction, into an old convent, and during the whole of this day received for food and bedding—*straw* only.—Finding himself wet and feverish, and possessing neither dry clothes or a bed, Mr. Robinson requested, as a favour, that he might be allowed to sleep for the first night at any house in town, observing to his keepers that he could not run away; and offering, in case of compliance with his entreaty, to defray not only his own expence, but that of the sentinel who might be placed over him.—He was peremptorily refused.

Soon after Lady Anne Fitzroy, and her brother Mr. Wesley, arrived here. He who recollects the former courtesy and gallantry of this once polished nation will scarcely believe, that an attempt could be made to immure a young, helpless, and beautiful woman, within the walls of a common prison. "The age of chivalry is indeed no more!"[6] By much supplication, and after considerable difficulty, her ladyship obtained permission to hire an apartment in an adjoining house, and to be served by a *traiteur*[7] with what she wanted for herself and her attendants. She was, however, forbidden to hold any communication with the people of the town, and a sentinel was placed over her to enforce the order. In the process of her confinement, liberty of walking in a garden, at the back of her prison, was granted to her ladyship; and this signal indulgence was followed up with leave to walk in the town, or to be carried in a sedan which she had borrowed, guarded, however, by her sentinel, lest her machinations might endanger the republic. The humane beneficence exerted by Lady Anne and her brother, to all ranks of their poor countrymen in captivity, are proclaimed here in terms of the most enthusiastic applause and gratitude. Misery, in whatever shape it appeared, excited their compassion, and called forth their bounty. They supplied the unhappy sufferers in the common prison with raiment, bedding, and food, without which assistance many of them must have perished.—You will observe, by one of my former letters (which, long ere this you must have received) that I had not the good fortune to see her ladyship. Admiral Bligh was more lucky, when he carried his son, in last January, on board the ship she was in, to receive her protection. We have known, for some time past, that they arrived safely in England.

Were it necessary to continue the subject, after what you have read, I am sorry to say, that it is in my power to adduce many more instances of premeditated systematic neglect, cruelty, and oppression, with which prisoners have been treated in this part of France during the present war. Many of the evils they have endured must indeed be placed to the account of Precini, the commissary, the same blockhead whose indecent democratic manners, in a company of ladies, so much disgusted me soon after I came to this place. This man has at length been superseded, and his office filled by a very plain honourable character, who extends to all in his department not only strict justice, but every fair and consistent indulgence, which the ameliorated state of public sentiments allows. The dismission of his predecessor, which was of the unceremonious kind, we chiefly owe to the representations made by Captain Kittoe, who had long witnessed his iniquity, and combated it, after a long struggle, successfully. The defence which this gentleman made at the *club* (or popular society) of the town, before which he was denounced, for "harsh and unjust usage of the prisoners of war," shall, however, be recorded in his justification. He did not deny that he had issued to them bad and unwholesome provisions; but this, he said, was only in compliance with orders he had received; in proof of which he named a representative, who had publickly directed, that the store-houses at Brest should be searched for damaged biscuit, "which," said he, "is good enough for those —— of Englishmen!" Had the charges against him turned on this single point, he must, therefore, have been acquitted of them; but it was clearly proved against him, that he had been guilty of innumerable acts of oppression and peculation.

While Precini locked up and cheated the prisoners, there were not wanting others to sport with their misery. I dare say you have often read, in extracts taken from the Paris news-papers, of a noisy speaker in one of the sections, distinguished by his ridiculous assumption of the name of BRUTUS.[8] This man is now a private sentinel, although but a few months since he was a general officer, and commanded the troops here. He was (like Tribout) originally a barber. During his command he took great delight in harassing the prisoners, and adding to their distresses. In one of these freaks an unlucky prognostic occurred of the decline of this great man's glory. Some Englishmen who had broken out of prison, in order to effect their escape, were retaken, and brought back. To amuse himself, Brutus ordered them to be shackled with the heaviest irons which could be procured, and in this condition marched them several times round the prison-yard; in the centre of which, encompassed by his satellites, he stood, enjoying their pain and aukward movements. A Guernsey-man, who was of the number, as they passed by the General, looked him full in the face, and cried, *"Chacun à son tour."*[9] At the moment it caused only an increase of the universal merriment; but the prediction seemed to be in some measure verified, when, soon after, Brutus's truncheon was taken from him, and a musquet put in its place.

This letter will be forwarded to you by Mr. Robinson, the gentleman whose name is so often mentioned in it. After a captivity of eighteen months, he has received permission, in consideration of his wounds, to return to England, on condition of sending back a French officer of equal rank to himself.—Adieu.

LETTER X

Quimper, 30th April, 1795.

At length the clouds of misfortune begin to separate, and a gleam of hope (though remote) breaks athwart the gloom, and points to England; whence I have lately received letters from those who are dearest to me, in which class I need not say you are included. You were right to be so brief and guarded in your expressions; although, as it happened, your letter reached me unopened, through a private channel. I observe what you say to me of the steps you are taking to bring about my exchange. Several Englishmen whom I know have lately effected theirs; and to my great joy (though I shall deeply feel the loss of his society and protecting influence) the Admiral every day expects an order to arrive from the maritime agent at Brest, for his liberation. A Captain Courand, who, on the 1st of June, commanded Le Sans Pareil, of 84 guns, is to be exchanged for him, and is now in France, pressing the committee of public safety to ratify the agreement, and forward the necessary passport. You must observe, that Admiral Bligh is exchanged for a *Captain*, because at the time of our sailing from England, in September last, he bore only that rank, in which capacity he commanded the Alexander, and consequently as such only could be exchanged. Innumerable are the obstacles which I foresee to prevent my accompanying him, when his passport shall arrive; but, as I am on very good terms with the commissary, I shall at least endeavour to obtain leave to go to Brest, in order to solicit permission from the representatives there to pass over into England, for the purpose of procuring a French officer of my rank to be returned in exchange for me. If success attend my petition (of which I am not in utter despair, as it will be backed by the interest of the Admiral) I shall be the bearer of my own letter; and if I miscarry, he will convey to you this sequel of the adventures and observations of your friend.

Deprived as you are in England of all communication with this country, except through the circuitous route of Switzerland and Germany, I often hear you ask me, What are the present politics and sentiments of the French? A man at the distance of five hundred miles from the metropolis can poorly answer such a question; but if you will be contented with a description of what the politics and sentiments of the people of Quimper and its neighbourhood are, according to the best information which I can procure; and accept of a string of opinions, derived from conversing with strangers, and from reading news-papers and fresh publications, as a solution of your enquiry, behold me ready to contribute to the extent of my ability to your gratification.

Here the friends of royalty, federalism, and an undivided commonwealth, struggle against each other with reciprocal vibrations. Federalism is, however, on the decline, and its supporters, attached as they are to the local prejudices which they contend for a continuation of, perceive the impossibility of carrying their point, and are fast melting into the two other great masses. Royalism, though bent to the earth, is not crushed. Its partizans are still numerous, and its hopes sanguine, too sanguine, I fear, for accomplishment. My political principles are, you see, unchanged since we parted; and I still think a limited monarchy the best of governments. Had I been born a Frenchman, I should have struggled as hard for the revolution of 1789, as I should have resisted with all my might that of 1792. Much as I hate despotism, I am scarcely less a foe to democracy; a sentiment which accords pretty well with those of my royal friends here. Since I have resided among the French, I have met with only one person, a lady (whose husband had once a place in the household,[1] and has emigrated) who has expressed to me a wish to see the old system restored. She, poor woman, cannot separate the splendour of a court, and the unlimited power of a king, from the prosperity and happiness of the people, always describing the latter as a direct and necessary consequence of the former. I am surprized to find that the royalists prefer Count d'Artois to his brother, Monsieur.[2] They call the Count a bold and decided character, although they do not spare his former profligate dissipation. To the little Louis, "*le monarque au berceau*," as they call him, they look rather with regret than expectancy, not unmingled with apprehension, lest violence or treachery should be used against him; but this fear I think groundless, because his preservation will best serve the interest of those whom he is among. I am assured that his morals are corrupted, and his health destroyed.—Unhappy infant! what a lesson on the instability of human grandeur does he furnish!

> "Un faible rejetton—entre les ruines
> *De cet arbre fécond, coupé dans ses racines.*"
> HENRIADE, 7th Canto.[3]

The royalist party is strongest in the country, and the republican in the town. The most numerous class of inhabitants in the latter, the little housekeepers, find their importance increased, and their vanity flattered, by becoming members of clubs and political societies, and being admitted into municipal posts and honours. Doubtless, even in this part of France, which has long been regarded with a jealous eye by the government, the royalists are not equal in number to their formidable antagonists: they will, however, I am confident, fly to arms, if ever a favourable opportunity of attacking their oppressors be presented to them. Whenever I find myself (which sometimes happens) in a little knot of these good people, almost all of whom have either fathers, brothers, sons, husbands, or other near relations emigrated; and when I listen to the downfall of the convention, and hear them, by the restoration of a king, restore themselves to their forfeited honours and estates; it brings to my remembrance what passed, seventeen years ago, among the loyalists of Maryland, where I was then, as now, a prisoner of war. I hear similar fallacious calculations made, unsupported expectancies indulged, and ardent resolutions adopted, to end, I fear, in similar disappointment. The paper-money, divisions and mistrusts of parties, my own situation at both periods, and other circumstances, render the parallel very striking to me. To dash, with rude hand, the cup of consolation[4] from the lips of these unfortunate people, were the extreme of cruelty; but when they appeal to me, by asking whether armies of Englishmen and emigrants may not be expected to execute their airy speculations, I cannot become a partner of the deceit, by administering to the delirium. Whatever might once be the opening presented to us for the attacking of France in her vitals, by a co-operation with the armies of La Vendée, that season is passed, never to return.[5] To commence, at this declining period of the contest, such a system, were almost to proclaim, that while we believed it possible to subjugate France by a coalition of exterior force, we disdained to profit by the arms of Frenchmen, in a cause which we called their own. Besides, if a publication, which is stuck up in all parts of the town, dated the 1st of *Floreal*, at Rennes, and signed by ten representatives and twenty-two *Chouan*[6] chiefs, with Caumartin[7] at their head, may be believed, the Vendéans have made their peace,[8] and submitted to the republic, after having for more than two years caused the most powerful diversion in favour of her external enemies. But this my friends here intreat me to despise; and, when I point out to them its marks of authenticity, assure me, that Charette will never lay down his arms, but on the condition of royalty being re-instated; that he is only temporizing, and will soon break out stronger than ever. I listen in silence, and know not which way to turn my faith.—What shall I say of this extraordinary character, Charette! who, whatever be his future intentions, has hitherto, certainly, displayed extraordinary powers of mind, and Antæus-like[9] arisen fresh from every fall. I am acquainted with two people who personally know him, and describe his talents, courage, and perseverance, in terms of enthusiastic admiration. The French do not scruple to affirm (but here I suspect their love of exaggeration, not unmixed with national vanity, to preponderate) that the war of La Vendée has cost to the republic more men than all her foreign conflicts united. If, instead of men, perplexity and vexation were substituted, the account would be more credible.

The proclamation which announces a conclusion of the war of La Vendée is not the only one, which strikes at this moment the public eye, in Quimper. His Prussian Majesty, Frederic William, our good and faithful ally, has, we are told, also made his peace with the republic.[10] When I recollect his threatening bombastic language, and the mighty irruption made into Champagne, not quite three years ago, by this pigmy in the shoes of a giant, I can compare him to nothing but the month (April) I write in, which is said to come in like a lion and go out like a lamb. The French themselves cannot help adverting to his former menaces, and sneering at them, when compared with his present meekness and tender concern for the effusion of human blood. The preamble of the proclamation states, that, "in Pilnitz, a part of his Prussian Majesty's dominions, the first partitioning treaty of the territory of France was executed. That now the republic has demonstrated to kings and ministers, that she is not only victorious but invincible, she will prove to them that she is generous, and willing to grant peace, upon terms consisting with her dignity, to all her enemies. And, that henceforth the ability of her government, not only to conclude, but to guarantee, treaties and alliances, ought not to be doubted, &c. &c."—A peace with Spain, likewise, is reported to be in great forwardness; so that it is probable, before the end of this year, England alone will have the contest to maintain; and well, I trust, it will be maintained by our victorious fleet?

Letter X: April 1795

If then the coalition be on the point of its dissolution, and Charette has laid down his arms, either we must abandon the subjugation of France, or seek for other means to accomplish it, which, if they exist at all, are internal. Nothing can be more dazzling and imposing than the great success of the French against their foreign enemies, and the seeming ease with which the vast machine of the republican government moves; but this smooth exterior conceals a hollow and ulcerated inside. The numberless abuses subsisting in the multiplied public offices, which defy control or abolition (what think you of its being asserted in the convention, that in the post-office department more than *thirty-nine thousand* persons receive salaries?); the depreciation of *assignats*, which proceeds in a ratio continually increasing, a piece of money, which eight weeks since sold for 140 livres, now fetching 400; and, above all, the enormous public expenditure, which almost defies computation; are causes of the most serious alarm to the supporters of the revolution. The last of them, if not checked, must produce a national bankruptcy, and overturn this government, as it did the monarchy; but whether to give birth to a new form of democracy, or to the restoration of a king, who shall say!

By the report of the new financier, Johannot, made to the convention—

	livres.	
The national expence of the month of *Nivôse* last was	423,374,450 - or -	£.18,522,632
The receipt of taxes in the same month was	57,168,733 - or -	2,501,132
Excess of expenditure, rejecting shillings and pence, and reckoning a livre at $10\frac{1}{2}$ d.	366,205,717 - or -	£.16,021,500

In the succeeding month, *Pluviose*, the difference was still more enormous: it exceeded the receipt by 443,164,244 livres, or £.19,388,435. "The trappings of royalty" would poorly keep pace with this unprecedented profusion, which is hourly increasing, by the inevitable augmentation of salaries to all the public servants, both civil and military. The naval officers have had a considerable addition to their pay since I left Brest; and, as a signal to all beneath, the stipend of the members of the convention has been increased from eighteen to thirty-six livres a day.

I do not pretend to know the nature and extent of the present taxes; but I remember the favourite scheme of a heavy land-tax, in lieu of all others, was trumpeted forth at the commencement of the revolution, not that it dates its birth at so recent a period. Our principle of taxing consumption, they treated with great contempt; but I have reason to believe they will soon adopt it, as I have lately read a most spirited and ingenious attack on Cambon,[11] and some of his predecessors, in which it is extolled. The most considerable of the present imposts is a duty of 20 *per cent.* on all lands and houses. This was calculated to produce 260 millions, and makes the annual value of landed property (including buildings) to be 1300 millions of livres. Let us suppose (dreadful supposition!) that a third part of this is sequestrated, and in the disposal of the government. Call this 440 millions; and farther, let us presume, that all these houses and lands will be sold at 25 years purchase (which, if the nature of a part of the property, and the fears of reclamation, particularly of the estates of the later emigrants, be considered, is perhaps too much) the amount will be 11 milliards.[12] This is the calculation of the most sanguine of the French with whom I have conversed on the subject; and even this, terrifying as it is to compute or read, seems likely to be insufficient. Johannot reckons, the national means at 15 milliards 226 millions, even after the allowances, which justice and humanity dictate, shall be deducted from them; and proposes to coin immediately 150 millions of copper, in order to afford support to the declining credit of *assignats*. I need not tell you, that I possess no *data* to formally controvert this statement of the financier; but I beg leave to observe, that his whole report, which I have carefully read, is conceived in those sanguine and flattering terms, which appear to me to have sprung from a pre-concerted determination of exhibiting the favourable side of the picture, and keeping the people in good-humour. I have heard it publickly derided, and have been told that both its premises and conclusions are false. In addition to the allowance which he hints is to be made to the relations and creditors of emigrants, under certain restrictions, is to be placed a complete restitution of the properties of the Brissotine party, and all who suffered under the tyranny of Robespierre: at least such expectations have been holden out in the convention. He also states, that there are now eight milliards of *assignats* in circulation, and that only three milliards more need be added to them. For the justness of this last declaration his word must be taken, as he does not tell us why he limits to this sum the future emission.—Query, How are the creditors of the old government to be considered, when the day of liquidation shall arrive? A lottery, it seems, is projected, of all the forfeited houses; and the scheme, at least here, appears to be relished.—There is yet another source of revenue, of a delicate nature, which I sometimes hear and read boasted of:—requisitions from the conquered countries; and confiscations of the church lands in the Austrian Netherlands.—How far these will be practicable to any great amount, I leave to you to determine. Remember, that the comparatively trifling levies, which have been already made upon the Belgians, are said to have rendered the French name odious in that country.

But little facts sometimes impress conviction on the mind, when a laboured detail has failed.—Until lately there were not any *assignats* in circulation of more than two thousand livres each in value; but, on the petition of the army contractors, *assignats* of ten thousand livres each have been fabricated, "in order to lessen the *expence of carriage*, which is become enormous."—One of the Paris papers, two months ago, assigned as a reason for raising its price, the increasing value of paper, which was then 80 livres a ream. "How," asks the editor, "can it be otherwise, when government, by contract, is everyday supplied with six thousand reams for its consumption in printing off *assignats*!!"

All *assignats* of the value of more than 100 livres, bearing the effigy of Louis XVI. were proscribed some time since, except in the purchasing of national domains. This was one of the last piratical manœuvres of Cambon, and was every way worthy of the financier of Robespierre. However it somewhat contributed to lessen the immense load of circulating paper.

When I sum up the component parts of this stupendous system, and contemplate it in the aggregate, I must confess myself to be staggered, and almost ready to pronounce against the ability of this wonderful[13] people to continue the contest in which they are engaged. But, after revolving the subject in every point of view in which it presents itself to my mind, I am decidedly of opinion, that not even a national insolvency would produce the effect, which some of the powers combined against them sought in its commencement. The dismemberment of France cannot be accomplished, without the extermination of its inhabitants, even though Mr. Playfair[14] write a second profound disquisition to demonstrate its necessity and practicability; and how far a "*bellum internecinum*,"[15] against twenty-four millions of people is either in its principle to be desired, or in its accomplishment to be expected, may at least exercise the casuistry of humble searchers of truth, like you and me.

That the French wish for peace, cannot be doubted by those who are in a habit of reading their daily chronicles, and listening to their sentiments; but even this event, desirable as they feel it to be, they will not purchase at the expence of the integrity of the empire, or by suffering any power, or combination of powers, on earth, to dictate to them what shall be their form of government, or even to interfere in the most inconsiderable point about their internal regulations. Such, upon my honour, I believe to be the unalterable determination of a large majority of the French nation. A peace with us they especially covet. I shall not now stay to examine what are the impediments on our side to its completion. We are accused of wishing to monopolize the trade of Europe to both the Indies. According to the latest accounts I have read from one of them, notwithstanding our rapid conquests in the beginning, the tide of victory seems to be so far balanced, as to render the event dubious; and even if we finally succeed in that quarter, it may become a question, whether "*le jeu vaut la chandelle.*"[16] The yellow fever, and the resistance of a million of men, suddenly awakened to a perception of their rights, are antagonists not to be despised. "Emancipate the negroes, and the commercial ascendancy of England is for ever destroyed," said Danton.[17] My opinion is very different; and I am persuaded, that if the Charibean islands were at this moment independant states, our shipping would not be less numerous (for our immense capital would flow into other channels) nor would sugar, rum, coffee, and Barbadoes water, be less attainable to administer to our luxury. If the opulence of England be founded on the basis of African slavery; if the productions of the tropics can be dispensed to us only by the blood and tears of the negro, I do not hesitate to exclaim—"Perish our commerce;" let our humanity live!

By the way, I am often asked, why we joined against them in a confederacy, whose aims (they say) were as irreconcileable to each other, as to justice. This query I have so little satisfaction in answering, that, for the sake of argument, and to prevent being totally overborne, I retort it upon them, and accuse them of being the aggressors: a contest in which nothing is gained or lost, for both affirm, and both deny.

It is, nevertheless, certain in the mean time, that a hatred of us, as a nation, is universally diffused among the favourers of the revolution. When declaiming on this head, their extravagance is sometimes not unentertaining. They have collected, and believed, without examination of their absurdity, a number of wild and ridiculous tales about us: such as that there existed a scheme to set the Duke of York upon the throne of France; that Marat and Robespierre were in the pay of Mr. Pitt, and acted by his directions, &c. &c. They stun one, indeed, with repetitions of the name of Mr. Pitt, and execrations of his politics, which, I often tell them, is the highest compliment they can pay him. "His father," said an orator in the convention, "infused into him, in his infancy, his hatred of France, and, like Hamilcar[18] of old, swore him to eternal enmity against the French name." But, perhaps, another great man, whose share in provoking the war, and sounding the knell of peace, has not been inconsiderable, may feel disappointed on being told, that his name in this part of France is never mentioned, and is even unknown. The splendid pebble, with which Mr. Burke,[19] after the first revolution, endeavoured to perturb the lake of French tranquillity, has not yet spread its undulations to this distant shore.—To descend from Mr. Burke to his vaunted antagonist Tom Paine,[20] I was, on coming into France, curious to learn what had become of this wandering demagogue, whom the delirium of the moment had rendered conspicuous. For a long time I could get no intelligence of him: to some his name was new; and others, with difficulty recollecting it, said he was guillotined. My enquiries remained unsatisfied, until I chanced to read in a news-paper a decree of the convention for his release from arrest, with other deputies of the party of Brissot. From this time, until a few days since, I had ceased to think about a being, whose name was never mentioned; when a news-paper again presented it to me, in a report of Courtois to the convention, dignified by the title of "founder of liberty in the two worlds." Notwithstanding this consolatory panegyric, I am of opinion that Mr. Paine is not destined to shine on the theatre of French politics. But whither shall he retire to better his fortune, and re-lume his fame? America would *now* prove a sterile and unproductive soil for the transplantation of such a genius; while ungrateful Europe (the French dominions excepted) shutting every avenue against him, bids him wander, like a second Cain, without an asylum, or a resting-place.

To return to my subject.—The present period is certainly an interesting one in the history of the revolution. The convention is not popular, and every day loses ground, in the affection of the people. You can form no adequate idea of the closeness with which its proceedings are scrutinized, and the asperity with which they are attacked, in the news-papers, and in private circles. Since I have resided among the French, freedom of opinion and speech has made an extraordinary progress. Heads which, six months ago would have "'bided but the whetting of the axe," now declaim unintimidated, and unrestrained. Has the proposition of Merlin de Thionville,[21] for the dissolution of the convention, and the election of a national assembly, yet reached you? It was strongly defended, and strongly reprobated. For the present, Merlin has been prevailed upon to withdraw his motion; but, I think, it will be resumed soon: the royalists eagerly long for it, and predict, from the moment it shall be decreed, the restoration of monarchy, provided the election be free and general; but this is not expected, as a proposal, in case it must be adopted, has been already started, to oblige the people to elect a majority of the present legislators. In the mean time the new constitution is loudly clamoured for by the republicans. Sieyes,[22] who is at length emerged from behind the curtain which had so long concealed him, and others, are said to be preparing it; and a very beautiful metaphysical theory of impracticability, I doubt not, it will prove. Let this be as it may, I dread an agitation of these questions, and become doubly desirous to get out of France before they are started; for, during the time of the election, we shall at least be locked up and half starved, if no worse befal us.

But another question, which involves more important consequences than at first appear, *viz*. Whether the leaders of the

Letter X: April 1795

ancient committee of public safety, Barrere, Collot d'Herbois, and Billaud de Varennes (Vadier having escaped) shall be tried, or not? has during the last six weeks almost absorbed every other consideration.[23] It was, in fact, an experiment of the strength of the two parties, the moderates and terrorists, which divide the convention. The latter are generally supposed to be completely overthrown; but, in my opinion, the middle step, of inflicting, without a trial, the punishment of exile (some say to Cayenne, others to an island on the coast of Brittany) upon culprits whose crimes exceed credibility, is not only unjust, but evinces something like a compromise. The royalists, the Brissotines, and all others who have been lately freed from confinement, greatly dreaded the escape of these monsters, in the consequent triumph of their party. Poor Madame Kérvélligan, while it was pending, did us the honour, with some more ladies, to dine with us. You cannot picture to yourself terror like her's, lest the moderates should be defeated. She took from her pocket a paper, and read to us from it, with great encomiums, the speeches in the convention of Legendre, Isnard, and others who had declaimed against the *prevenus*;[24] while she was enraged in an equal degree against those who had defended them, and resisted the return of the proscribed deputies (her husband is of the number) into the bosom of the convention, until they should be purified by trial. Lecointre[25] of Versailles was not spared upon this occasion. Mr. Kérvélligan is now in Paris; and who can wonder at her perturbation? Of the seventeen months which he lay concealed, she was shut up eleven a close prisoner in the *château* of Brest. If she do not hear from him by every post, she is miserable; not knowing, in the present temper of the times, who may be spared in a popular commotion. She and others declared to me, while the struggle lasted, that so exasperated were the two parties against each other, that they should not be surprised to hear, that they had had recourse to arms, and butchered one another in the senate-house. The days and nights of the 12th and 13th of *Germinal*[26] were particularly terrible. The convention during the whole of them remained at its post, most of the members being armed with pistols to prevent assassination. In this commotion, of which part of a narrative, written by one who was on the spot, has been read to me, the cry of "*Vive Louis dix-sept!*" was once or twice heard, but it was faintly uttered, whilst "*Vive la republique,*[27] and give us a constitution!" resounded on every side.

Immediately after this disturbance was quelled, expresses communicative of the event were dispatched into all the districts. The courier to this place arrived a little before noon on the 9th instant, and the drum was forthwith beat in every quarter of the town, inviting all "*good citizens*" to repair at two o'clock to the cathedral, to hear the account from Paris read, and to adopt measures in consequence of it. Being assured of not giving offence, I went at three to the place of appointment, and found the municipality, and about 150 people of the lower order, including a few officers, several soldiers, and many women, collected. They were listening to a man who was mounted into the pulpit, and reading to them a *bulletin*, stating the circumstances of the attempt which had been committed on the national representatives, and of its suppression; also the names of certain members whose arrest had been decreed; and lastly, that General Pichegru[28] was called in, to preserve by an armed force the peace of Paris from the machinations of royalists and terrorists. Every body wore their hats, and no insult was offered to us Englishmen, several of whom were present. When the reading was finished, an address to the convention was voted, on the patriotism and energy they had displayed; and several people got into the pulpit, and spoke in their turns. From these orators, a blacksmith was universally allowed to bear away the palm, haranguing with great fluency against the terrorists, and surprizing his auditors by the keenness of his sarcasms, and the justness of his observations. The speech of one who ascended the tribune was simply, "*Vive la republique!*" which was received with many plaudits. In conclusion they decreed, that the members of the ancient committee of *surveillance* of the town (which has long been suppressed) shall be deemed suspected persons, be disarmed, and obliged to appear every day before the municipality; and that henceforth they shall not be eligible to any office of trust or power in their commune.

A mention of the committee of *surveillance* leads me to bring you acquainted with that infernal institution, which, of all engines that ever were placed in the hands of a government, was surely the most effectual to over-awe the citizens, and to promote the cause of despotism. The number and cost of this host of licensed spies were not less extraordinary than their power, which authorized them, without assigning any reason but a suspicion of incivism, to enter the houses of all the inhabitants, whom they pleased to say had been denounced to them; to seize upon their persons, in order to deliver them over to the revolutionary tribunal; and to break open their cabinets, and inspect their papers. There are in France forty thousand communes, and every commune had its committee, which, upon an average, contained ten members, the number in part depending upon that of the inhabitants. The salary of every member was five livres a day.

If therefore we multiply	- -	40,000
	by	10
the number of members will be		400,000
		5
and the expence per day	- -	2,000,000 livres;
which multiplied by	- - -	365
makes the annual expence	- -	730,000,000 livres, or, at
$10\frac{1}{2}$ *d.* each, £.31,937,500.		

Liberté, Egalité, fraternité, ou la mort.

Les Sans-culottes composant le comité de Surveillance et Révolutionnaire de quimper ... au Représentant du peuple près ... de la marine à Brest.

Représentant

D'après l'entretien qu'un de nos collegues a eu avec toi, en présence des commissaires du District et de la municipalité, nous te prévenons que nous avons arrêté de faire mettre dans la même maison tous les prisonniers anglois qui sont dans nos murs, et de leur interdire toute communication au dehors.

Cette mesure est d'autant plus sage que déjà plusieurs d'entr'eux avoient tenté de s'enfuir, et s'étoient sauvé jusqu'à dix lieues de notre cité.

Nous te préviendrons de nos mesures ultérieures à leur égard, qui seront toujours dictées

par le plus pur Républicanisme, et
pour l'intérêt et la Sûreté publiques.

Salut et fraternité

Lemoyne Rose Raoulin

Cariou

Secrétaire

Montagne

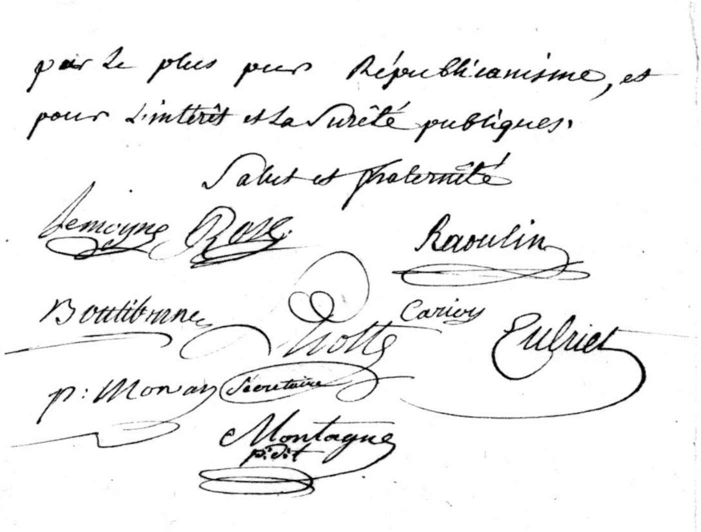

Plate 7: Letter from 'the *sans-culottes*' of the Quimper Committee of Surveillance to Representative Prieur de la Marne at Brest, undated. The letter informs the Representative (using the egalitarian second-person pronoun *tu*) that all English prisoners of war in the town are now to be housed in one building and forbidden communication with the outside world. Committee-member 'Montagne' has changed his name from 'Le Roy'. *Source*: Archives départementales du Finistère, 8 L 82.

The committee of *surveillance* of Quimper consisted of twelve members, whose names and occupations were as follows:

Botibon,	retail shopkeeper,	Rose,	barber
Harier,	butcher,	Roland,	merchant's clerk,
Moreau,	musician,	Morivan,	hog-butcher,
Becam,	taylor,	Le Moine,	gardener,
Cariou,	taylor,	Montaigne,	brazier,
Keroch,	barber,	L'Hot	printer's devil.

They were to a man the creatures of the creatures, ten gradations deep, of the committee of public safety. In such hands were the liberties and lives of Frenchmen deposited! Even on the day I write, the institution is not totally abolished, but is momently expected to be so. It is still retained in towns which contain forty thousand inhabitants, or more, but is seldom allowed to exercise its powers.

The number of persons guillotined in Quimper was only four, two priests and two women. The *guillotine* was kept in the cathedral, but performed its office on the parade. It was customary to send to Brest those who were denounced, which was more convenient than to try them on the spot, where witnesses might have established their innocence: of this class there were many victims. I was told, when at Brest, that 172 persons of both sexes had been executed there. The operation is said to have been performed on 32 of the number in somewhat less than nineteen minutes.

It is impossible to pronounce the word *guillotine*, without associating with it its grand mover Robespierre, that modern Procrustes,[29] who fought to contract or extend to the standard of his own opinion, a mighty people; before whom neither elevation of virtue or talents could erect a shield, or insignificancy of birth and situation creep beneath a shelter. Without aiming to become his defender, I must, however, be permitted to observe, that many of the relations, which, on authority seemingly good, I every day hear and read of his towering ambition and capricious cruelty, are too extravagant to be credited, and, if true, too degrading to our nature to be repeated. In the general horror and indignation excited by his remembrance, I am sensible (especially among this declamatory people) that truth will often be sacrificed to passion. There is, besides, a second reason, that increases the distrust with which I listen:—to screen themselves from odium, all the subordinate tyrants fix upon him, and attribute to his orders, the innumerable butcheries and acts of oppression which they have perpetrated.—They who were once his closest imitators, are now loudest in their outcries against his memory; which, in many instances, is loaded with the crimes of his contemporaries. I had not been taken twenty-four hours when Captain Le Franq, either from credulity, or a wish to impress me with an early belief of his not being attached to a sinking party, told me, among similar tales, that Robespierre had, in the town-hall of Paris, caused himself to be proclaimed, "Maximilian the First, Emperor of the French." Upon finding that a man, whose relative rank and situation in life entitled him to respectable sources of information, could thus, either from ignorance, prejudice, or a less laudable motive, be guilty of so gross a misrepresentation, it became doubly incumbent upon me to restrain my belief.

However outrageous the execrations of the French now are on hearing his name, they do not surpass the adulation with which they once approached the idol of his power. I wish I could send to you the *Gazette Nationale* of the 30th of *Pluviose*, which belongs to a collection of news-papers that I have access to, and contains a report of the 16th of *Nivose*, made to the convention by Courtois, in the name of the committee appointed to examine the papers of Robespierre. Never before was flattery so gross and servile used as some of these productions, which were addressed to him from different districts, *communes*, and popular societies. The statue inscribed to the "*immortal man*," and the poetic incense afterwards offered at his shrine by Boileau, fade before it. He is called in them the glorious, incorruptible Robespierre, who covers, as with a shield, the republic by his virtues and talents; who joins to the self-denial of a Spartan, or a Roman of early date, the eloquence of an Athenian. Even his tenderness and humanity of disposition are praised. One man congratulates himself on a personal resemblance of him; and another, at the distance of 600 miles, is hastening to Paris, to feast his eyes with a sight of him. He is compared, not by an individual but by a body of people, to the Messiah, "*annoncé par l'Etre Supreme, pour reformer toute chose;*" and afterwards he is said to manifest himself "*comme Dieu, par des merveilles.*"[30] On some occasion a *Te Deum*[31] was performed for him, the burthen of the ditty being, "*Vive Robespierre! Vive la Republique!*"—I feel ashamed to transcribe any more of these impious and contemptible absurdities. I beg of you, however, to remark, when Courtois's report shall fall into your hands, that amidst the papers which have been scrutinized of this extraordinary personage, though incontrovertible evidence of his restless and sanguinary disposition appears, yet nothing bearing the marks of an arranged plan for mounting a throne, or erecting himself into a dictator, was found. Some trifling hints are once or twice thrown out, which the reporter does not fail to magnify; but Robespierre, if he ever really entertained such a project, was too circumspect to commit it to writing; and knew too well the loose nature of man to entrust his secret, until it were matured in his own mind, and could tempt to confederacy by its probability of accomplishment. I never reflect on the sudden and total apostacy of the French from this man and Marat, without indulging a hope that the versatile levity of sentiment, and unceasing desire of change, which characterize the nation, will at length point, in a spirit of repentant loyalty, founded on an unconquerable determination to be free, to the descendants of their kings. And this hope I am always willing to sustain, by calling to mind our restoration of Charles the Second; but at the same time I confess, that (at least for the present) my observations pronounce it to be rather a conclusion which I desire, than a consummation which I expect.

By posterity then must Robespierre be judged. No scrutiny will reach his virtues, however it may exalt his genius. Vigour of mind he undoubtedly possessed, and he joined to it (except in moments of inebriation, to which he was sometimes addicted) profound dissimulation; but there exist unquestionable proofs, that he was a poltroon, which single flaw in his composition rendered his downfall certain. A combination of other causes might have prolonged his elevation, but could not have preserved it to the end of his existence. On how many occasions did Cromwell's personal intrepidity, and firmness of nerve, uphold him and his authority!

We owe candour more to a review of the worst than of the best of characters; and no man was ever more entitled to an indulgence of it than Robespierre.

The papers of the other members of the committee, of which Robespierre is believed to have directed all the springs, are also laid open, and are equally curious and shocking as his. There are among them orders, ready signed and sealed, for bringing to trial, and executing, those whose names might be inserted in the blank spaces. Juries, a venerable institution derived from *us*, have hitherto had very little claim to the gratitude of the French. In a report made to the convention by Saladin,[32] in the name of the committee of 21, on the 13th of last *Ventose* (3d March) it is stated, that the managers of the committee of public safety, Barrere, Collot, Billaud, &c. held every evening conferences with the public accuser and the president of the revolutionary tribunal, who rendered to them an account of their proceedings, and received their instructions for the work of the next day.—On the following account you may also rely. A judge and jury were sent to Paris, from a place 200 miles distant from it, to give an account of their principles, for having condemned two men to ten years imprisonment, who, in the opinion of a representative who was present in the court, ought to have suffered death. The crime of the prisoners was, having said, that "they wished to see the tree of liberty of their commune cut down."—The sentence was ordered to be quashed; they were tried again; and guillotined.

An extract of a letter, signed Darthè, found, after his execution, in the cabinet of Le Bas, is as follows. "*Le comité de salut public a dit à Le Bon, qu'il esperait que nous irions tous les jours de mieux en mieux. Robespierre voudrait que chacun de nous pût former un seul tribunal, et empoigner chacun une ville de la frontiere."*[33] After this gentle wish (allowing it to have been uttered) which breathes more closely that of Caligula[34] than any other that modern biography affords, you will, perhaps, think I have been too lenient to the memory of Robespierre. Remember, I only wish to apportion his share of guilt. The convention, by banishing the triumvirate, "until they can be tried at a period of more tranquillity," not only demonstrate a fear of the Jacobin party, but a secret apprehension lest many of themselves should be implicated in the transactions which such an enquiry would unfold. Hence the violent opposition to a publication of their papers by many of the moderate party, as well as that of their opponents. How indeed, in consistency, could those men, from whom they derived their powers, now turn their accusers?

To conclude an odious and debasing subject. The *"noyades, fuzilades, and republican marriages"* of Carrier at Nantes;[35] joined to the exploits of Collot d'Herbois at Lyons, who chained together, at one time, four hundred people, in the great square of the city, and fired upon them with grape-shot, until they were exterminated; with many others equally diabolical, which shall not pollute my page, almost tempt one to believe, that a majority of the nation were at one time accomplices in its crimes and miseries. They have, indeed, at length awakened from their delirium, and sigh at the dreadful retrospect.

I have written until my paper is exhausted, my eyes bedimmed, and my imagination haunted by racks, wheels, and *guillotines* dyed in human gore.—Therefore good night! and adieu until to-morrow, when I will resume my pen!

LETTER XI

Quimper, 1st May 1795.

AMIDST such scenes as I was yesterday condemned to describe, it were impossible but an universal corruption of manners must follow, and it has accordingly arrived. That the French should pant to be free, who can doubt, or who can blame? But it has happened to *them*, as it must to every people who are suddenly hurried into extremes, without the national mind being in any degree prepared for the change which has taken place. This people possesses not the stability of character, or the austere self-denying virtues, of the ancient republicans. Many of the present leading demagogues of the convention do not even affect a common regularity of manners; and, if the public journals, which do not spare them by name, may be believed, wallow in the most scandalous sensuality. I read the other day a description of a drunken scene between one of the Merlins[1] and a brother deputy, which was pourtrayed with much humour. I mention this to shew you, that the editors of news-papers here are not more afraid of the executive power than on your side of the water. When I compare the present number of the convention to what it was at its institution, not three years since, and recollect the causes,—self-murder, public execution, desertion, and banishment—which have occasioned the diminution, I stand petrified with amazement and horror. What stronger proof of the depravity of this legislative assembly can be adduced than their perpetual deliberate acts of treachery towards each other, in betraying private conversations, which have passed among themselves? Their annals are full of it. How many of their members have been hurried by it to the *guillotine*; and how many more have been supplanted in the public favour by the informers!

Letter XI: May 1795

The thirst for dissipation is not lessened; but whence the means which enable many of the French to pursue it in its present form are derived, is a mystery. If the excessive and daily increasing price of commodities be considered, nothing is more inexplicable than how those who have only stipulated incomes contrive to subsist upon them. I live with the most rigid frugality, and yet cannot bound my expences within less than 250 livres a week. It is certain that false *assignats* abound; and the tongue of malevolence has not scrupled to assert, that many of them have been issued from the national treasury, "in order to lessen the public debt, when the day of presentation for payment shall arrive." Remember, I do not pretend to state this as more than the whisper of party. It is evident that the habits which this plenty of the medium of exchange, however obtained, creates, are destructive of all industry. This little town is crowded by men and women, who, like the Athenians, do nothing from morning to night "but tell and hear of some new thing."[2] The national fickleness demonstrates itself no less in private than in public opinion. In Paris alone, in the month of last *Nivose*, 223 divorces took place, 198 of which were solicited by the *wives*. Nothing is more specious than a facility of divorce. To render the chain of union indissoluble were, indeed, to realize the punishment of Mezentius;[3] but to permit its separation upon every trifling and momentary caprice, is to corrupt society in its source. You know that marriage is here a civil contract only, which I have seen entered into at the *bureau* of the municipality, and which consists merely in the parties declaring, before certain witnesses, their wish to be united, and entering their names in a register; but of late all but flaming republicans have thought it necessary to strengthen the engagement, by privately superadding the ceremony of the church.[4]

The national taste has suffered equal degradation. The dramas of Racine, and the odes and epistles of Boileau,[5] are supplanted by crude declamatory productions, to which the revolutionary spirit has given birth. The French have been almost as ingenious as ourselves. It was a discovery reserved for the present age, that Pope[6] was a mere versifier; and that the immortal compositions of the two before-mentioned writers are harmonious tinklings only, devoid of fire of fancy, and elevation of genius.[7] There has been a report presented to the convention, on the *Gothicism*[8] which has overspread the land, and exterminated in its fury more than two thirds of the works of art and taste, which ennobled France. It will be handed down to posterity, in the chronicles of the revolution, as a fact that marks the spirit in which it has been conducted.

Notwithstanding the various arms by which religion has been persecuted, she again begins to lift her head. A report, presented by Boissy d'Anglas,[9] from the united committees of public safety, general security, and legislation, to the convention, containing ten articles in favour of public worship, has been adopted and decreed. By these the republic acknowledges no national religious institution; nor grants salaries to the priesthood; nor furnishes any place for the performance of worship, &c. &c.; but it expressly forbids, under pain of punishment, every one from preventing his neighbour from the exercise of his devotion.

In consequence of this decree on the back of the proclamation issued by Guesno and Guermeur, and of assurances from the constituted authorities that they shall not be molested, the moderate catholics here assemble on every Sabbath in the cathedral, the use of which (as an indulgence) is granted to them; but the more rigid, fearless of the law (which forbids it) hold little meetings at each other's houses, where the non-juring clergy officiate. This is known to the police; but the predilection of the country people, who flock in great numbers to these assemblies, renders it convenient to wink at them, and has hitherto restrained all attack upon them.

I went upon Easter Sunday to the cathedral, and found a numerous congregation there. The altar was lighted up by twelve large waxen tapers; the holy water was sprinkled upon the congregants; and the incense was burnt, with the accustomed ceremonies; but even here democratic spleen manifested itself in disturbing what it is no longer allowed to interdict. In the most solemn part of the service, the *Marseillois Hymn* was heard from the organ: that war-whoop, to whose sound the bands of regicides who attacked their sovereign in his palace marched; and which, during the last three years, has been the watch-word of violence, rapine, and murder*! How incongruous were its notes in the temple of the Prince of Peace! A blackguard-looking fellow close to me, whom I knew, by his uncombed hair, dirty linen, ragged attire, and contemptuous gestures, to be a *veritable sans-culotte*, joined his voice to the music, and echoed, "*Aux armes, citoyens!*"[10] Fear alone kept the people quiet; and of its influence in this country I have witnessed astonishing proofs, which demonstrate, beyond volumes of reasoning, the terror inspired by the revolutionary government.

As the observance of the Sabbath advances, the *Decadis* sink into contempt. I had heard much of civic feasts and other patriotic institutions celebrated upon them; but since I have been here, nothing of the sort has occurred. The national flag is displayed on the public offices, and if there is no pressure of business, the clerks have a holiday. A few zealous republicans also shut up their shops; but at present for one shop shut on a *Decadi*, there are six on a Sunday; for, however their owners may differ on political questions, a sense of religion is not extinguished in the mass of the people, even of the town. I have, nevertheless, been assured, that six months ago, to have shewn this mark of respect for the Sabbath would have been a certain mean of drawing down the resentment of the predominant faction. On every *Decadi* the laws are appointed to be read in the

---

* I was once carelessly humming, at a fire-side, the *Carmagnole*; when a lady, suddenly interrupting me, exclaimed, "For God's sake cease that hateful tune! It brings to my remembrance nothing but massacres and guillotines."

cathedral, and the municipality attend. I had once the curiosity to go to this meeting, and found the number of auditors, which I counted, exclusive of the reader, and those who attended officially, to be twenty-seven persons, of whom, to my surprize, five were old women.

Were I not bound to attend an appointment at twelve o'clock, in the event of which I am deeply interested, methinks it were a curious speculation (to which I incline) to try to develope what will be the probable state of France, when peace with all her neighbours shall be restored to her. The thinking part of the nation survey, not without alarming anticipation, the consequence of a million and a half of armed men, to whom a habit of indolence is become familiar, being turned loose upon a country whose specie has disappeared, whose foreign commerce is annihilated, and whose manufactures must be *born again*, for hardly a trace of their having ever existed remains: add to this, that the government, by being no longer revolutionary, will lose its strong executive spring: and that the people are split into innumerable parties, which hate each other with irreconcileable inveteracy.

National prejudices and political antipathies I consider as a vile state engine, which, in the hands of a few crafty men, has for more than five thousand years wrought the misery of the human race. Englishmen and Frenchmen, the Charib and the Hindoo, the philosopher of Europe and the naked savage whose wanderings I have witnessed at Botany Bay, shall one day, I presume in humble confidence to trust, be assembled before the "living throne," of a common Father; and look back on that diminutive speck, which in the boundless ocean of infinity nothing short of divine irradiation could make visible to their eyes;—to review with unqualified contempt, sorrow, and repentance, those false principles, and sanguinary conclusions, which rendered it unto them a theatre of contention and horror, and caused their days to be "few and evil!"[11]

Letter XI: May 1795

If such be my sentiments, I have no right to wish calamity to France. I do not.—May she conclude peace with her neighbours; and labour to settle her own government; and render happy her numerous children! But when I look forward to the completion of such an event, I think I foresee so many long years of havoc, which have yet to urge their course in this devoted country, that I will drop the curtain, and hasten to meet ——— ———. Adieu.

LETTER XII

Plymouth, 11th May, 1795.

My Dear ——,

Congratulate me. The circumstances which led to my obtaining permission to come to England, prove me fortunate beyond example; and as I think them honourable to French generosity, I shall not omit to record them.

I arrived here yesterday, in a little Danish brig bound to Copenhagen, which ran off the Sound, and made a signal for a pilot. One of the Cawsand[1] boats in consequence pushed out to us, and received Admiral Bligh, his two young gentlemen, and myself. We were soon landed; and I am happy to tell you that I found[2] —— —— —— —— —— —— —— —— —— —— —— —— —— —— —— ——

The packet which accompanies this will explain to you my hopes, and the measures which I intended to pursue, at the time it was written. The Admiral's liberation and passport arrived on the 2d instant; and, on his request for his *aid-de-camp* and interpreter to accompany him, the good commissary made no scruple of furnishing me with a passport to go to Brest, upon pledging myself to return, in case my application to the representatives might be rejected. Having bidden adieu to my friends, I set out on the following morning on horseback, with the Admiral and the two boys in a carriage, the best the town afforded, without springs, and with traces made of ropes. Our sudden departure was in consequence of knowing that an embargo, which had subsisted for some time, was just taken off, and that several American vessels were ready to sail for England. We travelled about thirty-six miles, through a country which is full of young promising corn, indicating a plentiful crop, and

Letter XII: May 1795

appearing not to have suffered from wanting husbandmen to sow it. About four o'clock we reached a village, whence there is a ferry about ten miles across to Brest. Here we embarked, with more than a dozen country people, who were carrying the produce of their farms to the next day's market. Only one of them could speak French, who satisfied the curiosity of the rest about us. They made their supper of *crape*, and were abundantly thankful to us for a remnant of a piece of cold veal which we had brought with us, some bread, and a little wine, which they ate as luxuries. Owing to a contrary wind, it was midnight before we got abreast of the harbour's mouth; when we learned, by hailing a vessel, to our unspeakable mortification, that all the Americans had sailed in the course of the day. The circumstance of having missed, by being a few hours too late, an opportunity, the fellow of which might not arrive for months, joined to the apprehensions and perplexity of men in our situation, on entering into a garrison-town like Brest, at so unseasonable and suspicious an hour, rendered our feelings very unenviable. We wanted the boatmen to land us at the town, and to shew us to an inn, where we might be accommodated with beds; but this they peremptorily refused to do, telling us, that we might every moment expect to be hailed by one of the forts, and ordered on shore to give an account of ourselves. This happened, as they had foretold, in a few minutes, when we were summoned through a speaking-trumpet to land within some pallisades at the point of the dock-yard. A serjeant and a file of men received us, and conducted us immediately to their officer at the guard-house, a tall well-looking young man; who after having inspected our passports, and listened to our wishes, very civilly offered to accommodate us as well as he could in his guard-room, or, if this proposition were not agreeable to send a serjeant with us to knock up an inn. We were grateful for his politeness, and begged to accept the latter, requesting permission to leave our baggage under his care until morning, which was complied with, and a serjeant was directly sent away with us. We had, however, but just passed one of the barriers of the dock-yard, when we were stopped by a municipality patrole, who, notwithstanding our conductor's explanations and remonstrances, carried us all forthwith to their guard-house, and gave us to understand, that we must pass the night there as well as we could. This treatment enraged us; and I bade them recollect that they were offering an unnecessary indignity to a *"General Anglais,"*[3] who had not entered Brest without ample and sufficient authority, and who would certainly represent their interference and impertinence, on the next morning, to his friend Admiral Villaret, and the members of the convention on mission here. This resolute tone, to which the Admiral desired me to give full force, had quickly its effect, and this *bourgeois* collection of tinkers and taylors thought proper to send us under an escort to a neighbouring inn; but it was now become so late, that, after having knocked at the door for more than half an hour, we were obliged to return to the guard-house, and take up our lodging there: the Admiral sitting up, on a bench, by the fire, and the two youngsters and I lying down on the guard-bed with the soldiers.

In the morning we took our leave with very little ceremony, and repaired again to the inn, where we found admission. After breakfasting, and rendering our dress as decent as we could without our baggage, we went, as we had been directed at Quimper, to the office of the maritime agent, and produced our passports. He received us very properly, and furnished us with tickets to shew in case of being stopped—an event not unlikely to happen to English officers walking in their uniforms about the streets of Brest. Our next visit was to Monsieur Villaret, whose reception of Admiral Bligh, and whose undeviating conduct to us both while we remained here, was friendly, polite, and flattering in the extreme. I had never before seen him, and had now the honour to be introduced to him by Admiral Bligh, as his *aid-de-camp*. His frank and gentlemanlike manners at once

Letter XII: May 1795

won my esteem. He appears to be between forty and fifty years old, is of an engaging countenance, well made, of a middle size, and has a military carriage. Upon hearing where we had left our baggage on the preceding evening, he directly dispatched his own coxswain for it, and it was brought to us safe and entire. But his goodness to me (as the friend of an officer whom he so highly respected for his gallant defence of his ship, as Admiral Bligh) must be particularly stated to you. No sooner was the predicament in which I stood made known to him, than he offered his interest to back my application to the representatives; and insisted that we all should immediately set out to their office to undertake it. Upon our arrival there, we were introduced to one of them, Champeaux, an old man, who at Admiral Villaret's intercession consented at once, without starting a difficulty, to my being allowed to accompany my Admiral, and promised me a passport.

Our only difficulty now was to find a conveyance. Admiral Bligh therefore expressed a wish to his friend that he might be suffered to hire a boat, which he would engage to send back immediately on being landed on the nearest part of the English shore. This proposition (which, considering the times, was rather of a delicate nature) was acceded to by Monsieur Villaret; who added, that he would take care that she should be properly fitted and victualled for us: however in the afternoon a lucky occurrence prevented us from putting his generous zeal to serve us to farther proof:—An American gentleman, who knew our situation, brought a little Danish master of a brig to our inn where we had dined (Admiral Villaret being engaged to the representatives) with whom we presently concluded an agreement for our passage. As the Dane wished to depart on the next day, it became again necessary to trouble Monsieur Villaret to urge the completion of our passports for sailing out of the harbour; and for this purpose he appointed to meet us at nine in the evening, at the house of the representatives. Thither, at the hour agreed upon, we repaired, and found him. He conducted us into a spacious garden, and introduced us to the representatives, Topsent, Vernon, and Harmand,[4] who received us with great cordiality; and when they learned that Admiral Bligh had been all day in town, chided Admiral Villaret for not having brought us with him to dine with them. These gentlemen, however, declined taking any part in granting the passports until the arrival of their colleague Champeaux, who was momently expected. We, therefore, continued walking on the terrace, and conversing on general subjects, which unavoidably led to the grand and only enquiry that seems to agitate the minds of Frenchmen:—the politics of the day, as connected with the revolution.—They spoke in respectful terms of our national character, and pathetically lamented the war between England and France, calling it an unhappy and fruitless contest to both parties. It was, they said, past human comprehension to account for the ceaseless implacable enmity between two nations, which by their valour, opulence, and enlightened character, were fitted to hold the balance and dictate the tranquillity of Europe. I listened in silence. These men had no *sans-culottism* about them, either in their manners, language, or dress; the two first were civil, moderate and correct, and the latter was gentlemanlike and respectable. Had it been my desire, it was not my interest, to interrupt or oppose them. I ventured, however, once or twice to slightly demur at one of their propositions, in order to draw out their sentiments more fully; which occasioned these words (from Vernon, I think) to be repeated with emphasis, "*France will be a republic! and England neither shall, nor ought to, interfere in our internal concerns.*" This conversation made a deep impression upon me, and was, I am confident, introduced in order that the Admiral (to whom I interpreted it) might communicate it on this side of the water. It differed but little from others which I had often heard on the same subject during my captivity; but the rank and situation of the speakers from whose lips it fell, render

Letter XII: May 1795

it memorable to me.—Finding that Champeaux did not come home, about ten o'clock we retired to our inn, being first given to understand, that I might be sure of meeting him in his office at six o'clock next morning, being the hour at which he always entered upon business.

At a few minutes before six on the following day I renewed my visit, and waited but a short time before I was admitted to Monsieur Champeaux. He was sitting in his office, in an elbow-chair, dressed in a flannel jacket abominably filthy, and smoking a short black pipe, exactly such an one as the old women in Ireland carry about in their mouths. It brought to my mind Sir William Temple's descriptions of those old burgomasters, who formerly, with so much plainness, wisdom, and integrity, conducted the affairs of the Batavian republic.[5] I had no more reason to complain of my reception now than on the preceding day. He told me that he did not wonder at my impatience, and that I should wait for what I wanted only until a clerk should come in. "But," added he, "our clerks are *fainéants*."[6] Ah! thought I, if this honest gentleman could take a peep, at this early hour, into an English public office, where vigilance for the common weal never slumbers!—His affable compliance removed a mountain from my mind. I now took an opportunity of presenting Admiral Bligh's compliments to him, and requesting, as an acknowledgment of his politeness, that he would name some French officer, a prisoner in England, whose release he might be interested about, and that he might depend on his being sent home. The old man bowed, and, recollecting himself for a moment, wrote down the name of a *Quarter Master*, who was taken in l'Atalante frigate, and is now in prison at Kinsale in Ireland, begging that I would give it to the Admiral with his thanks, and perfect reliance on his good faith. I continued to wait; but no clerk entering, although some other company did, I slipped out, and planted myself on the stair-case, where I had not remained long before a grave sober official-looking character came forward.—"Pray, sir," said I, "do you belong to the office?"—"Yes, citizen."—I told him my business in few words, and having been similarly situated in an English office, when I begged his assistance, looked as if I would be *grateful*. "Are you sure, citizen, that you have seen the representative?" —"Perfectly sure."—"The representative Champeaux?"— "Yes."—"Then follow me, and your business shall be done."— With a bounding heart I accompanied him into his office. When he had finished writing the passports, he took them in to the representative to be signed and sealed, and I amused myself as well as impatience, not unmingled with fear, lest some unforeseen impediment should be started, would allow, by looking about the room in which I was left alone. Opposite the door was written, in large characters, "Whatever servant of the republic shall accept of a fee or gratuity, for transacting the public business, shall forfeit his place, and be farther punished." There was also stuck up on the wall a satirical print of certain characters among us, who shall be nameless, in very ludicrous attitudes and situations.—He soon returned with the passports completely executed, and presented them to me, in such a manner as convinced me, that to have offered a reward to him, for having simply performed his duty, would have been construed into an insult, and perhaps have been attended with unpleasant consequences to myself.

I hurried to the Admiral with my credentials, and we lost no time in getting on board, and urging our departure from the port, which to our unutterable joy took place about eleven o'clock last Tuesday. A northerly wind prevented us from arriving here till yesterday.

The shortness of my residence in Brest, and the state of hurry and anxiety in which it was passed, almost preclude me from offering to you any remarks about it. It is very strangely laid out, on the side of a hill, and long flights of steps connect different parts of the town. It is certainly much larger than either

Letter XII: May 1795

Portsmouth or Plymouth, and contains some handsome public buildings, exclusive of the naval arsenal, which, you may be sure, I did not enter after the first night, when it was too dark to make any observations. The French are said to be making vigorous preparations here; but when we ran through Brest-Water, there were only nine or ten sail of the line ready, or nearly ready, for sea. As we sailed along, I cast a look of exultation at my old jail La Normandie. At the harbour's mouth we were boarded by a guard-boat, the officer of which offered not any interruption to us, upon seeing our passports.

I had almost forgotten to mention that before we embarked we heard that Le Franq, the captain of Le Marat, was cashiered, for being a *Robespierrist*; and that he, with many others, was obliged to shew himself twice a day at the office of the municipality, as a caution against his elopement. We did not see him, and by no means thought him entitled to much commiseration.—Admiral Villaret gave us the information.

To the civility of Mr. Anderson, the American consul, we were indebted, not only now, but when we were formerly at Brest. My two old friends of the prison-ship, on hearing of my arrival, found me out, and came to sup with us at our inn.

Our expences ran very high during our short stay at Brest. We dined, at a very middling ordinary,[7] at fifteen livres a head; and for tolerable wine after dinner were charged nineteen livres a bottle; every other article being proportionably extravagant.

I wait here only for —— —— —— —— —— ——
Expect to see me in town in a week.—Adieu.

WATKIN TENCH.

THE END

NOTES TO LETTERS

LETTER I

[1] Shakespeare, *Othello* I.iii.136 (*William Shakespeare: The Complete Works*, edited by Stanley Wells and Gary Taylor (Oxford: Oxford University Press, 1986), p. 931). Being 'taken by the insolent foe' is an episode in 'the story of [his] life' which Othello tells to Desdemona and to the Venetian Senate. Tench is associating himself with Othello as soldier-storyteller.

[2] Given that they are fighting the French, Tench may have Caesar's *Gallic War* (*De Bello Gallico*) specifically in mind, and is in any case linking Bligh and Caesar as soldier-chroniclers.

[3] See Appendix 2.

[4] Nielly, Joseph-Marie (1751–1833). Appointed *contre-amiral* under Admiral Villaret-Joyeuse (see n.4, Letter III, p. 141) by Jean Bon Saint-André in 1793 (see n.12, Letter IV, p. 144; commended by the Convention for the capture of the *Alexander*.

[5] The Convention's decree of May 1794, that no British prisoners should be taken, was probably not widely acted upon, but it reflects the special character of the war by 1794 when both sides were trying to 'incite revolt within the other', and saw themselves as engaged in a moral crusade which relieved them from 'any obligation to comply with the restraints that eighteenth-century conventions imposed on belligerents' (Norman Hampson, *The Perfidy of Albion: French Perceptions of England during the French Revolution* (London: Macmillan, 1998), pp. ix, xiii). In the period of Tench's captivity, the question of how British prisoners should be treated is clearly still an intensely political and very contentious one.

[6] Milton, *Paradise Lost* (1667), XI.489–98 (*The Poems of John Milton*, edited by John Carey and Alastair Fowler (London and New York: Longman, 1968), pp. 1007–8). The Archangel Michael shows Adam in a vision the consequences of the Fall, representing the misery of humankind's fallen state as a hospital where

> ... despair
> Tended the sick busiest from couch to couch;

NOTES TO LETTERS

> And over them triumphant death his dart
> Shook, but delayed to strike, though oft invoked
> With vows, as their chief good, and final hope.
> Sight so deform what heart of rock could long
> Dry-eyed behold? Adam could not, but wept,
> Though not of woman born; compassion quelled
> His best of man, and gave him up to tears
> A space, till firmer thoughts restrained excess.

[7] *Citoyen, tels sont mes ordres. Je suis républicain!*: Citizen, those are my orders. I am a republican.

[8] Bligh, Richard Rodney (1737–1821). At this point – November 1794 – Bligh did not know that he had been promoted from Captain to Rear-Admiral in July 1794.

[9] Named after Jean Paul Marat (1744–93), Paris-based revolutionary leader, editor of the radical democratic *Ami du peuple*. His assassination by Charlotte Corday in July 1793 was followed by a cult of his name. The successive naming and renaming of the ship reflected changes in the political climate: originally *Tigre*, it became *Marat* in 1793, *Formidable* in 1795 and (after its capture by the British in June 1795) HMS *Belleisle*.

[10] Le Franq, promoted by Jean Bon Saint-André in 1793, had previously been among the junior officers who had written urging him to appoint Admiral Villaret-Joyeuse as commander-in-chief of the navy: 'the firmness and the talents of citizen Joyeuse render him worthy of your choice: we will never fear a firm man, this is necessary to command a fleet. We are true *sans-culottes* and republicans who want [a republic] one and indivisible'; quoted in W. S. Cormack, *Revolution and Political Conflict in the French Navy, 1789–94* (Cambridge: Cambridge University Press, 1995), 271–2.

[11] gorget: 'a gilt crescent-shaped badge, suspended from the neck, and hanging on the breast, formerly worn by officers on duty' (*OED*).

[12] *état major*: military staff.

In a British line-of-battle ship (such as the *Alexander*) 'the commissioned officers berthed . . . in the space at the after end of the main deck called the wardroom, which was partitioned off from it by a light bulkhead' (N. A. M. Rodger, *The Wooden World: An Anatomy of the Georgian Navy* (London: Fontana/Harper Collins, 1986), p. 66).

[13] Tench may be referring to his experience as a prisoner of the French in Maryland in 1778, during the War of Independence; we have no knowledge of any previous visits to France itself.

NOTES TO LETTERS

[14] *mousses*: ship's apprentices.

[15] These are all marks of revolutionary egalitarianism. Removing your hat was associated with deference; the red cap of liberty, initially asssociated with the insurgent common people of Paris (the *sans-culottes*), subsequently became a symbol of the Republic itself.

[16] Louis Michel Le Peletier, Marquis de Saint-Fargeau (1760–93), aristocratic convert to Jacobinism, educational and penal reformer, killed by a royalist assassin. The 'prints of two heads' may be derived from studies of them as republican martyrs by the great neo-classical painter and Jacobin member of the Convention, Jacques Louis David (1748–1825). Paintings of the two men by David – of Le Peletier on his deathbed and of Marat dead in his bath – hung in the Convention on either side of the speaker's chair, till they were removed in February 1795.

[17] Maximilien Robespierre (1758–94), the revolutionary leader most closely associated with the Committee of Public Safety and the Terror. He followed Rousseau's classically inspired conception of a 'republic of virtue' in which citizens would subordinate their private interests to the demands of participation in the institutions of the state. 'If the aim of popular government in peacetime is virtue, then the aim of popular government at a time of Revolution is virtue and terror at one and the same time: virtue, without which terror is disastrous; terror, without which virtue is impotent' (speech to Convention, 5 Feb 1794). Robespierre's arrest (9 Thermidor/27 July) and execution the next day marked the beginning of the end of Jacobin power.

[18] œconomy: the management (rather than the economy) of a household or state (or ship). The management of the French ship as Tench describes it here would be comprehensively offensive to British officers. In the British Navy the right to walk the quarter-deck ('a deck above the main deck, running from the stern about half-way along the length of the ship') was restricted to sea officers and was an important indicator of that status (Rodger, *The Wooden World*, pp. 428, 24–5). Commissioned officers ate in the wardroom, the men on the lower or gun deck (Rodger, p. 61), nobody on the upper deck. As for cleanliness, British officers had often reacted similarly to the perceived dirtiness of pre-Revolutionary French ships (p. 105).

[19] *aux prières*: to prayers.

[20] Marseilles Hymn: the *Marseillaise*, written by Rouget de Lisle in April 1792 as the 'Chant de guerre pour l'armée du Rhin' (marching song of the Rhine Army), and taken up by republican soldiers from Marseilles marching to Paris in July 1792. It became the national anthem on 14 July

1795. While calling the song a 'hymn' – and the secular ritual in which it is sung, 'prayers' – is ironic (certainly on Tench's part); it is also part of the serious attempt to 'transfer sacrality' from the Catholic Church to the Republican State (see Maria Ozouf, *Festivals and the French Revolution*, trans. Alan Sheridan (Cambridge, Mass: Harvard University Press, 1975), pp. 263–82).

[21] *Carmagnole*: a revolutionary song and/or its accompanying dance, especially popular as a marching song of the revolutionary armies until banned by Napoleon in 1800. Composed in 1792, its fervent and ferocious words were frequently altered and added to in response to revolutionary events.

[22] English or British (or allied) land victories over French forces: at Agincourt (1482), Blenheim (1704) and Minden (1759).

[23] British naval heroes: Admirals Edward Russell (1653–1727), Edward Hawke (1705–81), George Rodney (1719–92) and Richard Howe (1726–99). All were involved in victories over the French, including Hawke and Howe at Quiberon Bay (1759) and Howe on 1 June 1794 ('the Glorious First of June'). Lord Howe, still commander of the Channel Fleet as Tench wrote (November 1794), was made Admiral of the Fleet and General of Marines in 1796.

[24] The Chelsea Royal Hospital for retired soldiers ('Chelsea Pensioners'); Greenwich Royal Hospital for retired naval officers (became the Royal Naval College in 1873).

[25] Tench's choice of historic events, and the language in which he describes them (with the King 'compelled' to sign Magna Carta) are pointedly Whiggish. Magna Carta (the Great Charter), was signed by King John at Runnymede in 1215, in response to baronial pressure. The Bill of Rights (1689) spelt out the conditions (including a Protestant succession and limitations on the royal prerogative) on which William of Orange (1650–1702) was offered the throne following the overthrow of the pro-Catholic and pro-French James II in the 'Glorious Revolution' of 1688.

[26] *Liberté, Egalité, Fraternité, ou la Mort*: Liberty, Equality, Fraternity, or Death. The phrase was displayed on most revolutionary monuments, documents and letters (see Plate 7).

[27] The Declaration of the Rights of Man and Citizen was proclaimed by the National Constituent Assembly on 26 August 1789. A liberal rather than democratic document, it asserted individual freedoms, and vested sovereignty in the nation (rather than the monarch).

[28] William Pitt (Pitt the Younger) (1759–1806). As British Prime Minister (1783–1801, 1804–6) Pitt spearheaded the war against

NOTES TO LETTERS

Revolutionary and Napoleonic France and the repression of political dissent within Britain itself.

[29] Alexander Pope, 'Epistle to Dr. Arbuthnot' (1735), line 36 (*Twickenham Edition of the Works of Alexander Pope*, edited by John Butt, IV, New Haven: Yale University Press, 1969, p. 98):

> To laugh, were want of Goodness and of Grace,
> And to be grave, exceeds all Pow'r of Face.

[30] 'Most [pre-revolutionary] naval officers were nobles' (Cormack, *Revolution and Political Conflict*, p. 42).

[31] Pierre-André de Suffren de Saint-Tropez (1729–88), a famously audacious naval commander in the Indian Ocean, 1782–3. A ship, *le Suffren*, was named after him.

[32] prize: a ship or property captured at sea.

[33] *pain d'égalité*: bread of equality. On 26 September 1793, Representative on Mission Fouché 'issued orders to the bakers at Moulins that they were in future to make only one kind of bread, known as "bread of equality", to be sold at a uniform price of three sous a pound, made possible by allotting a sum to compensate the bakers and recovering it from the rich' (Albert Mathiez, *The French Revolution*, trans. C. Phillips (London: Williams and Norgate, 1928), p. 385).

[34] Hottentots: a southern African people who had become a byword, among Europeans, for their supposed low level of civilization.

[35] *Le petit —— pleure quelquefois*: The little —— cries sometimes. It is probably the behaviour and physical condition of the boys rather than their age or social origin as such which upsets Tench. Many boys, of eleven and even younger, worked on British ships, some as apprentice officers (Rodger, *The Wooden World*, pp. 27–8, 68–9). Admiral Bligh's young son is probably on board in this capacity, and Tench's 'servant' (p. 6) could be a young gentleman of this sort.

[36] Shakespeare, *Macbeth*, I.vii.6–12 (*Complete Works*, p. 1105). Macbeth in soliloquy:

> . . . But in these cases
> We still have judgement here, that we but teach
> Bloody instructions which, being taught, return
> To plague th' inventor. This even-handed justice
> Commends th' ingredience of our poisoned chalice
> To our own lips.

NOTES TO LETTERS

[37] Ushant (Fr.: Ouessant), French island, about fourteen miles from the coast of Finistère. See Plate 1.

[38] *militaire*: military man.

[39] *Assignats* were paper currency introduced in 1789 to replace *specie* (actual coin) in commercial transactions. The main denominations of the currency were: louis = 24 livres; ecu = 3 livres; livre = 20 sols (or sous); sol = 12 deniers. The term 'franc' was sometimes used as a variant of livre, and this became more common after the Convention introduced the metric and decimal system on 7 April 1795. The *assignat* itself depreciated rapidly: 96 livres was the official cash-value of an *assignat* in November 1789, 24 in November 1794, but only 1 by November 1795.

[40] *Nous verrons!*: We shall see!

[41] Representatives on Mission (*Représentants en mission*) were deputies of the Convention sent out (from March 1793) to ensure the effective implementation of government policy in the provinces and the armed forces. After Thermidor the post was retained till April 1795, the Representatives now being used to purge Jacobins and ex-terrorists.

LETTER II

[1] *traitement*: allowance.

[2] For Tench's own role as a censor of prisoners' letters, on board the *Charlotte* in 1787, see *Sydney's First Four Years*, edited by L. F. Fitzhardinge (Sydney: Library of Australian History, 1979), pp. 11–12. However, comparisons of this sort – the ironies of the gaoler gaoled – do not appear to strike Tench himself.

[3] mounts a cockade: wears a cockade (rosette) of liberty. Tench's use of 'mount' here to mean 'put on, assume, display oneself as wearing (some special article of costume)' precedes *OED*'s first instance (from 1812).

[4] A johannes was the name by which the Portuguese gold coin, the *dobra de quatro escudos* or *peça* of Joannes V (1703–50) was known in the British American colonies, where it had been current.

[5] Shakespeare, *Timon of Athens*, IV.iii.387–9 (*Complete Works*, p. 1019). Timon, addressing his gold:

> Thou ever young, fresh, loved, and delicate wooer,
> Whose blush doth thaw the consecrated snow
> That lies on Dian's lap.

⁶ Shakespeare, *The Tempest*, IV.i.148–50 (*Complete Works*, p. 1335). Prospero to Ferdinand:

> These our actors,
> As I foretold you, were all spirits, and
> Are melted into air, into thin air.

LETTER III

¹ *Bretagne*: Brittany.

² *aide-de-camp*: an officer acting as confidential assistant to a senior officer.

³ *La Montagne*: The ship is named after the political faction known as the Montagne (the Mountain) a group of radical Jacobin deputies (Montagnards) who occupied benches at the top of the steep-banked Convention hall. Robespierre, Danton and Jean Bon Saint-André were Montagnards. The ship, originally named *Etats de Bourgogne*, was renamed *Montagne* in October 1793, *Peuple* in 1795, *Océan* later the same year.

⁴ Comte Louis-Thomas Villaret-Joyeuse (1748–1812). Appointed commander of the French fleet by Jean Bon Saint-André in 1793 for his competence and his record as a disciplinarian, and despite his aristocratic origins. The combination of being a Montagnard appointee and an aristocrat would explain 'the delicacy of his situation' after Thermidor, referred to in the next sentence.

Lord Howe, see Letter I, n.23, p. 138.

⁵ Modern accounts of Jean-François Renaudin and the *Vengeur* incident on 1 June 1794 corroborate Tench, but also stress the great courage of the French crew. See Robert Gardiner (ed.), *Fleet Battle and Blockade: The French Revolutionary War, 1793–1797* (London: Chatham Publishing in Association with the National Maritime Museum, 1996), p. 33; Philippe Henwood et Edmond Monange, *Brest: un port en revolution, 1789–1799* (Editions ouest-France, 1989), pp. 229–31.

⁶ darksome round: gloomy routine.

⁷ Some of the other surviving officers from the *Alexander* were later imprisoned in the Château de Brest. For Bligh's petitioning letter on their behalf see p. 69 and Plate 4.

⁸ Tench's coded observations, designed to be decipherable by himself later in Quimper, are presumably in fact the basis for parts of Letter IV,

written while he is still on *le Marat*, since 'That leisure which I so lately looked forward to at Quimper, seems likely to be afforded to me here.' The idea for the code may have come from his reading of Mary Wortley Montagu's *Turkish Embassy Letters* (1763) where, following a discussion of coded love-letters, she describes the heteroglossic discourse of members of her multilingual household in the Embassy district of Istanbul (Mary Wortley Montagu, *The Turkish Embassy Letters*, edited by Anita Desai (London: Virago, 1994), pp. 120–3). We do not know the languages, apart from French and Latin, of which Tench had a working knowledge. He tells us he 'cannot speak Welch' but clearly wishes to show that he knows some Welsh vocabulary (p. 87). 'The language of New Holland' is what would now be called the Sydney Language: the British colonizers of 1788 believed that the languages they heard in adjacent areas were dialects of the one language. 'Of the language of New South Wales I once hoped to have subjoined to this work [the *Account*] such an exposition, as should have attracted public notice; and have excited public esteem. But the abrupt departure of Mr Dawes . . . to encounter new perils, in the service of the Sierra Leona company, precludes me from executing this part of my original intention, in which he had promised to co-operate with me; and in which he had advanced his researches beyond the reach of competition' (*Sydney's First Four Years*, p. 291). See Jakelin Troy, 'By slow degrees we began . . . to understand each other . . . even in this the natives have the advantage', in *Exchanges: Cross-cultural Encounters in Australia and the Pacific*, edited by Ross Gibson (Sydney: Museum of Sydney, 1996), pp. 23–57.

LETTER IV

[1] *ad referendum*: for further consideration. Tench probably refers here to the lengthy conflict within the Dutch Estates-General which eventually concluded, in 1780, with a decision, by the bare margin of four provinces against three, to side with the American colonies against the British in the War of Independence.

[2] John Selden (1584–1654), jurist and politician. His *Mare Clausum, seu de Divinio* (1636), composed in 1616 at the command of James I, argued against the view that the high seas were open to all: rather, sea as much as land was subject to private property and 'the lordship of the circumambient ocean belongs to the crown of Great Britain as an indivisible and perpetual appendage'.

[3] The Delphic oracle's cryptic words referred to the wooden horse – with soldiers hidden inside it – which was presented as a gift by the Greeks to their Trojan enemies. The transfer of the image to describe the British navy was a commonplace ('The wooden walls are the best walls of this kingdom': Thomas, Baron Coventry, 1635).

[4] *Delenda est Carthago*: 'Carthage must be destroyed', a remark customarily attributed to Cato the Elder in the Roman senate. Longtime rivals, the ancient cities of Rome and Carthage (in North Africa) fought three wars – the so-called Punic Wars – between 265 BC and the destruction of Carthage in 146 BC. Jean Bon Saint-André had addressed the Convention in the following terms: 'The sea must become free like the land, and you can free both. Deploy therefore all the force and power which the People, whom you have the honour to represent, can give to exterminate the most miserable of its enemies, the speculators of London, the oppressors of Bengal, the disturbers of public peace in Europe. You have said that Pitt must pay for the crimes he has committed against all humanity. Your tribunes resounded with this war cry: *Carthage must be destroyed*. When the Romans wished to destroy Carthage, they created a more redoubtable navy than their enemy. Frenchmen, can you be less than the Romans? NO . . .', *Rapports des représentants du peuple envoyés à Brest et auprès de l'armée navale; par Jeanbon Saint-André* (Paris: Imprimerie Nationale [?Jan. 1794]), pp. 21–3, quoted in Cormack, *Revolution and Political Conflict*, p. 259.

[5] The French navy, with no major port in the English Channel, had begun construction of an artificial harbour at Cherbourg in 1783 but had abandoned the project in 1789 due to lack of funds.

[6] The Mediterranean naval harbour of Toulon was surrendered to the British by rebel French forces on 27 August 1793 and retaken, after the departure of the British, on 19 December.

[7] Bouguier: Pierre Bouguer (1698–1758), author of *Traité de navire* (1746), *Traité de navigation* (1753) and *Traité de la manœuvre des vaisseaux* (1757).

[8] *sans-culottes*: literally, without the knee-breeches worn by the aristocracy; a title adopted – initially in Paris in 1791 – by artisans and popular revolutionaries and those who claimed to speak for them. In Britain the term was commonly used to denote a violent revolutionary.

[9] In *Paradise Lost*, the devils build:

> . . . a bridge
> Of length prodigious joining to the wall
> Immovable of this now fenceless world

NOTES TO LETTERS

Forfeit to Death; from hence a passage broad,
Smooth, easy, inoffensive down to hell.
(X.301–5)

Adam and Eve are described as 'our grand parents', I.29 (*The Poems of John Milton*, pp. 941, 462).

[10] John Cartwright (1740–1824), gentleman reformer, leading member of the Society for Constitutional Information; a naval man (*c*.1758–70) and major in the Nottinghamshire militia. Tench has probably been reading Cartwrights's *Constitutional Defense of England, Internal and External*, published by Joseph Johnson in 1796. Tench's reference to the '*Saxon militia*' alludes (dismissively) to Cartwright's belief, widely shared by reformers, that ancient Saxon freedoms had been crushed by the 'Norman yoke'.

[11] This battle ('the Glorious First of June'), was the first major British naval victory of the war: six French line-of-battle ships were captured and one (the *Vengeur*) sunk.

[12] Jean Bon Saint-André (1749–1813) was the Montagnard naval expert. Formerly a Huguenot pastor and merchant sea-captain, he became a deputy in the Convention, member of the Committee of Public Safety, and *Représentant en mission* to the navy at Brest (October 1793–January 1794 and May–June 1794) where he ruthlessly but effectively reasserted discipline over and within the fleet. Arrested in 1795, he survived to become a prefect under Napoleon.

[13] *écrivain ou secrétaire*: writer or secretary.

[14] *Oh! le vilain —— !*: Oh, the dirty —— !.

[15] Admiral Sir George Montagu (1750–1829).

[16] *cum grano salis*: with a grain of salt.

[17] Lord Rodney: Admiral George Rodney (1719–92).

[18] *Fas est et ab hoste doceri*: 'It is proper to learn, even from an enemy,' Ovid, *Metamorphoses*, Book IV, line 428 (*Metamorphoses* (London: Heinemann, Loeb Classical Library, 1916), i, pp. 208–9).

[19] The Law of Suspects (17 September 1793) made the titles *citoyen* (citizen) and *citoyenne*, together with the informal singular form of address – 'tu' rather than 'vous' (see Plate 7) – compulsory in military and civilian life.

[20] *conseil de discipline*: disciplinary council (court martial).

[21] To run the gantlope (or gauntlet): a military and naval punishment in which 'the culprit had to run stripped to the waist between two rows of men who struck at him with a stick or a knotted cord' (*OED*).

[22] degradation: demotion.
[23] foremast-man: common sailor.
[24] One of the eight demands of the sailors who mutinied at the Nore (Thames estuary) in 1797 was 'that a more equal distribution be made of prize-money to the crews of his Majesty's ships and vessels of war' (quoted in G. E. Manwaring and Bonomy Dobrée, *Mutiny: The Floating Republic* (London: Cresset Library, 1935), p. 142).
[25] For the eighteenth-century British stereotype of the emaciated French – epitomized by Hogarth's *Calais Gate, or the Roast Beef of Old England* – see Linda Colley, *Britons: Forging the Nation 1707–1837* (New Haven and London: Yale University Press, 1992), pp. 32–7.
[26] Nielly, see Letter I, n.4, p. 135.
[27] The ten-day week (*décade*) ending in a secular rest-day (*décadi*) was introduced on 5 October 1793 at the same time as the Revolutionary Calendar.
[28] road: a piece of water near shore in which ships can ride at anchor (as 'roadsted' (roadstead), p. 37).
[29] The Popular Societies were a network of thousands of local political societies operating through France between 1789 and 1794. Jacobin in orientation, they were increasingly subordinate to the Convention and the Representatives.
[30] *Civisme* and *incivisme* – civic-mindedness and the lack of it – were a fundamental republican virtue and vice. Certificates of *civisme* – as proof of identity and public reliability – were first required of foreigners and then (by the 1793 Law of Suspects) of all citizens.
[31] *pilotins*: apprentices in the maritime service.
[32] *Décadis*: the secular rest-days, see note 27 above.
[33] The national flag of France adopted at the Revolution, consisting of equal vertical stripes of blue, white and red.
[34] Tench probably refers to the Cult of the Supreme Being, launched by Robespierre in the Convention on 7 May 1794. It was intended as an alternative both to the Catholic Church and to the iconoclastic atheism of the dechristianization movement, the effects of which in Quimper are described in Letter VII (pp. 71–2).
[35] Jacques-Louis Dupont (1755–1823), member of the Convention specializing in financial and educational matters; a militant atheist.
[36] However, the simile has not been traced.
[37] *Vive la Montagne! Vive les Jacobins!*: Long live the Mountain! Long live the Jacobins! The Jacobins, founded in May 1789, became the most powerful single political grouping in Revolutionary France. Centred on

the Jacobin Club in Paris (so named after the Jacobin convent in which they met) and with numerous associated clubs throughout France, they acted as a pressure group on and within the National Assembly and Convention. Initially broad in their range of revolutionary positions, from late 1792 they were increasingly associated with the Mountain and dominated by Robespierre and his policies. The Jacobin Club was finally closed on 12 November 1794, in the wake of Robespierre's downfall. In Britain in the 1790s, the term 'jacobin' was increasingly used in a broad and abusive sense to discredit radicals and liberals of all kinds.

[38] *à présent il faut crier, au diable la Montagne! A bas les Jacobins!*: now we have to shout, the Mountain to the devil! Down with the Jacobins!

LETTER V

[1] The winter of 1794–5 (the 'Grand Hiver') was the coldest of the century. Inaugurated by a savage frost on Christmas Eve – the same day that price controls on foodstuffs (the so-called '*le maximum*') were abolished – it intensified the sufferings of the people (as it did in Britain) and allowed the French cavalry to cross the frozen Rhine and defeat the Dutch navy.

[2] Lady Anne Fitzroy, sister of the future Duke of Wellington (Arthur Wellesley) and of the Earl of Mornington (Richard, later Governor-General of India), had been imprisoned in Quimper with another brother, probably Henry Wellesley (or 'Wesley', see Letter IX, p. 91, footnote).

[3] François-Joseph Bouvet de Précourt (1753–1832), French admiral who subsequently led the unsuccessful expedition to Bantry Bay (1796–7).

[4] Pierre-Jean Van Stable (1744–97), French admiral who broke the British blockade to lead the American grain convoy into Brest on 1 June 1794.

[5] l'Orient (now normally Lorient): south-east of Quimper, see Plate 1.

[6] Shakespeare, *Julius Caesar*, IV.ii.272–5 (*Complete Works*, pp. 697–8). Brutus to Cassius:

> There is a tide in the affairs of men
> Which, taken at the flood, leads on to fortune;
> Omitted, all the voyage of their life
> Is bound in shallows and in miseries.

NOTES TO LETTERS

⁷ Tench's analogies between the current war, the Punic War and the American War of Independence are based on the danger of wintering out. The Carthaginian general Hannibal (247–?183 BC) defeated the Romans at Cannae in Apulia, southern Italy, 216 BC. His subsequent wintering at Capua was widely seen as the turning-point of his own fortunes and those of Carthage. Allied forces crossed the French frontier at numerous points in spring–summer 1793; the Austrians defeated the French at the Belgian port of Valenciennes (21–3 May, 1793) and took the city on 28 July.

⁸ Unless the italicized '*I*' is a printing error, Tench is saying he is the only British officer on the ship able to read the French newspapers.

⁹ The cat woman is a recognized folk-motif, for instance in Aesop's *Fables*, but a version involving Jupiter has not been traced.

¹⁰ *frizeur*: (*friseur*) hairdresser.

¹¹ manes: the deified souls or honoured spirits of the dead.

¹² Joseph-Jeanne Marie-Antoinette (1755–93), Queen of France (1774–92), youngest daughter of Maria Theresa of Austria; imprisoned with her husband in August 1792, tried and executed in the autumn of 1793. Two powerful contemporary versions of the queen are in collision in this passage, each based principally on gender: the self-consciously chivalrous view famously articulated by Edmund Burke and the prevalent Republican view of her as corrupt and licentious.

¹³ The French took Amsterdam on 20 January 1795; by the Treaty of the Hague on 16 May, the United Provinces became the Batavian Republic, a 'sister republic' under French control. Prussia agreed a separate peace-treaty with France by the Treaty of Basle, 5 April 1795.

¹⁴ François Athanase Charette de la Contrie (1763–96), commander of counter-revolutionary forces in La Vendée (the *département* immediately to the south of Brittany, see Plate 1) from 1793. He made peace with the Republic in February 1795 at the Treaty of La Jaunaye, but rallied to royalism again with the Quiberon Bay expedition in June 1795; he was captured and shot in February 1796.

LETTER VI

¹ For an account of Lieutenant Robinson's experiences as a prisoner of war, see [Anon.], 'Narrative of an officer's imprisonment in France (1794)', in *Naval Yarns: Letters and Anecdotes*, edited by W. H. Long (Wakefield: EP Publishing, 1973), pp. 172–91; Adrien Carré, 'La prison-bagne des marins anglais', pp. 9–37.

NOTES TO LETTERS

² It is unclear whether 'his own countrymen' means 'other men from Provence' or 'other Frenchmen'.

³ 'The philosopher Aristippus, a follower of Aristotle, was shipwrecked on the coast of Rhodes, and observing geometrical diagrams drawn upon the sand, he is said to have shouted to his companions: 'There are good hopes for us; for I see human footsteps' (Vitruvius, *De Architectura*, Book vi (London: Heinemann, Loeb Classical Library, 1934), pp. 2–3).

⁴ A military engineer, a man trained in the construction of military works.

⁵ Thomas Gray's poem, 'A Long Story' (1753), describes 'an ancient pile of building', the work of 'faery hands' with 'Each panel in achievements cloathing/ Rich windows that exclude the light' (*The Complete Poems of Thomas Gray*, edited by H. W. Starr and J. R. Hendrikson (Oxford: Clarendon Press, 1966), p. 25, lines 2, 4, 6–7).

⁶ espaliers: fruit-trees trained up a lattice, or the lattice itself; the reference here could be to either or both.

⁷ clowns: a rather literary and condescending term for rural working people.

⁸ The highest concentration of Breton-speakers was in the three western departments of Finistère (*Penn-ar-Bed*), Morbihan (*Mor-Bihan*) and Côtes du Nord (*Aodoù-an-Hanternoz*); see Plate 2. In this western area, 'Breton was the language of the majority, and the rural areas were characterized by monolingualism . . . According to Coquebert de Montbret, in 1806 there were 995,558 people, out of a total of 1,385,936 in the three *départements* of Western Brittany who were able to speak Breton, a little more than 71 per cent of the population' (Rhisiart Hincks, 'The Breton language in the nineteenth century', in *Language and Community in the Nineteenth Century*, edited by Geraint Jenkins (Cardiff: University of Wales Press, 1999), pp. 369–95 (370, 372). As for Wales at the same period, 'Thomas Darlington estimated that 587,245 people lived in Wales in 1801 and that 80 per cent spoke Welsh', with the majority of these monoglot Welsh-speakers (John Aitchison and Harold Carter, *A Geography of the Welsh Language, 1961–1991* (Cardiff: University of Wales Press, 1994), p. 35).

⁹ The slogan was originally used in the Convention in December 1792, in the wake of French victories in Austria, to describe the official purpose of France's military interventions in other countries: the establishment of free and popular governments and the abolition of privilege.

¹⁰ Precini: properly Prépigui(?). See Carré, 'La prison-bagne des marins anglais', pp. 29–34.

[11] *dépôt*: depository, depot.

[12] For an account of Captain Kittoe's role in negotiating improved conditions for British prisoners of war, see Carré, 'La prison-bagne des marins anglais', pp. 20–34.

LETTER VII

[1] *cautionné*: stood surety for.

[2] *passe-dix*: a game played with three dice in which the object is to score more than ten.

[3] *Ma mère! Dix sols pour!—Ma tante! Quinze sols contre!*: My mother! Ten sols for!—My aunt! Fifteen sols against!

[4] Mademoiselle Kervélégan: the daughter of Augustin le Goaze de Kervélégan, see note 10 below.

[5] John Milton, *Paradise Lost*, IV, 869–71 (*The Poems*, pp. 664–5):

> And with them comes a third of regal port
> But faded splendour wan; who by his gait
> And fierce demeanor seems the prince of hell.

[6] Federalism – a provincial revolt against the centralizing and predominantly Parisian Montagnard regime – was seen by its opponents as a threat to '*la république une et indivisible*' (the republic one and indivisible). At its peak in summer 1793, it was especially strong in maritime provinces such as Brittany.

[7] *bons citoyens*: good citizens.

[8] *enragés*: a pejorative term, originally applied to the followers of Jacques Roux in the Paris sections, who demanded economic measures to protect the poor in the spring and summer of 1793.

[9] *cocarde blanche*: white cockade; an emblem of royalism (the Bourbon flag was white).

[10] Augustin le Goaze de Kervélégan (1748–1825), Breton deputy to the Convention. Associated with the Girondin (or Brissotin) faction (see note 11), Kervélégan escaped from house-arrest after the expulsion of the Girondins from the Convention in June 1793, helped to rally federalist forces in Caen (Normandy), and subsequently spent much of 1794 in hiding in Brittany. Reinstated to the Convention after 9 Thermidor (27 July 1794), he later became a member of the Council of Elders and the Legislative Body under the Directory.

NOTES TO LETTERS

[11] Brissotine party: a political grouping associated with Jacques Pierre Brissot (1754–93) with a preponderance of members from the Gironde (hence the alternative name of 'Girondins'). The grouping emerged, partly in reaction to the September Massacres of 1792, in opposition to the Montagnards who succeeded in purging them from the Convention in June 1793. Surviving Brissotin deputies (including the Breton, Kervélégan) were reinstated to the Convention in December 1794.

[12] the Mountain: the Montagne faction, see Letter III, note 3.

[13] Note the italics; Sunday evening parties would be a point on which a British Protestant might differ from both Catholic and anti-clerical French people; but not strongly enough, in Tench's case, to stay at home.

[14] *ton*: the prevailing fashion.

[15] *gens d'armes*: a national paramilitary police force dating from the sixteenth century; ancestor of the modern *gendarmerie*.

[16] *Conciergerie*: the Paris prison in which Marie-Antoinette also had been imprisoned.

[17] *Voila l'égalité!*: That's equality!

[18] M. C. Guesno had previously been a merchant, J. T. M. Guermeur a lawyer.

[19] The Representatives have established their offices in the same building – the erstwhile Bishop's House – occupied by the tavern where Tench drinks coffee and reads the Paris newspapers, the Lion d'Or (see Letter VIII, note 11, and Plate 5).

[20] See Plate 4.

[21] dight: adorned.

John Milton, *Il Penseroso* (1631), 158–60 (*The Poems of John Milton*, p. 146):

> With antique pillars' massy proof,
> And storied windows richly dight,
> Casting a dim religious light.

[22] On the sacking of the cathedral of Saint Corentin on Saint Corentin's Day 1793 (12 December), see Daniel Collet, 'La Révolution à Quimper', in Jean Kerhervé (ed.), *Histoire de Quimper* (Toulouse: Editions Privat, 1994), pp. 175–95.

[23] Shakespeare, *Measure for Measure*, II.ii.117–24 (*Complete Works*, p. 903). Isabella to (and of) Angelo:

> Merciful heaven,
> Thou rather with thy sharp and sulphurous bolt
> Split'st the unwedgeable and gnarled oak
> Than the soft myrtle. But man, proud man,
> Dressed in a little brief authority,
> Most ignorant of what he's most assured,
> His glassy essence, like an angry ape,
> Plays such fantastic tricks before high heaven
> As make the angels weep.

[24] The oath of allegiance under the Civil Constitution of the Clergy (1790). The proportion of 'refractories' (clergy refusing the oath) to 'constitutionals' was higher in the rural areas of the west than in any other part of France.

LETTER VIII

[1] Between the battle of Hastings (1066), when they helped the Normans to conquer England, and the marriage of Anne of Brittany to Charles VIII of France (1491), the Dukes of Brittany had indeed sided, in the conflicts between the French and English, sometimes with the former and sometimes with the latter. A treaty of 1532 bound Brittany definitively to France, while guaranteeing a degree of provincial autonomy which survived till 1789. Work on Quimper cathedral began in 1239, work on the town walls in 1240.

[2] See Plate 5 for a map of Quimper.

Voltaire, the pseudonym of François Marie Arouet (1694–1778), was a writer and social critic whose opposition to tyranny and religious bigotry led to his prolonged exile from France, part of it spent in Britain. The Republic came to see Voltaire and Jean-Jacques Rousseau (1712–78) as its principal ideological precursors. The historian Gabriel Bonnot de Mably (1709–85) was a classical republican whose *Observations sur l'histoire de France* (1765) compared the British polity favourably with France's absolute monarchy, as Voltaire's *Lettres philosophiques* (1734) had implicitly done.

[3] *maréchaux de France*: generals of France.

[4] The date of the overthrow of the monarchy.

[5] See the bilingual decree in Plate 6. The significance of such bilingual proclamations is a matter for debate. In a speech to the

Convention on 28 January 1794, Barère famously asserted that 'Federalism and superstition speak Breton', and there was an element in Republicanism which identified minority languages as a threat to the 'Republic one and indivisible'. Rhisiart Hinks argues that 'as in the case of licensing the translation of the Scriptures into Welsh in the sixteenth century, it is clear that it was felt that conveying the message justified using the language which, it was hoped, would eventually disappear' ('The Breton language in the nineteenth century', in Geraint Jenkins (ed.), *Language and Community in the Nineteenth Century* (Cardiff: University of Wales Press, 1999), pp. 369–95 (247)). However, 'the vigour of Barère's rhetoric should not lead us to ignore the *lack* of fervour with which Revolutionary administrations pursued the policy of linguistic nationalism' (Martin Lyons, 'Regionalism and linguistic conformity in the French Revolution', in Alan Forrest and Peter Jones (eds.), *Reshaping France: Town, Country and Region during the French Revolution* (Manchester: Manchester University Press, 1991), pp. 179–92 (188)).

6 It is hard to say whether Tench's choice of Cornwall and Wales as the appropriate points of comparison here is due to their reputation for poverty, their cultural and historic links, Tench's personal connections to them, or some combination of these factors. Nor is it clear whether 'England' is being distinguished from 'Cornwall and Wales' or being used as a synonym for Great Britain.

7 *Le peuple Français reconnait l'Etre Suprême*: The people of France acknowledge the Supreme Being.

8 In a major act of 'dechristianization', the cathedral of Notre-Dame in Paris had been renamed the 'Temple of Reason' in October 1793 and a public ceremonial held there on 10 November in which 'relays of patriotic maidens in virginal white paraded reverently before a temple of philosophy erected where the high altar had stood' (William Doyle, *Oxford History of the French Revolution* (Oxford: Oxford University Press, 1989), p. 261). The Temple of Reason at Quimper presumably stood on the Plateau de la déesse Raison (see Plate 5).

9 *neuf Thermidor* (9 Thermidor, Year II; or 27 July 1794) was the date of Robespierre's arrest (he was executed the following day). The phrase – or simply the word *Thermidor* – was subsequently used as the name for the major turning-point in the Revolution which the fall of Robespierre constituted. Thermidor was the eleventh month in the Republican Calendar which had been agreed by the Convention in October 1793 (backdated to the first day of the Republic, 22 January 1793), and which continued in use until 31 December 1806. The months were: *vendémiaire*

(the month of vintage); *brumaire* (the month of fog); *frimaire* (the month of frost); *nivôse* (the month of snow); *pluviôse* (the month of rain); *ventôse* (the month of wind); *germinal* (the month of germination); *floréal* (the month of flowering); *prairial* (the month of meadows); *messidor* (the month of harvest); *thermidor* (the month of heat); *fructidor* (the month of fruit) (Colin Jones, *The Longman Companion to the French Revolution* (London and New York: Longman, 1988), p. 428).

[10] *Ilium fuit*: Ilium is destroyed. 'Fuimus Troes, fuit Ilium et ingens/ Gloria Teucrorum' ('We are Trojans no more, Ilium is destroyed, and the great glory of the Trojans has passed'), Virgil, *Aeneid*, II.325 (London: Heinemann, Loeb Classical Library, 1916), pp. 316–17. Tench no doubt intends an effect of bathetic irony here, contrasting a brief and vulgar neo-classical Republic of Virtue both with the true pathos of the fall of Troy recorded in classical epic and with his own cultivated, Latin-speaking neo-classicism.

[11] The coffee-house was probably the Lion d'Or, occupying part of what had been the Bishop's Town House (see Plate 5). It had been a local base for the radical 'Hébertist' faction in 1793–4.

[12] The word may be simply part of a slogan, but could be a trace of the Quimper municipality's decision of 11 December 1793 to rename the town 'Montagne-sur-Odet'. The market-place in which the statue of Liberty stood was probably the Place de la République (see Plate 5).

[13] Calculous: 'of or pertaining to a calculus or the stone; diseased with the stone' (*OED*).

[14] The number of beggars in the streets in early 1795 will have been sharply increased by the lifting of price controls on basic foods – '*le maximum*' – which coincided with the onset of the hard winter. It is the effects of moving *away* from revolutionary egalitarianism that Tench may well be witnessing.

[15] *Noblesse bretonne*: the Breton nobility.

[16] A 'land' is 'one of the strips into which a corn-field, or a pasture-field which has been ploughed, is divided by water-furrows' (*OED*).

[17] This refers to the seed/yield ratio of the wheat crop, giving an increase of five or six grains for every one sown, a poor ratio by contemporary English standards, which averaged close to eight.

[18] *la racine Anglaise*: the English root.

[19] See Tench's 'survey of the cultivated land belonging to the public' (*Sydney's First Four Years*, pp. 247–59).

[20] countries: Tench may mean counties or regions, normal meanings of the word at that time.

[21] *crape*: properly, *crêpe* (*krampouezhenn*, in Breton and, therefore, to the 'peasants' themselves).

[22] James Boswell had made a comparable analogy in the Scottish Highlands, near Fort Augustus: 'We had a considerable circle about us, men, women and children, all M'craes, Lord Seaforth's people. Not one of them could speak English. I observed to Dr. Johnson, it was much the same as being with a tribe of Indians' (Samuel Johnson, James Boswell, *'A Journey to the Western Islands of Scotland', 'The Journal of a Tour to the Hebrides'*, edited by Peter Levi (1775, 1786; Harmondsworth: Penguin, 1984), p. 237). However, in the context of Tench's analogy between rural Bretons and urban Indians (Delhi) or Persians (Ispahan or, more commonly now, Isfahan), Tench's use of the word 'natives' to describe the former implies that the French-speaking population of Quimper are quasi-colonial latecomers rather than indigenous (but French-speaking) Bretons, an implication not present elsewhere in Tench's book. In its later and more systematically historicist manifestations (notably in the novels of Sir Walter Scott) such analogies sometimes implied that such peoples, while admirable in many ways, belonged essentially to the past. Balzac's study of the counter-revolution in Brittany, *The Chouans* (1829), which carries this implication, is modelled on Scott's *Waverley* (1814), with the Scottish highlanders played by Chouans and the Hanoverians played by the French Republicans.

[23] If Tench means that a bilingual gentry is one of the features which Wales and Brittany have in common at this period, his view may run counter to the stress in modern historiography on the 'anglicization' of the eighteenth-century Welsh gentry.

[24] *Cornouaille* (Breton, *Vro Gernev*), one of the ancient subdivisions of Brittany. The view that Welsh, Breton and Cornish derived from a single 'old British' language was pioneered by the Oxford scholar Edward Lhuyd (1660–1709) and is still the accepted view. Tench would probably know that *Caer* (castle) was also the Welsh name for Chester.

[25] Duelling was proscribed by Church and State in Britain, but was still widely practised among the upper classes.

[26] *charbon de terre*: literally 'earth coal', what we would now call simply 'coal'. Tench may mean that what the surgeon has analysed is not 'coal' in this sense. However, in the eighteenth century 'coal' more commonly meant charcoal, and mineral coal was commonly called 'pit coal' or 'sea coal'.

[27] Edward Gibbon, *The History of the Decline and Fall of the Roman*

Empire, vol.V (1788), edited by David Womersley (London: Allen Lane, The Penguin Press, 1994), vol. iii, p. 498.

LETTER IX

[1] Sir Frederick Morton Eden (1766–1809), British politician, diplomat and social investigator, principally remembered for his *State of the Poor* (1797).

[2] One autobiograhical narrative survives: Anon., 'Narrative of an officer's imprisonment in France, 1794', in *Naval Yarns: Letters and Anecdotes; comprising accounts of sea fights and wrecks, actions with pirates and privateers, etc., from 1616 to 1831*, edited by W. H. Long (Wakefield: EP Publishing, 1973), pp. 172–91.

[3] necessaries: 'necessary-houses', privies.

[4] Prieur de la Marne (1756–1827), member of the Committee of Public Safety and Representative on Mission to Brest with Jean Bon Saint-André from October 1793. See the letter addressed to him from the Quimper committee of *surveillance* on the subject of British prisoners of war (Plate 7).

[5] *Paradise Lost*, I.591–2, 594–9 (*The Poems of John Milton*, p. 497). Milton so describes Satan immediately after the latter's fall from Heaven when:

> . . . his form had yet not lost
> All her original brightness . . .
> . . . As when the sun new-risen
> Looks through the horizontal misty air
> Shorn of his beams, or from behind the moon
> In dim eclipse disastrous twilight sheds
> On half the nations, and with fear of change
> Perplexes monarchs.

[6] The captivity of Lady Anne Fitzroy is presented here as repeating the captivity of Marie-Antoinette and confirming Burke's interpretation of that event: 'I thought ten thousand swords must have leapt from their scabbards to avenge even a look that threatened her with insult. – But the age of chivalry is gone . . . Never, never more, shall we behold that generous loyalty to rank and sex, that proud submission . . . which kept alive, even in servitude itself, the spirit of an exalted freedom.' Edmund

Burke, *Reflections on the Revolution in France*, edited by C. C. O'Brien (1790; Harmondsworth: Penguin, 1968), p. 170.

⁷ *traiteur*: caterer.

⁸ L. Junius Brutus, by tradition the founder of the Roman Republic, supposedly executed his own sons when they were convicted of involvement in a royalist plot.

⁹ *Chacun à son tour*: everyone gets his turn (spoken by a Guernsey man and therefore a French-speaker).

LETTER X

¹ That is, in the royal household.

² Charles-Philippe, Comte d'Artois (1757–1836), the youngest brother of Louis XVI, became Charles X, King of France (1824–30). From 1789, Artois directed *émigrés* from Turin and then Coblenz. In October–November 1795 he led a British-backed expedition to the island of Yeu off Brittany which failed to link up with Charette. 'Monsieur' was the traditional courtesy title of the eldest of the monarch's younger brothers. At the date Tench is writing, this was the Comte de Provence (the future Louis XVIII); the title passed to Artois in 1796.

³ The allusion is to a passage from Canto 7 of Voltaire's epic poem *La Henriade* (1723) describing a previous Bourbon dauphin (the future Louis XV), and is the source of the description of the present dauphin (Artois's nephew, who had in theory been Louis XVII from 6 June 1793 and who was to die – aged ten – shortly after Tench wrote) as '*le monarque au berceau*' (the cradled monarch):

> ... O jours remplis d'allarmes!
> O combien les français vont répandre de larmes
> Quand sous la même tombe ils verrons réunis
> Et l'époux et la femme, et la mère et le fils!
> Un faible réjeton sort entre les ruines,
> De cet arbre fécond coupé dans ses racines.
> Les enfants de Louis descendus au tombeau,
> Ont laissé dans la France un Monarque au berceau.
> De l'Etat ébranlé douce & frêle espérance.

In one of many eighteenth-century English translations: 'What dire alarms have seiz'd the *French*,/ What loud laments I hear, what Weeping see?/ In the same Grave at once, hard Fate, are laid/ The Husband, Wife, and Mother, and the Son./ Among these Royal Ruins springs a Sprig/ That branches from the Tree, the Root cut off,/ The Sons of Lewis in their Tombs enclos'd,/ Have left to govern France a cradled King./ Sweet, but frail Hope of an unsettled State' (*Henriade*, . . . *translated from the French into English blank verse by John Lockman,* London, 1732). A new edition of *La Henriade* had appeared in 1790, 'printed by royal command for the edification of the dauphin'.

[4] 'Neither shall we give them the cup of consolation to drink for their father or for their mother.' *Jeremiah* 16:7.

[5] In fact, the Chouan leader (see note 6), Joseph-Geneviève, Comte de Puisaye, had been in London from September 1794 negotiating for a British and *émigré* invasion, which eventually took place at Quiberon in June–July 1795. If it had succeeded, Puisaye planned that Chouan forces would 'join up with 12,000 royalists . . . and then march via Concarneau, to Quimper to free the prisoners' (Puisaye, letter to Secretary Windham, 10 July 1795, quoted in Maurice Hutt, *Chouannerie and Counter-Revolution: Puisaye, the Princes and the British Government in the 1790s* (Cambridge: Cambridge University Press, 1983), Vol. 2, p. 305).

[6] The *Chouans* (a word derived from the nickname of one of them) were a peasant-based counter-revolutionary guerrilla movement in Brittany and other parts of north-western France. Beginning in 1791, after priests had been required to swear oaths in support of the Civil Constitution of the Clergy, *chouannerie* continued intermittently until at least 1799, sometimes – until 1796 – in alliance with the counter-revolutionary armies of La Vendée.

[7] Caumartin: Pierre-Marie Desoteux, Baron de Cormatin (1753–1812), commander of the royalist forces in Brittany following Puisaye's departure for England in July 1794.

[8] A series of treaties with the Vendéans between February and May 1795 was followed by a treaty with the Chouans at La Prévalaye, 20 April 1795 (1 Floréal, Year III).

[9] Antæus, son of the god Poseidon and the goddess Ge (Earth), a giant whose strength was renewed every time he touched his mother earth. Hercules eventually crushed him to death in the air.

[10] Prussia, having played an important part in the fighting in 1792–4, made a separate peace with France at the Treaty of Basle, 5 April 1795. Tench had earlier doubted such an outcome (p. 51).

[11] Joseph Cambon (1756–1820), Jacobin member of the Convention and finance minister under Robespierre.

NOTES TO LETTERS

[12] milliard: a thousand million.

[13] Tench uses 'wonderful' in the then normal sense of extraordinary.

[14] William Playfair (1759–1825), American entrepreneur and publicist in Paris who initially sided with the Revolution but after he left France wrote a hostile *History of Jacobinism* (1793) and in 1795 advocated the issue of forged *assignats* as a weapon against the Republic.

[15] *bellum internecinum*: civil war.

[16] *le jeu vaut la chandelle*: the game is worth the candle.

[17] Georges Jacques Danton (1759–94), leading Jacobin and member of the Committee of Public Safety. He initially supported the Terror but urged restraint from early 1794; he was executed on 5 April. He had spoken influentially in the Convention debate which preceded the decree of 4 February 1794 abolishing slavery in all French colonies. The decree cemented the alliance – initiated in August 1793 by Sonthonax, Commissioner on St Domingue and a Brissotin – between black and Republican forces in the struggle for control of the islands of the West Indies.

[18] Hamilcar (d. 229), Carthaginian general, father of Hannibal.

[19] Edmund Burke (1729–97), politician and polemicist. His *Reflections on the Revolution in France* (1790) – Tench's 'splendid pebble' – initiated the British pamphlet wars of the 1790s on the conservative side. Burke's previous reputation as a liberal Whig made his wholesale and bitter opposition to the Revolution of 1789 particularly challenging for other liberal Whigs, such as Tench.

[20] Thomas Paine (1737–1809), pamphleteer and international revolutionary. *Rights of Man* (1791–2), his reply to Burke's *Reflections*, was the single most potent influence on the development of British popular radicalism in the 1790s, as his *Common Sense* (1776) had been the most widely read pamphlet of the American Revolution. Tench returned from New South Wales at the height of Paine's influence. Moving to France to escape British government persecution, Paine became member for Calais in the Convention. Associated with the Girondins (Brissotins), he was expelled from the Convention with them and imprisoned in the Luxembourg from December 1793 to January 1795. Tench's prognosis is sour but roughly accurate: dissatisfied with the new order in France, Paine returned to America in 1803 to be scorned as an atheist and leveller, dying in poverty and isolation.

[21] Antoine-Christophe, Baron Merlin de Thionville (1762–1833), member of the Convention and Representative on Mission to the Vendée, played a key role in the overthrow of Robespierre.

NOTES TO LETTERS

[22] Emmanuel-Joseph, Abbé Sieyès (1748–1836), 'monk of the Revolution' (Robespierre), author of the influential pamphlet, *Qu'est-ce que le Tiers-état?* ('What is the third estate?') (1789) and an author of the Declaration of the Rights of Man.

[23] Bertrand de Barère de Vieuzac (1755–1841), member of the Convention and Committee of Public Safety, associated with the Montagnards but attacked Robespierre at Thermidor. Jean-Marie Collot d'Herbois (1749–96), dramatist, member of the Convention and Committee of Public Safety, responsible for brutal repression as Representative on Mission in Lyons, and an architect of Thermidor. Jacques-Nicolas Billaud-Varennes (1756–1819), member of the Convention and Committee of Public Safety but a Thermidorian conspirator. Marc-Guillaume-Alexis Vadier (1736–1828), member of the Convention, Thermidorian. All four were tried and sentenced to deportation in May 1795: Barère and Vadier escaped and survived; Billaud-Varennes and Collot d'Herbois were deported to Guinea.

[24] The *prévenus* (the accused) are Barère, Collot d'Herbois and Billard-Varennes. The two men 'declaiming' against them in the Convention were: Louis Legendre (1752–97), Parisian butcher who became a regicide member of the Convention but subsequently participated in the Thermidor coup and helped put down the 'Germinal' rising; M. Isnard (1751–1825), landowner and Girondin, President of the Convention from May 1793, in hiding from June 1793 to December 1794.

[25] Laurant Lecointre (1742–1805), Montagnard member of the Convention, violently anti-Montagnard after Thermidor.

[26] On 12 and 13 Germinal, Year III (1 and 2 April 1795), there were unsuccessful popular insurrections in Paris in the name of radical political and economic policies.

[27] *Vive Louis dix-sept! . . . Vive la république . . .*: Long live Louis XVII! . . . Long live the Republic . . .

[28] Charles Pichegru (1761–1804), general, commander of the Armies of the Rhine, the Moselle (with Hoche) and the North. Though he may have 'preserved the peace of Paris from the machinations of royalists and terrorists', from 1795 he was involved in the royalist plots which eventually led to his arrest and death.

[29] In Greek mythology, Procrustes – literally, 'the stretcher' – was a highwayman who tied travellers onto a bed and, depending on whether they were shorter or longer than the bed, stretched them or cut off their limbs until they fitted it perfectly.

[30] *annoncé par l'Etre Suprême, pour réformer toute chose*: foretold by

the Supreme Being, to reform all things; *comme Dieu, par des merveilles*: as God does, by marvels.

[31] From *Te Deum laudamus* ('Thee, God, we praise'), an ancient Latin hymn of praise, sung as a thanksgiving on special occasions.

[32] J.-B.-Michel Saladin (1752–1812), Montagnard member of the Convention who nevertheless opposed the proscription of the Girondins. He was arrested, but returned after Thermidor as an anti-terrorist.

[33] *Le comité de salut public a dit à le Bon, qu'il espérait que nous irions tous les jours de mieux en mieux. Robespierre voudrait que chacun de nous pût former un seul tribunal, et empoigner chacun une ville de la frontière*: The Committee of Public Safety said to Le Bon that they hoped things were getting better for us day by day. Robespierre wanted each of us to form a tribunal, and each to seize a frontier town.

Tench's reference here to the two Robespierrists – Augustin Alexandre Darthè (1769–97) and Philippe Le Bas (1765–94) – is puzzling, since the former was still alive when Tench wrote (though he was subsequently executed) and the latter had committed suicide on 9 Thermidor (27 July 1794).

[34] Caligula, Roman Emperor AD 37–41, notorious for cruelty, mental instability and extravagance.

[35] Jean-Baptiste Carrier (1756–94), Representative on Mission to Nantes, responsible for particularly brutal acts of systematic repression, including death by firing-squad (*fusillades*), and mass drownings (*noyades*) in the Loire at Nantes. There were also accounts of young men and women tied together naked and then drowned (*republican marriages*).

LETTER XI

[1] Merlin de Thionville (see Letter X, n.21, p. 158) or Philippe Antoine Merlin de Douai (1754–1838).

[2] 'For all the Athenians and strangers which were there spent their time in nothing else but, either to tell, or to hear, some new thing.' *Acts*, 17:21.

[3] In Virgil's *Aeneid*, Mazentius was the king of the Tyrrhenians who put criminals to death by tying them face to face with dead bodies.

[4] A law of 20 September 1792 legalized divorce which, it was argued, 'follows from individual liberty, which would be lost in any indissoluble commitment'. Women were given equal status in suing for divorce. Moves to make divorce more difficult, especially for women, followed

NOTES TO LETTERS

Thermidor, but it was the Napoleonic Civil Code of 1804 which, while retaining divorce, 'made it much more difficult to obtain, especially for women' (Lynn Hunt, *The Family Romance of the French Revolution* (London: Routledge, 1992), p. 162).

[5] Jean Racine (1639–99), French neo-classical dramatic poet, author of *Phèdre*, *Athalie* and other tragedies.

Nicolas Boileau (1636–1711), French critic and poet, associate of Racine and Molière.

[6] Alexander Pope (1688–1744), English poet, conservative satirist, translator of Homer's *Iliad* and *Odyssey*. His *Essay on Criticism* was modelled on Boileau's *L'Art poétique*.

[7] Joseph Warton had influentially criticized Pope and 'his model Boileau' in these terms, arguing that 'we do not ... sufficiently attend to the difference there is betwixt a Man of Wit, a man of Sense, and a True Poet', the former two types lacking 'creative and glowing imagination' (Joseph Warton, *An Essay on the Genius and Writings of Pope* (London, 1756), pp. iv–v). Reissued in 1782, Warton's essay came to be associated with early Romanticism.

[8] It is not clear to what report to the Convention Tench is referring or whether '*Gothicism*' is his term or the report's. He may be referring to the translation into French, in the 1790s, of British novels by Horace Walpole and Ann Radcliffe, and to the beginnings of stage melodrama in Paris; but 'Gothicism' is being used very broadly here, in a way that links an artistic tendency and the physical destruction of traditional cultural artefacts.

[9] François Antoine, Comte de Boissy d'Anglas (1756–1826), a member of the Convention opposed to regicide, became a member of the Committee of Public Safety after Thermidor and helped to draw up the Constitution of Year III.

[10] *Aux armes, citoyens!*: To arms, citizens!

[11] As the penultimate paragraph of his last letter written from France, this passage echoes sections in the closing chapters of the *Account* where he compared 'a savage roaming for prey amidst his native deserts' with the idealized view of the savage imagined by 'European philosophers' such as Rousseau; he then urged 'those who have been born in more favoured lands, and who have profited by more enlightened systems [to] compassionate, but not despise, their destitute and obscure situation. Children of the same omniscient paternal care, let them recollect, that by the fortuitous advantage of birth alone, they possess superiority; that untaught, unaccommodated man, is the same in Pall Mall, as in the

wilderness of New South Wales' (*Sydney's First Four Years*, pp. 291, 293–4). Tench now, in less optimistic mode, situates the global imperial conflicts of his time within a biblically derived eschatology, looking back five thousand years to the Creation and forward to humankind's assembly before the 'living throne' of the Creator, as prophesied in Revelation. After the loss of the North American colonies, the British Empire consisted (in addition to Canada) of some West Indian islands (home of 'the Charib'), New South Wales, and parts of India (home of 'the Hindoo'), so that Tench is here drawing Britain, her empire and her principal imperial rival together into a grand redemptive narrative encompassing the whole of time and space.

LETTER XII

[1] Cawsand is on the western (Cornish) side of Plymouth Sound.

[2] He probably refers here to those members of his wife's family who lived in Devonport (adjoining Plymouth on the eastern (Devon) side of the River Tamar), possibly including his wife Anna Maria herself. Devonport may have been Tench's home-town.

[3] *General Anglais*: English general.

[4] J. B. N. Topsent had previously been a merchant sea-captain, J. B. Harmand a lawyer.

[5] 'Those Families which live upon their Patrimonial Estates in all the great Cities, are a people differently bred and manner'd from the Traders, though like them in the modesty of Garb and Habit, and the Parsimony of living . . . The chief End of their Breeding is to make them fit for the service of their Countrey in the Magistracy of their Towns, their Provinces, and their State . . . Nor do these families . . . usually arrive at great or excessive Riches . . . They content themselves with the honour of being useful to the Publique, with the esteem of their Cities or their Country, and with the ease of their Fortunes.' Sir William Temple, *Observations upon the United Provinces of the Netherlands*, edited by Sir George Clark (1673; Oxford: Clarendon Press, 1972), pp. 83, 84–5.

[6] *fainéants:* lazy.

[7] ordinary: 'eating-house or tavern where public meals are provided at a fixed price' (OED).

APPENDIX 1

RELATION D'UNE EXPEDITION A LA BAYE BOTANIQUE, SITUEE dans la Nouvelle Hollande, sur la côte Meridionale, nommée par le Capitaine Cook, NOUVELLE GALLES MERIDIONALE. AVEC des Observations sur les Habitants de cette Contrée, & la liste de l'Etat Civil & Militaire, au Port Jackson, traduit de l'Anglais; du Capitaine WATKIN TINCH [sic]; PAR C**. P**.[1] *A PARIS*, Chez KNAPEN Fils, Libraire-Imprimeur, au bas du Pont Saint Michel. 1789.

TRANSLATOR'S NOTE[2]

This moment, when the assembled Nation is about to reform all branches of the administration, is clearly the right time to make known a volume which studies the creation of a Colony designed to return to the Nation those men whose crimes led to their dismissal from her breast.

Concerned men, at least, consider that the penal laws should be less harsh. They know that institutional vices are the causes of most crimes. But what should be done with those guilty men whose life is preserved by such less harsh laws? And with those who are not condemned to lose their lives by the present legislation? Should they be left to rot in prison, where they will become still more perverse? This would not meet the Law's intention, which seeks only to punish in order to correct. If the Magistrate is forced to open the prisons which can no longer hold these unfortunates, should he let them return to society in the hope that they will become better? Given the all-too-frequent occurrence of unfortunate cases, we must give up this hope: this is not the place to discuss the reasons.

Finally, should one put criminals to work on public projects within the Society they have offended? This method would certainly fulfil one of the first intentions of good legislation. It is, however, a method which is difficult to put into practice. It does not seem to hold the same advantages for the Nation as the method which the English[3] have considered that they must substitute for it. This people, who we would do better to copy in their political conduct than in their fashions, have just sent a Colony of 775 criminals to Botany Bay in New Holland.

The idea of using a land to establish agricultural Colonies is not new. It is the means used to make it successful, however, that we venture to

APPENDIX 1

present here as innovative: for example, the choice of the site, and the care which the English take of the guilty men – an attitude which is not simply an expression of physical compassion that can vary in different circumstances and that can be mistaken. No, philosophical compassion is the basis for their policies: their attitudes are more permanent because they are based on a calculation of the elements of each individual's happiness and of that of society. We venture to hope that such a fine example will be followed by the French, who are second to none in their compassion and humanity.

The details contained in this narrative are all the more interesting as they record the experience of the most daring, the most far-flung institution yet founded by Europeans. Captain Cook has given us some information about the site of this colony, although he only passed through it.

(Translated from Charles Pougens's original French by Sharif Gemie)

APPENDIX 2

From the *London Gazette*, 31 January–3 February 1795.

Admiralty-Office, February 3, 1795

A Letter from Rear-Admiral Bligh, late Captain of His Majesty's Ship the Alexander, to Mr. Stephens, (a Copy of which is as follows) was received at this Office the 30th of last Month.[1]

On Board the Marat, at Brest, November 23, 1794.

SIR,

The arrival of the Canada must long since have informed their Lordships of my Misfortune, in losing His Majesty's Ship Alexander, late under my Command, having been taken by a Squadron of French Ships of War, consisting of Five of Seventy-four Guns, Three large Frigates, and an armed Brig, commanded by Rear-Admiral Neilly; farther Particulars and Details I herewith transmit you, for their Lordships Information. We discovered this Squadron on our Weather Bow, about Half past Two o'Clock, or near Three, in the Morning on the 6th Instant, being then in Latitude 48 deg. 25 Min. North, 7 deg. 53 Min. West, the Wind then at West, and we steering North-East; on which I immediately hauled our Wind, with the Larboard Tacks on Board, and without Signal, the Canada being close to us. We passed the strange Ships a little before Four o'Clock, the nearest of whom at about Half a Mile distant, but could not discover what they were. Shortly after we bore more up, let the Reefs out of the Top-Sails, and set Steering-Sails. About Five o'Clock, perceiving, by my Night-Glass,[2] the strange Ships to stand after us, we crowded all the Sail we could possibly set, as did the Canada, and hauled more to the Eastward. About Day-break the Canada passed us, and steering more to the Northward than we did, brought her on our Larboard Bow. Two ships of the Line and Two Frigates pursued her; and Three of the Line and One Frigate chased the Alexander. About Half past Seven o'Clock the French Ships hoisted English Colours. About a Quarter past Eight o'Clock we hoisted our Colours, upon which the French Ships hauled down the English, and

APPENDIX 2

hoisted their's; and drawing up within Gun-Shot, we began firing our Stern Chaces at them, and received their Bow Chaces. About Nine o'Clock, or shortly after, observing the Ships in pursuit of the Canada, drawing up with her, and firing at each other their Bow and Stern Chaces, I made the Canada's Signal to form a Head for our mutual Support, being determined to defend the Ships to the last Extremity; which Signal she instantly answered, and endeavoured to put it in Execution by steering towards us; but the Ships in Chase of her, seeing her Intentions, hauled more to Starboard to cut her off, and which obliged her to steer the Course she had done before. We continued firing our stern Chaces at the Ships pursuing us till near Eleven o'Clock, when Three Ships of the Line came up, and brought us to close Action, which we sustained for upwards of Two Hours, when the Ship was become a complete Wreck, the Main-Yard, Spanker-Boom, and three Top-Gallant-Yards shot away, all the lower Masts shot through in many Places, and expected every Minute to go over the Side; all the other Masts and Yards were also wounded, more or less, nearly the whole of the Standing and Running Rigging cut to Pieces, the Sails torn into Ribbands, and her Hull much shattered, and making a great Deal of Water, and with Difficulty she floated into Brest: At this Time the Ships that had chased the Canada had quitted her, and were coming fast up to us, the Shot of one of them at the Time passing over us. Thus situated, and cut off from all Resources, I judged it adviseable to consult my Officers, and accordingly assembled them all on the Quarter-Deck; when, upon surveying and examining the State of the Ship, (engaged as I have already described) they deemed any farther Resistance would be ineffectual, as every possible Exertion had already been used in vain to save her, and therefore they were unanimously of Opinion, that to resign her would be the Means of saving the Lives of a Number of brave Men. Then, and not till then, (painful to relate) I ordered the Colours to be struck; a Measure which, on a full Investigation, I hope and trust their Lordships will not disapprove. Hitherto I have not been able to collect an exact List of the Killed and Wounded, as many of the former were thrown overboard during the Action, and, when taken Possession of, the People were divided, and sent on Board different Ships, but I do not believe they exceed Forty, or thereabout. No Officer above the Rank of Boatswain's Mate was killed. Lieutenant Fitzgerald, of the Marines, Mess. Burns, Boatswain, and McCurdy, Pilot, were wounded, but in a fair Way of doing well.

    The cool, steady, and gallant Behaviour of all my Officers and Ship's Company, Marines as well as Seamen, throughout the whole of the Action, merits the highest Applauses; and I should feel myself deficient in my Duty, as well as in what I owe to those brave Men, were I to omit requesting you will be pleased to recommend them in the strongest Manner to their Lordship's Favour and Protection; particularly Lieutenants Godench, Epworth, Carter, West and Daracott; Major Tench, Lieutenants Fitzgerald and Brown of the Marines; Mr Robinson the Master, together with the Warrant and Petty Officers, whose Bravery and good Conduct I shall ever hold in the highest Estimation. I have hitherto been treated with great Kindness and Humanity, and have not a Doubt but that I shall meet with the same Treatment during my Captivity.

      I am, with great Respect,
       SIR,
       Your most obedient and
        Most humble Servant,
         R. R. BLIGH

Philip Stephens, Esq;
Secretary of the Admiralty.

APPENDIX 3

From the *Analytical Review*, Vol. XXIV, September 1796.

ART. II. *Letters written in France, to a Friend in London, between the Month of November 1794, and the Month of May 1795.* By Major Tench, of the Marines, late of his Majesty's Ship Alexander. 8vo. 224 pages. Price 4s. in boards. Johnson. 1796.[1]

The strange mixture of wisdom and folly, of generous actions and atrocities, and of sufferings and success, which a neighbouring country has exhibited during the last six years, the wonderful changes it has undergone, and the immense multitude of important events which it has compressed within so narrow a circle, have naturally attracted our attention strongly towards it, but our means of information have of late been very inadequate to our curiosity. Our *regular* tour writers, shut out by the war, and the jealousy of both governments, have been unable, like Mr. Burke, to find France upon the map; and have been forced to leave the rich mine to be partially explored by interlopers, whom the fortune of war, or some other casualty, has cast upon the coast. Of this number is the author of the present work. He was taken with admiral Bligh in the Alexander, and carried into Brest, after the ship had sustained a long action against a very superiour force.

One of the first things that struck the major, after having been taken out of his own ship, was the total want of cleanliness on board the french one, to which he was removed. [P. 10.][2]

'Nothing short,' says he, 'of the evidence of my senses could, nevertheless, have made me believe, that so much filthiness could be quietly submitted to, when it might be so easily prevented. Indeed, a ship is in all situations very unfavourable to scrupulous nicety; but no description can convey an adequate idea to a british naval officer, who has not witnessed it, of the gross and polluted manner in which the french habitually keep all parts of their vessels, if I may judge from what I see in this. And to complete the jest, captain Le Franq has more than once boasted to us of the superior attention which he pays to the cleanliness of his ship.'

Nor is his account of the french officers on board the Marat much more favourable. He gives a number of instances of their want of information, delicacy, and liberality, and in the course of them introduces the following traits and reflections which are deserving of remark.

[Pp. 25–7.]—'When the question of the relative naval strength of the two nations is agitated, which it often is, I am tempted to cry out to my country, in the words of the grecian oracle,—"Trust to your wooden walls." I am more confirmed in this opinion from reading every day in the *bulletins* of the astonishing successes of this people, both in the Pyrenees and on the frontiers of Holland [. . .] On the celebrated measure of making them a present of four ships of the line, and six thousand of their best seamen, which were sent to Brest and Rochfort from the Mediterranean, they often make themselves merry, and us serious, by pointing out the ships as they now lie near to us, equipped and ready for sea; and by affirming, that the supply of men thus received enabled them to fit out those cruizing squadrons which have so sorely distressed our commerce.'

The above blunder is not the only one the author lays to the charge of our naval administration. He speaks with indignation of our suffering the american convoy under admiral Vanstable to enter Brest, at a moment when it's capture would have been of the greatest detriment to the enemy, and when they had nothing to oppose to our efforts but the crippled and mutilated squadron left them by lord Howe. His own observations on this subject are strengthened by the following conversation, which he reports to have passed between an english officer and the french admiral Villaret de Joyeuse. [P. 40.]

' "Were you not astonished to see me chase you, on the 9th of june last, with my crippled fleet?"—"Yes," was the answer.—"My only reason for it was, if possible, to drive you off our coast, as I momently expected the appearance of the great american convoy, the capture of which would have ruined France at that juncture. Why you did not return to the charge, after running us out of sight, you best know. Had you kept on your station two days longer, you must have succeeded, as, on the 11th of june, the whole of this convoy, beyond our expectation, entered Brest, laden with provisions, naval stores, and west indian productions." '

At the curious phenomenon of the french fleet keeping the sea for five or six weeks very shortly after the action of the 1st of june, and their intercepting our trade without molestation, the major glances in a less direct manner. [P. 48.]

'Cut off as I am from all communication with english politics, I shall not presume to guess at the causes which have retained our fleet in harbour. But some of those which have not retained it, I shall venture to state. It was not the weather, for that was uninterruptedly fine until the 25th of january. It was not the wind, for that during the same period was always easterly, here at least, and our distance from Plymouth is barely 45 leagues. It was not a want of information, for (to my knowledge) exclusive of other channels, two english gentlemen, who escaped from this place in a boat at least as early as the 8th of january, must have arrived in England by the 12th or 13th.'

On the sailing of the fleet for the above cruize, the author, who had already been removed from the Marat to the Normandie, an old ship fitted up for the reception of prisoners, and had thence been brought back to the Marat again, was once more confined to the prison-ship. There he 'suffered every mental punishment which low minded rancour and brutal ignorance could inflict, and every physical hardship which a rigorous winter, and occasional deficiencies of food could produce.' During the whole month of january he did not see a fire, and on Christmas day was one of fifteen english officers, with admiral Bligh at their head, whose dinner consisted of eight very small mutton chops, and a plate of potatoes. A threat, however, of complaining to admiral Villaret, produced better fare; whence it was evident, that their ill treatment was rather attributable to the low agents of government, than to government itself; and that the allowance made to prisoners [*le traitement*] was embezzled by the officers of the prison-ship, who are described as a set of worthless wretches, except two who filled civil posts, and who were men of honourable characters and compassionate hearts.

A stay of several months in the port of Brest enabled the author to obtain a considerable insight into the french naval institutions, a number of which he details to his readers. Several of them appear to be worthy the consideration of our government, especially their regulations respecting prize-money. [P. 34.]

'A captain receives but in a proportion of 5 to 1 to a foremast-man; a captain of troops, and a naval lieutenant, as 4 to 1; a naval ensign, subaltern of troops, surgeon, and commissary, as 3 to 1; midshipmen, boatswains, gunners, etc. as 2 to 1; and quarter-masters, and the lowest rank of officers, as $1\frac{1}{2}$ to 1.'

Not only do we think with the major, that a distribution somewhat similar is 'very desirable in a country where, hitherto, this important part of the reward of naval toils has been apportioned with the most cruel and insulting contempt of the feelings and necessities of the lower orders,' but we are of opinion, that it's adoption, by holding out an encouragement to our seamen to enter voluntarily into the king's service, would do away the necessity of recurring to the odious practice of pressing, by which the gallant defenders of a free country are reduced to a condition little better than that of slaves.

During their confinement, admiral Bligh and the author had been several times flattered with hopes of being sent on their parole to

Quimper, and several times disappointed. At length, however, they were suffered to enter the land of promise; from the misery of a prison ship they were removed to the comforts of a neat and respectable house; and from the contemplation of the disgusting uniformity of manners of a set of sea *sansculottes*, they were enabled to extend their observations to more varied scenes of life, and to note the demeanour of the different classes of a people who had recently thrown off the yoke of despotism. When all the orders of society are shaken together by a political convulsion, similar to Cromwell's usurpation, or the revolution of France, a number of ridiculous characters never fail to force themselves into notice. Every man of flippant tongue, impudent disposition, and adventuring spirit turns reformer, strutting in office with all the vulgar importance of "brief authority." Several personages of this description are pourtrayed by the major with considerable humour. Sometimes indeed, we think him too severe upon the floating follies of the day, but when he hangs up in effigy a citizen Precini, a commissary of prisoners, whose brutal manners, so far from being redeemed by the probity that should characterize a republican, are accompanied by a knavish inclination to defraud the victims of war of their scanty allowance, the entertainment we receive is unmixed with commiseration. [Pp. 65–6.]

'At one of these routs,' says he, speaking of this Precini, 'I saw a specimen of genuine democratic manners, which all who aim to become great men in the state affect to imitate [. . .] A courtier of Versailles at his toilet, surrounded by paints, patches, and perfumery, was, in the eye of reason, a ridiculous and contemptible animal; but the most effeminate essenced *marquis*, that ever consulted a looking glass, was surely preferable to this indecent blockhead.'

After reciting a number of facts, that serve to characterize the nation and the moment, the author enters into some short speculations concerning the probable event of the contest in which we are engaged, and the failure of french paper-money, and concludes them by the following observations, which do honour to his penetration, and to his philanthropy. [Pp. 107–8.]

'When I sum up the component parts of this stupendous system, and contemplate it in the aggregate, I must confess myself to be staggered, and almost ready to pronounce against the ability of this wonderful people to continue the contest in which they are engaged [. . .] If the opulence of England be founded on the basis of african slavery; if the productions of the tropics can be dispensed to us only by the blood and tears of the negro, I do not hesitate to exclaim—"Perish our commerce;" let our humanity live!'

Many of the more voluminous publications, that have appeared concerning french affairs, have been so filled with extraneous matter, with journals of senatorial debates, and with extracts from books already known in this country, that the author's work has been the least part of itself—*minima est pars puella sui*.[3] Little of this sort is to be found in the volume before us. In the facts the major relates, he is for the most part, personally concerned, and his observations, though they frequently want novelty, are such as those facts naturally suggest. He writes with the cheerful ease, and in the agreeable and unaffected style, that distinguishes the author and the gentleman, and has, upon the whole, afforded us more information and entertainment than the small size of his book led us to expect. We cannot however, help observing, that some of his conclusions are drawn with that hastiness, and that careless ease, for which military men are so often remarkable.

M.

Notes to Appendices

APPENDIX 1

[1] C** P** is Charles Pougens. His reference to 'the assembled Nation' ('la Nation assemblée') points to a probable publication date after the proclamation of the National Assembly on 17 June 1789.

[2] This note, originally in French, was written by Pougens to accompany his own French translation of Tench's original. Pougens's capitalization has been retained.

[3] In common with most French authors, Pougens uses the term *Anglais* (English) to designate all inhabitants of the British Isles (Sharif Gemie).

APPENDIX 2

[1] 'A court-martial was automatic when any naval ship was lost' (Brian Lavery, *Nelson's Navy: The Ships, Men and Organisation, 1793–1815* (London: Conway Maritime Press, 1989), p. 217). Bligh's account of the battle – a technical and meticulous blow-by-blow account of the events which led to his decision to surrender the *Alexander* – is clearly intended as a vindication, written in anticipation of court-martial. In the event, he was honourably discharged. The *Naval Chronicle* commented that 'Admiral Bligh's defence of the *Alexander* has never been surpassed in our naval annals; and, had it been his good fortune to have had with him, in that unequal conflict, such a force as might have attacked the French squadron with any fair estimate of success, the result will not be questioned by any one who is conversant with the superiority of British nautical skill and courage' (*The Naval Chronicle: The Contemporary Record of the Royal Navy at War, Volume 1, 1793–98*, edited by Nicholas Tracy (London: Chatham Publishing, 1998), p. 114). The *London Gazette's* capitalization (conservative by comparison with the capitalization of Tench's *Letters* and the *Analytical Review*) and spelling have been retained.

[2] A nautical term for 'a short refracting telescope especially constructed for use during the night' (*OED*).

APPENDIX 3

[1] The original spelling and capitalization have been retained but some of the longer quotations have been shortened. The review is reproduced in *The Works of Mary Wollstonecraft*, edited by Marilyn Butler and Janet Todd (London: Pickering, 1991, Vol. I), pp. 467–72, where the editors identify 'M' (see p. 172) as a signature used regularly by Wollstonecraft as a reviewer for the *Analytical Review*.

[2] Page references are to the present edition.

[3] 'Auferimur cultu; gemmis auroque teguntur / omnia; pars minima est ipsa puella sui': 'We are won by dress; all is concealed by gems and gold; a woman is the least part of herself', Ovid, *Remedia Amoris*, ll. 342–3 (*The Art of Love and Other Poems* (London: Heinemann, Loeb Classical Library, 1929), pp. 178–9).

BIBLIOGRAPHY

WRITINGS BY WATKIN TENCH

A Narrative of the Expedition to Botany Bay; with an account of New South Wales, its productions, inhabitants, etc. To which is subjoined, a List of the Civil and Military Establishments at Port Jackson, By Captain Watkin Tench, of the Marines (London: printed for J. Debret, opposite Burlington-House, Piccadilly, 1789).

A Complete Account of the Settlement at Port Jackson, in New South Wales, including an accurate description of the situation of the colony; of the natives; and of its natural productions: taken on the spot, By Captain Watkin Tench, of the Marines (London: sold by G. Nicol, Pall-Mall, and J. Sewell, Cornhill, 1793).

Letters Written in France to a Friend in London, between the month of November 1794, and the month of May 1795. By Major Tench of the Marines, late of his Majesty's ship Alexander (London: printed for J. Johnson, St Paul's Church-Yard, 1796).

WORKS CITED OR ALLUDED TO IN TENCH'S *LETTERS*

Bible (Authorised version, 1611).
Bouguer, Pierre, *Traité de navire* (Paris, 1746).
Bouguer, Pierre, *Traité de navigation* (Paris, 1753).
Bouguer, Pierre, *Traité de la manœuvre des vaisseaux* (Paris, 1757).
Burke, Edmund, *Reflections on the Revolution in France*, edited by C. C. O'Brien (1790; Harmondsworth: Penguin, 1968).
Caesar, Julius, *De Bello Gallico* (London: Heinemann, Loeb Classical Library, 1917).
Cartwright, John, *A Constitutional Defense of England, Internal and External* (London: J. Johnson, 1796).
Gibbon, Edward, *The History of the Decline and Fall of the Roman Empire*, edited by David Womersley (1776–88; London: Allen Lane, the Penguin Press, 1994).
Gray, Thomas, 'A Long Story' (1753), *The Complete Poems of Thomas Gray*, edited by H. W. Starr and J. R. Hendrikson (Oxford: Clarendon Press, 1966).

London Gazette (1665–).

Milton, John, 'Il Penseroso' (1631), *Paradise Lost* (1667), *The Poems of John Milton*, edited by John Carey and Alastair Fowler (London and New York: Longman, 1968).

Ovid, *Metamorphoses* (London: Heinemann, Loeb Classical Library, 1916).

Playfair, William, *A History of Jacobinism* (London, 1793).

Pope, Alexander, 'Epistle to Dr. Arbuthnot' (1735), *Twickenham Edition of the Works of Alexander Pope*, edited by John Butt, 11 vols. (London and New Haven: Methuen, Yale University Press, 1961–9).

Selden, John, *Mare Clausum, seu de Divinio* (London, 1636).

Shakespeare, William, *William Shakespeare: The Complete Works*, edited by Stanley Wells and Gary Taylor (Oxford: Oxford University Press, 1986): *The Tragedy of Julius Caesar*; *The Tragedy of Hamlet, Prince of Denmark*; *Measure for Measure*; *The Tragedy of Othello, the Moor of Venice*; *The Life of Timon of Athens*; *The Tragedy of Macbeth*; *The Tempest*.

Temple, Sir William, *Observations upon the United Provinces of the Netherlands*, edited by Sir George Clark (1673; Oxford: Clarendon Press, 1972).

Virgil, *Aeneid* (London: Heinemann, Loeb Classical Library, 1916).

Vitruvius, *De Architectura* (London: Heinemann, Loeb Classical Library, 1934).

Voltaire, *La Henriade* (Paris, 1723).

WORKS CITED BY THE EDITOR

Aitchison, John and Carter, Harold, *A Geography of the Welsh Language, 1961–1991* (Cardiff: University of Wales Press, 1994).

Anon, *Fragmens* [sic] *du dernier voyage de la Pérouse* (Quimper: P. M. Barazer, prairial an v. [1797]).

Anon., 'Narrative of an officer's imprisonment in France, 1794', in *Naval Yarns: Letters and Anecdotes; comprising accounts of sea fights and wrecks, actions with pirates and privateers, etc., from 1616 to 1831*, edited by W. H. Long (Wakefield: EP Publishing, 1973).

Archives départementales du Finistère, several documents as cited in text.

Austen, Jane, *Mansfield Park* (1814; London: Oxford University Press, 1970).

Balzac, Honoré, *The Chouans*, trans. H. A. Crow (1829; Harmondsworth: Penguin, 1972).

Bohls, Elizabeth A., *Women Travel Writers and the Language of Aesthetics, 1716–1818* (Cambridge: Cambridge University Press, 1995).

Boileau, Nicolas, *L'Art poétique* (1674).

British Critic: A New Review, 42 vols., 1773–1813.

BIBLIOGRAPHY

Butler, Marilyn, *Jane Austen and the War of Ideas* (Oxford: Oxford University Press, 1975).

Cambry, Jacques, *Voyage dans le Finistère ou état de ce département en 1794 et 1795*, edited by D. Guillou-Beuzit (1799; Quimper: Société archéologique du Finistère, 1999).

Carré, Adrien, 'La prison-bagne des marins anglais à Quimper 1794–1796: aspects méconnus de la Révolution en Basse-Bretagne', *Bulletin de la société archéologique et historique de Nantes et de Loire Atlantique* (1982), pp. 9–37.

Collet, Daniel, 'La Revolution à Quimper', in Jean Kerhervé (ed.), *Histoire de Quimper* (Toulouse: Editions Privat, 1994).

Colley, Linda, *Britons: Forging the Nation 1707–1837* (New Haven and London: Yale University Press, 1992).

Cormack, W. S., *Revolution and Political Conflict in the French Navy, 1789–94* (Cambridge: Cambridge University Press, 1995).

Doyle, William, *Oxford History of the French Revolution* (Oxford: Oxford University Press, 1989).

Dunmore, John, 'Utopie française, auteur anglais?', *Dix-Huitième siècle*, 26 (1994), pp. 409–506.

Eden, Frederick Morton, *The State of the Poor* (London, 1797).

Edwards, Gavin, 'Watkin Tench and the cold track of narrative', *Southerly*, 60, 3 (2000), pp. 74–93.

Favret, Mary A., *Romantic Correspondence: Women, Politics and the Fiction of Letters* (Cambridge: Cambridge University Press, 1993).

Gardiner, Robert (ed.), *Fleet, Battle and Blockade: The French Revolutionary War, 1793–1797* (London: Chatham Publishing in Association with the National Maritime Museum, 1996).

Gentleman's Magazine, 70 vols. (1731–1800).

Gibson, Ross (ed.), *Exchanges: Cross-cultural Encounters in Australia and the Pacific* (Sydney: Museum of Sydney, 1996).

Gury, Jacques, 'En marge d'une expedition scientifique: Fragments du dernier voyage de La Perouse [1797]', *Dix-Huitième siècle*, 22 (1990), pp. 195–237.

Gury, Jacques, 'Fragments en quête d'auteur', *Dix-Huitième siècle*, 26 (1994), pp. 507–9.

Hampson, Norman, *The Perfidy of Albion: French Perceptions of England during the French Revolution* (London: Macmillan, 1998).

Hemingway, Joseph, *A History of the City of Chester* (Chester, 1831).

Henwood, Philippe, and Monange, Edward, *Brest: un port en revolution, 1789–1799* (Brest: Editions ouest-France, 1989).

Hincks, Rhisiart, 'The Breton language in the nineteenth century', in Geraint Jenkins (ed.), *Language and Community in the Nineteenth Century* (Cardiff: University of Wales Press, 1999), pp. 369–95.

BIBLIOGRAPHY

Hunt, Lynn, *The Family Romance of the French Revolution* (London: Routledge, 1992).

Hutt, Maurice, *Chouannerie and Counter-Revolution: Puisaye, the Princes and the British Government in the 1790s* (Cambridge: Cambridge University Press, 1983).

Johnson, Samuel, and Boswell, James, *'A Journey to the Western Islands of Scotland', 'The Journal of a Tour of the Hebrides'* (1775, 1786; Harmondsworth: Penguin, 1984).

Jones, Colin, *The Longman Companion to the French Revolution* (London and New York: Longman, 1988).

Lavery, Brian, *Nelson's Navy: The Ships, Men and Organisation, 1793–1815* (London: Conway Maritime Press, 1989).

Mably, Gabriel Bonnot de, *Observations sur l'histoire de France* (Geneva, 1765).

Manwaring, G. E., and Dobrée, Bonomy, *Mutiny: The Floating Republic* (London: Cresset Library, 1935).

Masson, Philippe, *Les sépulcres flottants: Prisonniers français en Angleterre sous l'Empire* (Brest: Editions ouest-France, 1987).

Mathiez, Albert, *The French Revolution*, trans. C. Phillips (London: Williams and Norgate, 1928).

Mitchell, Adrian, 'Watkin Tench's sentimental enclosures', *Australia and New Zealand Studies in Canada*, 11 (June 1994), pp. 23–33.

Monthly Review; or, Literary Journal, 108 vols., 1790–1825.

Montagu, Mary Wortley, *Turkish Embassy Letters*, edited by Anita Desai (1763; London: Virago Press, 1994).

Ovid, *The Art of Love and Other Poems* (London: Heinemann, Loeb Classical Library, 1929).

Ozouf, Maria, *Festivals and the French Revolution*, trans. Alan Sheridan (Cambridge, Mass: Harvard University Press, 1975).

Paine, Thomas, *Rights of Man* (1791–2; Harmondsworth: Penguin, 1979).

Paine, Thomas, *Common Sense* (1776; Harmondsworth: Penguin, 1998).

Philp, Mark, 'Republicanism', in Iain McCalman (ed.), *An Oxford Companion to the Romantic Age: British Culture 1776–1832* (Oxford: Oxford University Press, 1999), pp. 673–4.

Pope, Alexander, 'An Essay on Criticism' (1711), *The Iliad* (1715–20), *The Odyssey* (1725–6), *Twickenham Edition of the Works of Alexander Pope*, edited by John Butt, 11 vols. (London and New Haven: Methuen, Yale University Press, 1961–9).

Racine, Jean, *Phèdre* (1677), *Athalie* (1691), *Théâtre complet*, edited by M. Pal (Paris: Garnier, 1960).

Rodger, N. A. M., *The Wooden World: An Anatomy of the Georgian Navy* (London: Fontana/Harper Collins, 1986).

BIBLIOGRAPHY

Scott, Walter, *Waverley; or, 'Tis Sixty Years Since* (1814; Oxford: Clarendon Press, 1981).

Sieyès, Emmanuel-Joseph, *Qu'est-ce que le Tiers-état?* (1789; Geneva, 1970).

Tench, Watkin, *Sydney's First Four Years, being a reprint of 'A Narrative of the Expedition to Botany Bay' and 'A Complete Account of the Settlement at Port Jackson' by Captain Watkin Tench of the Marines*, edited by L. F. Fitzhardinge (Sydney: Library of Australian History, 1979).

Tench, Watkin, *1788, comprising 'A Narrative of the Expedition to Botany Bay' and 'A Complete Account of the Settlement at Port Jackson' by Watkin Tench*, edited by Tim Flannery (Melbourne: Text Publishing Company, 1996).

Thompson, J. M. (ed.), *English Witnesses of the French Revolution* (Oxford: Basil Blackwell, 1938).

Tracy, Nicholas (ed.), *The Naval Chronicle: The Contemporary Record of the Royal Navy at War*, vol. 1, *1793–1798* (London: Chatham Publishing, 1998).

Voltaire, *Lettres philosophiques* (1734; Oxford: Blackwell, 1946).

Voltaire, *The Henriade*, trans. John Lockman (London: C. Davis, 1732).

Warton, Joseph, *An Essay on the Genius and Writings of Pope* (London: J. Dodsley, 4th edn., 1782).

Williams, Gwyn A., *Artisans and Sans-Culottes: Popular Movements in France and Britain during the French Revolution* (London: Arnold, 1968).

Williams, Helen Maria, *Letters Written in France, in the Summer of 1790, to a Friend in England* (London: J. Johnson, 1790).

Wollstonecraft, Mary, *The Works of Mary Wollstonecraft*, edited by Marilyn Butler and Janet Todd (London: Pickering, 1991), Vol. 1.

INDEX

Acquilon, L' 46
Act of Union (1707) xxxi
Adamant 10n.
Aeneid 160n.3
Agincourt, battle of 12, 138n.22
aide-de-camp (*aid-de-camp*) 22, 127, 141n.2
Alexander xiii, xviii, xx, xxv, xxxiv, 5n., 8, 10n., 30, 35, 39, 46, 49, 68, 99, 135n.4, 136n.12, 141n.7, 165–7, 168, 173
Alsace 90
America 5n., 26, 48, 109–10, 158n.20
America 53
American War of Independence xvi, 48, 136n.13, 142n.1, 17n.7, 158n.20
Amsterdam xiv, 147n.13
Analytical Review xx, xxx, 168, 173
Anderson, Consul 134
Anglicanism xxvi, xxxiii, xxxii
Anne, duchess of Brittany 74, 151n.1
Antæus 103, 157n.9
Antigua xxxviiin.21
Aristippus 148n.3
Art poétique, L' 161n.6
assignats xiii, xiv, 17, 20, 55, 62, 80, 82, 83, 93, 104, 106, 107, 122, 140n.39, 158n.14, 172
Astrolabe xxxviiin.10
Atalante, L' 132
Atlantic Fleet xiv, xx
Audacieux, L' 46
Austen, Jane xxvii–xxviii, xxxviiin.17
Austria xii, 147n.7, 148n.9
Austrian Netherlands 106
aux armes, citoyens 124, 161n.10
aux prières 11, 137n.19

Balzac, Honoré de 154n.22
Bantry Bay 146n.3
Barbados 108
Barère (Barrere) de Vieuzac, Bertrand de 111, 119, 151–2n.5, 159n.23, 159n.24
Basle, Treaty of 147n.13, 157n.10
Bastille, the xi, xxiii
Batavian Republic 132, 147n.13; *see also* Holland

Belgium 106
Belleisle 136n.9
Bentinck, Captain 22
Bertram, Sir Thomas xxxviiin.21
Betsy 55–6
Billaud-Varennes (Billaud de Varennes), Jacques-Nicolas 111, 119, 159n.23, 159n.24
Blenheim, battle of 12, 138n.22
Bligh, Admiral Richard Rodney xv, xviii, xix, xx, xxxviiin.12, 5n., 7, 9, 10, 17–18, 19, 22–3, 25, 35, 42, 44, 45, 49, 52, 53, 54–5, 67–8, 69, 71, 86, 97, 99, 100, 127, 129–32, 133, 136n.8, 139n.35, 141n.7, 165–7, 168, 170, 171, 173
Boileau, Nicolas xxxiv, 117, 122, 161n.5, 161n.6, 161n.7
Boissy d'Anglas, François Antoine, Comte de 123, 161n.9
Bonaparte, Napoleon xiv, xxxviiin.21, 138n.21, 144n.12
bonnet rouge 10, 13, 140n.3
bons citoyens 63, 149n.7
Boswell, James 154n.22
Botany Bay xi, xv, xvi, xxxviiin.10, 125, 163
Bouguer, Pierre 28, 143n.7
Bouvet de Précourt, Admiral François-Joseph 45, 146n.3
Brest xi, xviii, xxi, xxii, xxvi, xxxv, xxxviiin.10, 5, 10, 11, 14, 15, 17, 19, 22, 25, 27, 30, 36, 39, 40, 44, 49, 55, 58, 68, 69, 76, 79, 83, 86, 88, 92 and n., 93, 94, 95, 97, 99, 105, 111, 114–15, 127, 128, 129, 133–4, 141n.7, 144n.12, 146n.4, 155n.4, 165, 168, 169, 170
Breton (language) xviii, xx, xxxii, 59, 77, 148n.8, 151–2n.5, 154n.21, 154n.22, 154n.24
Brimaudière, Mademoiselle xx, xxii, 53, 62
Brimaudière, Monsieur 66–7
Brissot, Jacques Pierre 66, 109, 150n.11
Brissotins xxiv, 64, 106, 109, 111, 150n.11, 158n.17; *see also* Girondins
Bristol 47

INDEX

Britain xii, xvi, xx, xxiii, xxvii, xxxi, xxxiii, xxxvi, 13, 27, 37, 89, 138–9n.28, 143n.9, 145–6n.37, 154n.25, 161–2n.11
British Critic xxxviin.7
Britons: Forging the Nation 1707–1837 xxxi, 145n.25
Brittany (Bretagne) xiii, xviii, xix, xxxii, 22, 53, 58, 59, 67, 74, 82, 95, 111, 141n.1, 147n.14, 148n.8, 149n.6, 149n.10, 151n.1, 154n.22, 154n.23, 154n.24, 156n.2, 157n.7
Brown, Lieutenant 167
Brutus xxxiv, 98, 156n.8
Burke, Edmund xi, xxvii, 109, 147n.12, 155–6n.6, 158n.19, 158n.20, 168
Burley, Mr 53
Burns, Mr 166

Caen 149n.10
Calais 158n.20
Calais Gate 145n.25
Caldwell, Colonel 61
Caligula 120, 160n.34
Cambon, Joseph 105, 107, 157n.11
Cambry, Jacques xix, xxxvii–xxxviiin.10
Camperdown xiv
Canada 10n., 165–6
Cannae, battle of 48, 147n.7
Cape St Vincent xiv, 10n.
Capua 48, 147n.7
Caribbean islands 108
Carlisle, Lord 90
Carmagnole xxix, 12, 65, 124, 138n.21
Carrier, Jean-Baptiste 120, 160n.35
Carter, Lieutenant 167
Carthage 26, 143n.4, 147n.7
Cartwright, John 29n., 144n.10
Castile (Castille) 89
Castle Howard 90
Caumartin, *see* Desoteux
cautionné 62, 149n.1
Cawsand 127, 162n.1
Cayenne 111
Champagne 103
Champeaux xxxv, 130, 131, 132, 133
Channel, the xvi, xxxiv, 17, 27, 143n.5
Channel Fleet xiii, xiv, xvi–xviii, xx, 138n.23
charbon de terre 88, 154n.26
Charente, Le 5n.
Charette de la Contrie, François

Athanase xiv, 51, 68, 70, 102–3, 104, 147n.14
Charles I, King of England xxxviiin.15
Charles II, King of England xxvii, 118
Charles VIII, King of France 74, 151n.1
Charles-Philippe, Comte d'Artois (Charles X) 101, 156n.2
Charlotte xvi, 140n.2
Chatham xx
Chelsea Royal Hospital 12, 138n.24
Cherbourg 27, 143n.5
Chester xv, xxxvin.4, xxxviin.7, xxxviiin.15, 154n.24
Chouans xiii, xiv, xix, 102, 154n.22, 157n.5, 157n.6, 157n.8
Chouans, The 154n.22
Civil Constitution of the Clergy, the xxiii, 151n.24, 157n.6
civisme 145n.30
Coblenz 156n.2
cocarde blanche 64, 149n.9
Colley, Linda xxxi, xxxi, 145n.25
Collot d'Herbois, Jean-Marie 111, 120, 159n.23, 159n.24
Committee of Public Safety xxiv, 119–20, 124, 137n.17, 144n.12, 158n.17, 159n.23, 160n.33, 161n.9
Committees of Surveillance xxiv, 113–16, 155n.4
Common Sense 158n.20
Complete Account of the Settlement at Port Jackson, A xiii, xv, xvi, xxiii, xxxiii, xxxv, xxxvin.2, xxxvin.4, xxxviin.7, xxxviiin.8, 141–2n.8, 161–2n.11
communes 117
Concarneau 157n.5
Conciergerie 66, 150n.16
Conseil, Captain 55, 56
conseil de discipline 31–2, 144n.20
Constitutional Defense of England, Internal and External, A 144n.10
Convention, La 45
Cook, Captain James 164
Copenhagen 127
Corday, Charlotte 136n.9
Cornish (language) 154n.24
Cornouaille 87, 154n.24
Cornwall (Britain) xxxvin.4, 76, 86, 152n.6
Cornwall (Brittany), *see* Cornouaille
Côtes du Nord 148n.8
Courand, Captain 99

INDEX

Courtois 109, 117, 118
crêpe (*crape*) 86, 128, 154n.21
Cromwell, Oliver xxvii, 119, 171

Danton, Georges Jacques xxiv, 108, 141n.3, 158n.17
Daracott, Lieutenant 167
Darlington, Thomas 148n.8
Darthé, Augustin Alexandre 119–20, 160n.33
David, Jacques Louis xxxiv, 137n.16
De Bello Gallico 135n.2
Décadis (*Decadis*) 40, 124–5, 145n.27, 145n.32
Declaration of the Rights of Man and the Citizen, The xi, xxiii, 13, 138n.27, 158n.22
Delcher 15
Delhi 87, 154n.22
Denbigh xv
dépôt 61, 148n.12
Desoteux, Pierre-Marie, Baron de Cormatin (Caumartin) 102, 157n.7
Devonport xvi, xx, 162n.2
Devonshire 85, 86
Diadème, Le 31
Directory, the xiv, 149n.10
Droits de l'Homme, Les 5n., 46
Dupont, Jacques-Louis 40, 145n.35
Dutch republic, *see* Holland

East India Company 14
East Indies 8, 108
écrivain ou secrétaire 29, 144n.13
Eden, Sir Frederick Morton 91, 155n.1
émigrés xx, 157n.5
England xv, xvi, xxi, xxii, xxxi, xxxiv, 3, 8, 13, 15, 20, 22, 25–6, 27, 28, 30, 48, 51, 53, 76, 78, 84, 88, 90, 97, 98, 99, 100, 103, 108, 127, 131, 132, 151n.1, 152n.6, 157n.7, 170, 172
English (language) xxxvin.4, 8
enragés 63, 149n.8
Entreprenant, L' 29, 46
Eole, L' 46
'Epistle to Dr. Arbuthnot' 139n.29
Epworth, Lieutenant 167
espaliers 57, 148n.6
Espion, L' 61
Essay on Criticism, An 161n.6
Essay on the Genius and Writings of Pope, An 161n.7
état major 32, 136n.12

Etats de Bourgogne, Les 141n.3
Europe 3, 17, 27, 88, 90, 108, 125, 131

Festival of Reason xiii, 152n.8
Finistère xix, xxii, 140n.38, 148n.8
Fish, Captain George xxii
Fish, Sarah xxii
Fitzgerald, Lieutenant 166, 167
Fitzroy, Lady Anne 45, 53, 91n., 96–7, 146n.2, 155n.6
Formidable, Le 136n.9
Fort Augustus 154n.22
Fouché, Joseph 139n.33
Fougueux, Le 46
Fragmens [sic] *du dernier voyage de la Pérouse* xiv, xxxviiin.10
Fraternité, La 5n.
Frederick, Duke of York 109
Frederick William IV, King of Prussia 103
French (language) xviii, xxxi, xxxii, 25, 59, 87, 128, 141–2n.8, 154n.22
frizeur 50, 147n.10, 152–3n.9
fuzilades (*fusillades*) 120, 160n.35

Galaup, Jean François de, Comte de La Pérouse xi, xvi, xxxvii–xxxviiin.10
Gasparin, Le 46
Gazette Nationale 117
General Anglais 129, 162n.3
gens d'armes 66, 150n.15
Gentille, Le 5n.
Gentleman's Magazine xv, xxxviin.1
Germany 89, 100
Germinal rising 159n.24
Gibbon, Edward 89, 154–5n.27
Gironde, the 150n.11
Girondins xii, xiii, xxiv, 149n.10, 158n.20, 159n.24, 160n.32; *see also* Brissotins
Glorious First of June/Combat de prairial xiii, xviii, 29–31, 70, 138n.23, 144n.11
Glorious Revolution (1688) xi, xxvi, xxvii, 138n.25
Godench, Lieutenant 167
gorget 9, 33, 136n.11
Gothicism xxxi, xxxiv, 123, 161n.8
Greenwich Royal Hospital 12, 138n.24
Grey, Thomas 148n.5
Guermeur, J. T. M. 67–8, 69, 72, 83, 123, 150n.18, 150n.19

INDEX

Guesmo, M. C. 67–8, 69, 72, 83, 123, 150n.18, 150n.19

Hague, the, Treaty of 147n.13
Hamilcar 109, 158n.18
Hamilton, Captain 10n.
Hamlet 41
Hannibal 48, 147n.7
Harmand, J. B. 131, 162n.4
Hastings, battle of 151n.1
Hawke, Admiral Edward 12, 138n.23
Haygarth, Thomas xxxviin.7
Henriade, La 101, 156–7n.3
Hill, Hannah, *see* Sargent, Hannah
Hincks, Rhisiart 151–2n.5
Historical and Moral View of the French Revolution, An xiii
History of Jacobinism, A 158n.14
History of the Decline and Fall of the Roman Empire, The 154–5n.27
Hoche, Lazare xiv, 159n.28
Hogarth, William 145n.25
Holland xii, xvi, xxxiii, xxxv, 26, 51, 142n.1, 147n.13, 169; *see also* Batavian Republic
Howe, Admiral Richard (Lord Howe) 12, 22, 30, 138n.23, 169

Il Penseroso 150n.21
incivisme (incivism) 39, 113, 145n.30
Indomptable, L' 45
Ireland xxxv, 37, 47, 61, 132
Isfahan (Ispahan) 154n.2, 287
Isnard, M. 111, 159n.24

Jacobin, Le 45n.
Jacobin Club xiii, xxiv, xxv, 42, 145–6n.37
Jacobins xxiv–xxv, xxxviin.7, 42, 120, 137n.16, 137n.17, 140n.41, 141n.3, 145n.29, 145–6n.37, 146n.38, 157n.11, 158n.17
James I, King of England 142n.2
James II, King of England 138n.25
Jean Bart, Le 5n., 45, 47
Jemappe, Le 46
Jersey 48
Johannot 104, 105–6
John, King of England 12–13, 138n.25
Johnson, Joseph xx, xxiii, xxxviin.7, 144n.10, 173
Johnson, Samuel 154n.22
Julius Caesar xxii, 5n., 135n.2

Julius Caesar 146n.6

Kersalaun, Marquis de 56, 58, 60
Kervélégan (Kérvélligan), Madame 65, 111; *see also* Le Goaze de Kervélégan, Augustin
Kervélégan (Kérvélligan), Mademoiselle xxiv, 63, 65, 149n.4
Klingly, General 90
Kinsale 132
Kittoe, Captain 61, 67–8, 97, 149n.12
krampouezhenn, see *crêpe*

La Jaunaye, Treaty of 147n.14
La Pérouse, *see* Galaup, Jean-François de
La Prévalaye xiv, 157n.8
La Vendée xiii, xix, 67, 79, 102, 103, 147n.14, 157n.6, 157n.8, 158n.21
Latin xv, xxxii, xxxiv, 26, 141–2n.8, 153n.10
Law of Suspects (1793) 144n.19, 145n.30
Le Bas, Philippe 119, 160n.33
Le Franq, Captain xxvi, 8, 9, 10, 11, 13, 14, 15, 17, 19, 25, 29, 31, 33, 42, 45, 117, 134, 136n.10, 168
Le Goaze de Kervélégan (Kérvélligan), Augustin 64–5, 111, 149n.4, 149n.10; *see also* Kervélégan
Le Peletier (Pelletier), Louis Michel, Marquis de Saint-Fargeau 11, 137n.16
Lecointre, Laurant 111, 159n.25
Legendre, Louis 111, 159n.24
Letters Written During a Short Residence in Sweden, Norway and Denmark xiv, xxiii
Letters Written in France in the Summer of 1790 to a Friend in England . . . xi, xxii–xxiii
Letters Written in France to a Friend in London xiv, xv, xvi, xviii, xx–xxi, xxii–xxiii, xxviii, xxxi, xxxv, xxxvin.3, xxxviin.5, 1–134 *passim*, 168–72, 173
Lettres philosophiques 151n.2
Lhuyd, Edward 154n.24
Liberté, Egalité, Fraternité, ou la Mort 13, 138n.26
Lisbon 91n.
Liverpool xxxvin.4, xxxviin.7
livres 33, 44, 62, 104, 105, 106, 107, 113, 122, 140n.39

182

INDEX

London xvi, xx, xxi, xxii, xxxvin.4, 5, 14, 17, 143n.4, 157n.5
London Gazette xviii, 5n., 165, 173
'Long Story, A' 148n.5
Lorient (l'Orient) 46, 53, 72, 146n.5
louis 20, 83, 140n.39
Louis XIV, King of France 26, 107
Louis XVI, King of France xii, 50, 65, 147n.12, 159n.27
Louis XVII, King of France 112, 156n.3
Louis, Comte de Provence (Louis XVIII) 101, 156n.2
Luxembourg 158n.20
Lyons 120, 159n.23

Mably, Gabriel Bonnot de 74, 151n.2
Macbeth 139n.36
McBride, Admiral 22
McCurdy, Mr 166
Madrid 26
Magna Carta 12–13, 138n.25
Majestueux, Le 45, 47
Mansfield Park xxix, xxxviiin.17
Marat, Jean Paul xiii, xxiv, 12, 109, 118, 136n.9, 137n.16
Marat, Le xix, xxiv, xxviii, xxx, xxxi, xxxiv, 5 and n., 8, 16, 19, 20, 22, 25, 46, 134, 136n.9, 141–2n.8, 165, 168, 170
Mare Clausum, seu de Divinio 142n.2
maréchaux de France 76, 151n.3
Maria Theresa, Empress of Austria 147n.12
Marie Antoinette, Queen of France xiii, 50–1, 147n.12, 150n.16, 155n.6
Marne, Prieur de la 95, 114–15, 155n.4
Marseilles 137n.20
Marseillaise (Marseilles, *Marseillois* Hymn) xxv, 12, 124, 137–8n.20
Maryland xvi, 102, 136n.13
maximum, le 146n.1, 153n.14
Mazentius (Mezentius) 122, 160n.3
Measure for Measure 150–1n.23
Mediterranean, the 10n., 27, 169
Merlin de Douai, Philippe Antoine 121, 160n.1
Merlin de Thionville, Baron Antoine-Christophe 110, 121, 158n.21, 160n.1
Mezentius, *see* Mazentius
militaire 17, 140n.38
Milton, John xv, xxxiv, 6, 28, 135n.6, 149n.5, 150n.21, 155n.5
Minden, battle of 12, 138n.22
Mitchell, Adrian xxi

Molière (Jean Baptiste Poquelin) 161n.5
Montagnards xxiv, xxv, xxvi, 141n.3, 141n.4, 144n.12, 149n.6, 150n.11, 159n.23, 159n.25, 160n.32; *see also* Montagne, La
Montagnard, Le 46
Montagne, La (political faction) 42, 64, 81, 141n.3, 145–6n.37, 146n.38, 150n.12; *see also* Montagnards
Montagne, La (ship) 22, 29, 35, 38, 45, 141n.3
Montagu, Admiral Sir George 30, 40, 144n.15
Montagu, Lady Mary Wortley xxiii, 141–2n.8
Montbret, Coquebert de 148n.8
Monthly Review xxxviin.7
Morbihan 148n.8
Mornington, Earl of 91n., 146n.2
Moulin 139n.33
mousses 9, 137n.14
Mutius Scævola, Le 45

Nantes 120, 160n.35
Napoleonic Civil Code 160–1n.4
'Narrative of an officer's imprisonment in France, 1794' 155n.2
Narrative of the Expedition to Botany Bay, A xi, xvi, xx, xxxi, xxxvin.2, xxxvin.4, xxxviin.8, xxxviiin.10
National Assembly (la Nation assemblée) xi, xii, xvi, xxiii, xxxiv, 138n.27, 145–6n.37, 173n.1
National Convention xii, xiv, xxiv, 80, 104, 109, 111, 118, 119, 121, 124, 135n.4, 135n.5, 137n.16, 140n.40, 140n.41, 141n.3, 143n.4, 144n.12, 145n.29, 145n.34, 145n.35, 145–6n.37, 148n.9, 149n.10, 150n.11, 151–2n.5, 152–3n.9, 157n.11, 158n.17, 158n.20, 158n.21, 159n.23, 159n.24, 159n.25, 160n.32, 161n.8, 161n.9
Naval Chronicle 173
Neptune, Le 46, 47
Nestor, Le 45
Neuf Thermidor, Le 45, 47
New Holland 24, 141–2n.8, 163
New South Wales xi, xii, xv, xvi, xx, xxi, xxii, xxxvi, 141–2n.8, 158n.20, 161–2n.11
Nielly (Neilly, Nieully), Contre-Amiral Joseph-Marie 5, 35, 39, 45, 135n.4, 145n.26, 165

INDEX

Noblesse Brétonne (bretonne) 84, 153n.15
Nore, the xiv, 145n.24
Normandie, Le xix, xxi, xxviii, xxxiv, 19, 22, 23, 44, 53–4, 55, 134, 170
Normandy 64, 85
North Sea Fleet xiv
noyades 120, 160n.35

Observations sur l'histoire de France 151n.2
Observations upon the United Provinces of the Netherlands 162n.5
Océan, L' 141n.3
Othello xxii, 135n.1
Othello 135n.1

pain d'egalité 15, 82, 139n.32
Paine, Thomas xii, xxvii, 109–10, 158n.20
Papillon, Le 5n.
Paradise Lost 135n.6, 143–4n.9, 149n.5, 155n.5
Paris xvi, 14, 38, 39, 47, 49, 58, 65, 81, 84, 98, 107, 111, 112, 117, 119, 122, 137n.15, 137n.20, 143n.8, 149n.6, 149n.8, 156n.14, 156n.17, 159n.26, 161n.8
Patriote, Le 46
passe-dix 62–3, 149n.2
Pennant, Thomas xxxviin.4
Penrhyn, Lord and Lady xxxviin.4
Pelletier, Le 5n., 46
Peuple, Le 141n.3
Philadelphia 20, 48
Pichegru, General Charles 112, 159n.28
Pilnitz 103
pilotins 39, 145n.31
Pitt, William 13, 30, 39, 91, 109, 138–9n.28
Playfair, William 107, 138n.28, 158n.14
Plouec, Marquise de xxix, 63, 66
Plymouth xiv, xx, 10 and n., 48, 74, 127, 134, 162n.1, 162n.2, 170
Pontenazan 92, 94–5
Pope, Alexander xxiii, xxxiv, 123, 139n.29, 161n.6, 161n.7
Popular Societies 29, 145n.29
Portsmouth xx, xxix, 10n., 134
Pougens, Charles xvi, xxxviiin.10, 164, 173
Prairial, combat de, *see* Glorious First of June

Precini (Prépigui) xxix–xxx, xxxi, xxxiii, 61, 97–8, 148n.10, 171
prévenus (prevenus) 111, 159n.24
Price, Fanny xxix, xxxviiin.21
Price, Mr xxix
Procrustes 116, 159n.29
Protestantism xxvi, xxxi, xxxii, xxxiii, xxxvi
Prussia xii, 51, 88, 147n.13, 157n.10
Puisaye, Joseph-Geneviève, Comte de 157n.5, 167n.7
Punic Wars 143n.4, 147n.7
Pyrenees 15, 26, 29, 35, 169

Queen Charlotte 31
Quiberon Bay xiv, 138n.23, 147n.14, 157n.5
Quimper xiv, xviii, xix, xx, xxii, xxiv, xxv, xxvi, xxix, xxx, xxxiii, xxxviin.6, xxxviiin.10, 22, 23, 25, 44, 45, 51–2, 53, 56, 60, 62, 64, 69, 70, 74–90, 91, 95, 96, 99, 100, 103, 114–16, 121, 122, 129, 141–2n.8, 145n.34, 146n.2, 146n.5, 150n.22, 151n.1, 151n.2, 152n.8, 153n.13, 154n.22, 155n.4, 171

Racine, Jean xxxiv, 122, 161n.5, 161n.6
racine Anglaise, la 85, 153n.18
Radcliffe, Ann 161n.8
Redoutable, Le 46
Reflections on the Revolution in France xi, xxvii, 155–6n.6, 158n.19
Relation d'une expédition à la Baye Botanique xi, xvi, 163–4
Renaudin, Admiral Jean-François 22–3, 45, 141n.5
Rennes 102
Republican Calendar xiii, xviii, 145n.27, 152–3n.99
'Republican Catechism, The' 40–1
republican marriages 120, 160n.35
Representatives on Mission xxiv, xxv, xxvi, 17–18, 140n.41, 144n.12, 158n.21, 159n.23, 160n.35
Republicain, Le 46
Revolution, La 45
Revolutionnaire, Le 45
Rights of Man, xii, 158n.20
Rio de Janeiro xxxi
Robespierre, Maximilien de xiii, xxiv, xxv, xxix, 11, 13, 29, 37, 40, 42, 49, 62, 64, 65, 66, 80, 81, 106, 107, 109,

INDEX

116–20, 134, 137n.17, 141n.3, 145n.34, 145–6n.37, 152–3n.9, 157n.11, 158n.21, 159n.22, 159n.23, 160n.33
Robinson, Lieutenant xxii, 53, 93–4, 95–6, 98, 147n.1, 167
Rochefort 27, 169
Rodney, Admiral George (Lord Rodney) 12, 31, 138n.23, 144n.17
Roman Catholicism xxvi, xxxi, xxxii, xxxiii, 41, 73, 123–4, 137–8n.20, 138n.25, 145n.34, 150n.13
Romanticism xxviii, xxxiv, 161n.7
Rome xxxiii, 48, 143n.4, 147n.7
Rouget de Lisle, C. J. 137n.20
Rousseau, Jean-Jacques 137n.17, 151n.2, 161–2n.11
Roux, Jacques 149n.8
Russell (Russel), Admiral Edward 12, 138n.23

Saint-André, Jean Bon xxvi, 29, 30, 135n.4, 136n.10, 141n.3, 141n.4, 143n.4, 144n.12, 155n.4
Saladin, J.-B.-Michel 119, 160n.32
Sans Pareil, Le 99
sans-culottes xxvii, xxxv, 28, 71, 80, 81, 124, 131, 136n.10, 137n.15, 143n.8, 171
Sargent, Anna Maria, *see* Tench, Anna Maria
Sargent, Hannah xvi
Sargent, Robert xvi
Schomberg, Admiral 22
Scilly, Isles of 47
Scipion, Le 45, 47
Scotland xxxi
Scott, Sir Walter 154n.22
Selden, John 25, 142n.2
September Massacres (1792) xii, 150n.11
1788 xv, xxxvin.2
Shakespeare, William xv, 14, 72, 135n.1, 139n.36, 140n.5, 141n.6, 146n.6, 150–1n.23
Sidebotham, Mr xxxviin.4
Sieyès, Emmanuel Joseph, Abbé 110, 159n.22
Society for Constitutional Information 144n.10
sols (*sous*) 90, 140n.39
Sonthonax 158n.17
Spain 103
specie 83, 125, 140n.39

Spithead xii, xiv, xvi, 17, 37
State of the Poor, The 155n.1
Stephens, Philip xxxviiin.12, 165, 167
Suffren (Suffrein) de Saint-Tropez, Pierre-André de 14, 139n.31
Suffren, Le 139n.31
Superbe, Le 46, 47
Supreme Being, Cult of the xiii, 145n.34, 152n.7, 159–60n.30
Switzerland 20, 100
Sydney 141–2n.8
Sydney's First Four Years xxiii, xxxiii, xxxvin.4, xxxviiin.19, 140n.2, 153n.19, 161–2n.11

Temeraire, Le 46, 47
Tempest, The 141n.6
Temple, Sir William xxxv, 132, 162n.5
Tench, Anna Maria xvi, 162n.2
Tench, Major Watkin xi, xii, xiii, xiv, xv–xxiii, xxiv–xxxvi, xxxvin.2, xxxvin.3, xxxvin.4, xxxviin.7, xxxvii–xxxviiin.10, xxxviiin.15, 1, 69, 135n.1, 135n.2, 135n.5, 136n.13, 137n.18, 137–8n.20, 138n.23, 138n.25, 139n.35, 140n.2, 141n.5, 141–2n.8, 142n.1, 144n.10, 145n.34, 147n.7, 147n.8, 150n.13, 150n.19, 152n.6, 153n.10, 153n.14, 153n.19, 153n.20, 154n.22, 154n.23, 154n.24, 154n.26, 156n.2, 156n.3, 157n.10, 158n.13, 158n.19, 158n.20, 160n.33, 161n.8, 161–2n.11, 167, 168–72
Terrible, Le 45
Terror, the xxiv, xxiv, xxvi, xxxi–xxxii, 137n.17, 158n.17
Thames 53, 93
Thermidor (*neuf Thermidor*) xxiv, 80, 137n.17, 140n.41, 141n.4, 149n.10, 152–3n.9, 159n.23, 159n.24, 159n.25, 160n.32, 160–1n.4, 161n.9
Thorn 10n.
Tigre, Le 5n., 46, 136n.9
Timon of Athens 140n.5
Tirannicide, Le 46
ton 66, 150n.14
Topsent, J. B. N. 131, 162n.4
Torbay 17
Toulon 27, 143n.6
Tourville, Le 46
Traité de la manoeuvre des vaisseaux 143n.7
Traité de navigation 143n.7

INDEX

Traité de navire 143n.7
traitement 19, 33, 44, 55, 93, 140n.1, 170
traiteur 96, 156n.7
Trajan, Le 46
31 de Mai, Le 46
Tribout, General 49, 98
Turin 156n.2
Turkish Embassy Letters xxiii, 141–2n.8

United Provinces, *see* Holland
Ushant 17, 47, 140n, 37

Vadier, Marc-Guillaume-Alexis 111, 159n.23
Valenciennes 48, 147n.7
Valmy xii
Van Stable (Vanstable), Admiral Pierre-Jean 45, 146n.4, 169
Vengeur, Le, 22, 23, 30, 141n.5, 144n.11
Vernon 131
Versailles xxix, xxx, 66, 111, 171
Villaret-Joyeuse, Admiral Comte Louis-Thomas xxvi, xxxv, 22, 23, 29, 35, 40, 44, 45, 129–31, 134, 135n.4, 136n.10, 141n.4, 169, 170
Virgil 160n.3
Voltaire (François Marie Arouet) 74, 151n.2, 156n.3
Voyage dans le Finistère ou état de ce département en 1794 et 1795 xix, xxxviiin.10

Wales xvi, xviii, xxxi, xxxvin.4, 59, 76, 86, 87, 148n.8, 152n.6, 154n.23
Walpole, Horace 161n.8
Warton, Joseph 161n.7
Waverley 154n.22
Wellington, Arthur, duke of 146n.2
Welsh (language) 87, 141–2n.8, 148n.8, 151–2n.5, 154n.24
Wesley (Wellesley), Henry 91 and n., 96, 146n.2
West, Lieutenant 167
West Indies xvi, xxxv, xxxvi, 108, 158n.17
Whiggism xxvii, xxxiii, 138n.25, 158n.19
William of Orange 13, 138n.25
Williams, Gwyn A. xxxv
Williams, Helen Maria xi, xxii–xxiii
Williams Wynn (family) xxxviiin.4
Williams Wynn, Sir Watkin (1749–89) xv
Williams Wynn, Sir Watkin (1772–1840) xv, xxxiii
Wollstonecraft, Mary xiii, xiv, xx, xxii, xxvii, xxx, xxxviiin.7, 168–72, 173
Wordsworth, William xxviii
Wynnstay xvi, xxxviiin.4

Yeu, island of 156n.2
Yorke, Philip xxxviiin.4

Zele, Le 46